# Gender and Modernity in Kerala

# Gender and Modernity in Kerala

## Politics, Praxes, Paradoxes

*Edited by*

Meena T. Pillai

Orient BlackSwan

The publication of this book was funded by Centre for Cultural Studies, University of Kerala.

GENDER AND MODERNITY IN KERALA:
POLITICS, PRAXES, PARADOXES

**ORIENT BLACKSWAN PRIVATE LIMITED**

*Registered Office*
3-6-752 Himayatnagar, Hyderabad 500 029, Telangana, India
*Email*: centraloffice@orientblackswan.com

*Other Offices*
Bengaluru, Chennai, Guwahati, Hyderabad, Kolkata,
Mumbai, New Delhi, Noida, Patna, Visakhapatnam


First published by Orient Blackswan Private Limited 2023

ISBN 978 93 5442 463 2

037715

*Typeset in* Minion Pro 11/13 *by*
Shine Graphics, Delhi 110 094

*Printed at*
B B Press, Noida

*Published by*
Orient Blackswan Private Limited
3-6-752, Himayatnagar, Hyderabad 500 029, Telangana, India
*Email*: info@orientblackswan.com

Dedicated to that most endearingly unconventional academic, Mundoli Narayanan, who inspired all our enquiries in this field while being the most unstinting critic and ally. The musketeer who combined critical rigour with mirth and madness in mounting a passionate brief, along with many of us, for making Kerala Studies a part of the English literature curriculum in Kerala.

# Contents

# Acknowledgements

This book is very dear to me, for much of it is a record of the exhilarating work my PhD scholars and I together did at the Centre for Cultural Studies, University of Kerala. Thus, it is to them, most of whom are contributors to this volume, that I owe much of this endeavour. I thank Murali and Gigy for joining my students and me in this long journey, for without them, particularly Murali, our attempts to understand this complex domain would have been partial at best. I thank the Syndicate of the University of Kerala and our former Vice Chancellor Professor V. P. Mahadevan Pillai for the gracious award of funds for innovative projects from the State Plan to the Centre for Cultural Studies, which helped me complete this project in time. I am deeply indebted to Professor Babu Cherian and the Benjamin Bailey Foundation whose unwavering trust in me kept me going through each stage of this intellectual journey. I have no words to thank Sreenath Sreedharan, Managing Editor, Orient BlackSwan, who combined utmost professionalism with ethics, empathy and punctuality, so much so that he made publishing a volume of this kind blend seamlessly with the joy, warmth and diligence of academia. My thanks to that genial young scholar Sidharth Joy, who keeps the Centre for Cultural Studies so vibrantly alive. Many thanks to my friends and colleagues, Babitha, Kalyani, Deepa, Lakshmipriya, Appu, among a host of others, who added in different ways and measures to the collegiality and felicity, so essential to those sailing on perilous projects such as these. Can never thank Pramod Nayar enough, for his friendly 'digs' across the years that kept me digging. I am profoundly indebted to my beloved colleague and friend, Vishnu Narayanan, for helping me pursue my academic lunacies while providing such staunch support in dealing with mundane bureaucracies. Utmost regards to Parvathy Chechi, for always believing in my work and me. Hugs to Shaji Jacob, Sunil Elayidom and P. Pavithran, for the deep bonds of friendship we cherished across decades, and also for nurturing my love for Kerala Studies and cultural studies. My love to my family for putting up with my deliriums and managing to hold me together amidst the often-dreary daily grind of life.

**Meena T. Pillai**

# Introduction

## *Gender, Modernity and Kerala*

MEENA T. PILLAI

Modernity is a complexly entangled phenomenon, with practices and discourses that originated in a distant past constantly shaping contemporary practices and discourses. The often-myopic logic that had marked earlier iterations of the 'modern' in India continue to be re-articulated in present-day debates, even as gendered aspirations and transgressions buried by such prescriptive modernities of the past continue to re-emerge and disrupt extant and emergent schemas for 'managing' and containing them. We are at a crucial juncture where questions around women's clothes, body, menstruation, education, everyday practices and so on, which earlier projects of modernity failed to bury, re-emerge as spectres that haunt and unsettle our present, necessitating a re-reading of India's multiple modernities. This study of a collection of gendered archives of modernity from a small strip of land like Kerala becomes significant in this context. While mainstream academic forays premise discourses with 'progress' as their favoured point of departure, modernity, as explored and theorised in this compilation (against the contextual specificities of Kerala), centres its investigative crux on marginalised, unexplored and less discernible gendered narratives. To this end, the volume draws upon archival materials that ranges from some of the earliest textual iterations of gender since Kerala's palpable engagements with modernity, to its variant contemporary digital representations.

This expansive collection of essays on gender and modernity attempts to survey, map and critique Kerala's varied engagements with the problematics of modernity vis-à-vis their complex sociocultural engagements with gender. Spanning a diverse geography, as also the rich material, cultural and critical terrains offered by Kerala, this academic foray into modernity seeks to address a broad array of subjects and experiences that dynamically mediate fomentations of the modern at different spaces and times from asymmetric social locations. It seeks to reread the existing corpus of literature on Kerala's geocultural transformations that map its shifts from the 'pre-modern' to the 'modern', foregrounding the argument that pivotal to the region's experience and engagements with modernity was a salience of gender. While modernity has been postulated as a shared sense of the new, it is imperative to view Kerala's many modernities as a process of careful negotiations with, and disembedding from, its many social and religio-ritualistic certitudes, alongside the strategic retainment or re-deployment of select 'convenient traditions'. The conflicts and negotiations between the two—the avowed and the disavowed gendered traditions and cultural idioms and their chequered cartographies—continue to frame and curate the region's contemporary social worlds.

This book attempts to bring under scrutiny Kerala's experience of modernity and its sociocultural manifestations, its ambiguities and paradoxes, by critically looking at gender as a performative, political and material experience that is intimately woven into the social fabric of the region. Through essays that critically interrogate modernity and its hegemonic underpinnings, this critical endeavour attempts to map the ways in which the gendered subject gets discursively imagined/formed amidst the region's multiple engagements with its own socio-political imaginaries and the world outside. The book aims to bring to the fore the ruptures and compromises which shaped the cultural as well as historical structures of thought and feeling, that have constituted (or continue to constitute) a sense of the 'modern', spelling out the attitudinal shifts—or its lack thereof—that define/circumscribe gendered desires, practices, utterances, acts and rituals. To this end, the book views 'modernity' as transient metaphors or points of reference that will bring into perspective the slow, nonlinear, often messy, contradictory, complex dialectics of sedimentation and innovation of ideas into practices, practices into cultures, and cultures into epistemic systems. It attempts to think through the myriad poles through which modernities are experienced, not in the sense of a linear shift—from the 'pre-modern' to the 'modern', and onto the 'post-' and 'hyper-' phases of the phenomenon—but rather as contextualised by the politics, paradoxes and practices through which *being modern/performing modernity* is inhabited and lived.

Most of the essays in this volume can be located under the ambit of cultural studies, in/of Kerala, opening new fissures and continuities that challenge established distinctions between canonical domains of learning and the emergent everyday, between hierarchical epistemologies and non-generic arenas of enquiry. In that sense, the volume looks at marginalised actors, 'disappeared' texts, buried contexts, epochal discontents, and unruly subjectivities that went into the historical and cultural (un)making of the region, which then become sites/archives of critical investigation. The fraught interpretative realms/modalities offered by what I call the non-disciplinary/counter-disciplinary terrains of cultural studies in Kerala open the scope for a radical restructuring of accepted pedagogies and research methodologies. Thus, the volume is also part of a larger project to address the ambivalences of theorising and practising cultural studies in the discursive cartographies of Kerala. In venturing beyond representative texts, canonical figures, favoured idioms and celebrated histories, this selection hopes to disturb/unsettle the constraints of dominant narratives in the field, facilitating nuanced critical engagements.

Furthermore, this compilation presents itself at a critical juncture in the region's history when, once again, the prescriptive conditions that evolved out of the gendered parameters of modernity are discursively being reappraised in the public sphere. If Kerala's modernity can and must be read as a chronologically evolving, polyvalent negotiation between revered, surviving archives of tradition and the rational–curious 'modern' citizen, an analysis of its gendered/gendering influences must venture beyond reductive projects that merely seek to map patterns of misogyny and incidents of patriarchy. Rather, such a project calls for a theoretically informed critical investigation into the pre-emptive logic that emphatically mediated the ideational filters by which gender has been read in the region, while accommodating the many omissions and under-archived sites of gendered oppression.

The volume's title shares an indebted resemblance to Rita Felski's book, *The Gender of Modernity*, and acknowledges her leitmotifs that run parallel to the principal undertakings and engagements of the book—refactoring the modernity of gender and the gendering of modernity. The attempt here is not to reify 'a feminist theory of the modern', or to enumerate an 'overarching meta-theory of modernity articulated from the vantage point of the present' (Felski 1995, 8–9). Rather, an effort is made to parse modernity as an ensuant and residual category located within the vernacular genderscapes. While gender assumes the discursive centre of the book, it is also interleaved by the ex-centric gender modernities revived as spectral traces. The 'spectrality' of gender is a crucial tangent that informs the cohabitations of tradition and modernity in Kerala.

The book also addresses the trenchant underpinnings of gendering subjects and their unequal lived experiences in a region grappling with multiple noetic forms of modernities. It enquires how projects trafficking modernity produced culpable locations of deferred and discrepant desires, constituting and reconstituting the register of otherness through curated sensibilities and ocular marginalisations. In many ways, this is an attempt at Felskian inquiry—'what if feminine phenomena, often seen as having a secondary or marginal status, were given a central importance in the analysis of the culture of modernity' (Felski 1995, 10). The essays in this collection revisit archives of vernacular cultural imaginary and memory to discursively engage with modernity's cis-gendered heteropatriarchal cartographies as charted through literary, cultural and lexical matrices. The resultant engagements are methods for exorcising the 'Malayali' historical amnesia, unsettling the myth of material, moral and gender parity that has come to occupy recent recapitulations of the region's trysts with modernity.

While strikingly varied in content, the ten inquisitive essays that comprise this collection find common ground in their archival depth and in their aims to evolve novel, unique, vernacular conceptualisations of modernity. Even as these essays straddle gender, Kerala modernity and their attendant methodologies, the book situates the modalities of gender in varying contexts, including, but not limited to, print modernity, vernacular and bilingual lexicography, twentieth-century theatre and its queer representations, women's travel narratives, early Malayalam novels and women's fictional worlds, early modern historiography, gastronomic cultures, sartorial moralities and reform movements, televisual patriarchies and digital misogynies. With a critical emphasis on forgotten archives, less explored narratives and non-canonised texts, this compilation investigates the variant utterances sedimented at the interstices of Kerala's sociocultural history using gender as a primary critical filter.

This exciting collection of essays has an ambitious sweep from the phobic and erotic in mediaeval myths around the monstrous feminine, to contemporary gender dissent by digital counter-publics. By critically situating the transgressive 'uncanny' feminine as the primary point of departure, this compilation problematises the modernist frameworks of Kerala that continue to be fraught with the spectral imaginings of gender. Acknowledging the persistent fluidities of gendered anxieties, this book inevitably thinks anew the paradigms of 'recency' and 'reason' that fail to account for the multiplicities entailed in the visions of modernity. Thus, it also becomes a re-positing and reclaiming of the desiring socii. The modalities of 'regional' modernity cannot be redacted from the interpellant subjectivities and intersubjectivities that get articulated against the ideations of pleasure and desire; this makes the reclaiming even more compelling.

The mobilities of traveling bodies are as important a vector as the genderedness of sewn-up bodies. The book's excavation of the gendered traveller bespeaks a strain of regional modernity that is both vernacular and cosmopolitan. The iterations of vernacular cosmopolitanism could also be traced in the idioms of a socio-affective space like a kitchen in Kerala, where complex transactions of different spatio-temporal registers have happened through different textual genres like the cookbook. In addition to the problematisation of such transactions, the book also intensifies the debates around the disruptive ruptures and coalescences that agents of global modernity, like television, facilitate in the lifeworlds of regional modernity. Even as the volume shies away from imbuing a homogeneity to Kerala's or India's many modernities, it does not foreclose itself from conversing with the cosmopolitan transactions either. Even though the compilation finds its cohesion in the vernacularising of the region's multiple modernities, its imaginaries are not parochial.

While the essays in the volume have consistently tried to engage with the multifaceted nature of Kerala's modernities and its changing relation with gender as an idea and as practice, they differ in the ways in which they 'confront', 'unsettle' and 'disquiet' the historical and the mundane, the collective and the subjective, the traditional and the new. To this end, the collection is divided into three sections.

The first section, titled 'Confronting Histories', locates the 'memory crisis' (Terdiman 1993) woven into feminist, Marxist and liberal recollections of the nineteenth- and twentieth-century narratives of progress and rationality—to retrieve the absented spectres of unruly desires, subjectivities and etymological limits. Against the givenness of aggrandising 'reason' that seems to have determined 'modern' typologies of women, gender, sexuality and sociality, the essays in the section offer critical contestations raising unbidden leaky seats of 'present-past' (Terdiman 1993) that scrutinise both collective and cultural memory.

The section begins with the essay, 'Return of the Uncanny *Yakshi*: Gendering the "Spectres" of Kerala's Modernities', which is an exploration of the *Yakshi* myths that infest Kerala's fraught engagements with the idioms of gender. For one thing, it is a recurrent image of the hauntological trace of the female that survived the sacrificial pyre of masculinised modernity; conversely, it is also a reminder of an unending and insatiable vengeance that 'repeats without being present in the first place' (Fisher 2018, n.p.). The 'unfinishedness' of modernity, as Habermas would put it, thus becomes an evocative reminder of modernity's own spectrality—one that 'insists without ever existing' (Fisher 2018, n.p.). By situating its discursive arc in the specific demography offered by Kerala, this essay, alongside others in the compilation, seeks to study the various fomentations and iterations of modernity in the region, pitching it in contrast with the 'ghastly' homogenisations of both the 'global' and the 'national'. Concurrently, the essay also tries to offer a framework within which could be invoked many of the gendered aspirations and transgressions around questions of women's desires, sexualities, bodies, sartorial choices, travel and reading, that form the subject of other essays in the volume, offering the possibility of reading them as spectres that come to haunt and unsettle the cartographies of the present.

Muraleedharan Tharayil's essay, 'Imaginations of Pleasure: Against a History of Desire in Kerala', seeks to address the performative antecedents that reappraised the perceptions of desire and sexuality in Kerala. This article critically subjects to study incidents as diverse as the theatre performances of the much-acclaimed Ochira Velukutty who enacted female roles, to the more contemporary instances of moral policing, accentuating the manifold routes of sexual desire and pleasure in Kerala. To this end, the essay studies not only disruptive desires but also the possibilities of dissent within seemingly non-subversive acts, thereby spelling out the ways in which structures of desire figure within the popular sociocultural imaginations of the region.

'Re-reading *Indulekha:* Intimate Hierarchies in the Ambiguities of Sanskritised Registers and Domesticated Social Space' by Arya K. attempts to explore how women's creative cultures were strategically excluded from the formal literary and aesthetic categories constructed by the canonical and patriarchal registers of genres like the novel in Malayalam. The essay studies *Indulekha* to understand how 'literariness', as a constructed attribute of the text, and 'discrete' patriarchal linguistic codes of the novel fashion the ideal woman and her aptitudes. By charting the ways in which androcentric modes of canonisation systematically excluded women's experiential, imaginative and affective histories, even as it sheds light on the fashioning of a distinctly middle-class savarna woman, the essay draws attention to the gendered paradoxes writ large within Kerala's literary modernity.

'Stree, Purushan, Napumsakan: Shaping Femininities and Effeminacies in Early-Nineteenth-Century Kerala' by Maalavika Ajayakumar is a critique of select lexicographic texts against the context of gender and Kerala's nascent modernity. She examines the imbrications of the lexical and ideological matrices in solidifying gendered markers of identity in Kerala by reading the entries pertaining to gender in the Benjamin Bailey dictionaries. This study attempts to trace the trajectory of gendered Malayalam terms, the essentialist criteria that buttress their definitions, and the socio-symbolic contexts and ideational filters that informed this process of 'gendered meaning-making' in early modern-Kerala.

The formative context of the second section, 'Unsettling Praxes', underscores the intimate contingencies of gendered bodies in lived ecologies of 'transformative' commitments coerced upon by/through projects of modernity. Focussing on the acts of women reading, writing, travelling, dressing, sewing and cooking, the section unravels the gendered performative economies of 'bargaining' with multiple talons of emergent modernities and their agents.

The section begins with Meera C.'s essay 'Fashioning the Reading Woman in Colonial Kerala: A Woman Reader's Memoir in Perspective', which investigates the fashioning of a historical woman reader in Kerala, charted against the ideations of femininity in late-nineteenth-century Kerala. It explores reminiscences of reading by women in relation to the fashioning of proper and respectable gendered subjects in the sociocultural moment under consideration, locating reading as a practice and a discursive site that visibilises gendered inhabitations and negotiations of modernity in the region.

In its bid to look at the gendered economies of travel and mobility, Sucheta Sankar V.'s essay 'Liminal Modernities: At the Intersections of Travel Discourses, Gender and Kerala (1880s–1920s)' explores discourses on travel in Kerala between 1880 and 1925, and offers novel readings on the 'gendered traveller'. It reflects on early travel discourses in Malayalam as a springboard for theorising the liminality and *in-betweenness* of modernity, specifically in the backdrop of the late nineteenth- and early twentieth-century Kerala. The essay postulates the interplay of gender within the protean mobility practices and emergent cultures of travel in the region, exploring its interventions in the fraught, dynamic relationship between travel and modernity.

Arya A., in her essay 'Sewing Malayali Christian Women: Missionary Makings of Sartorial Morality and "Modern" Domesticity in Travancore', draws on nineteenth-century missionary archives and proto-novels penned by Christian authors alongside a critical inspection into the 'sewing' cultures popularised by the mission to map how sartorial practices were mediated to fashion the category of the 'Malayali Christian Woman'. The essay dwells upon the twin projects of 're-sartorialisation' and 're-socialisation', contrived at the interstices of caste and religion, which reiterated gendered performance of labour and 'modern' domesticities.

'Cookbooks from Kerala: Creative Adaptations and Inscriptions of Alternative Modernities' by Gigy J. Alex emphasises how micro-narratives on food can be emplaced within the discourses on/of modernity and how the genre of the 'cookbook' could be read as a facilitator of modernity. Her study becomes significant in that it postulates a novel interpretive filter by premising cookbooks as cultural artefacts and 'gastronomic agents' that serve as potent sites within which alternate modernities can be moulded and affirmed.

The essays in the third section, 'Disquieting Continuities', shed light on newer and evolving aspects of Kerala's modernity—its trans-local possibilities following the advent of electronic media, and the new socialities that are imagined and discursively fashioned through this technologically mediated modernity. This section attempts to study the various ways in which women's bodies and their gendered performances become new enunciatory sites that embody the negotiations between modernity and tradition. To this end, the essays in this section delve into how continuities are 'disquieting' and 'disquieted' through two familiar, yet fraught, historical events that have (re)defined women's domestic and social agency—the advent of television modernity following the introduction of television in Kerala, and the networked gender resistances that the emergence of a digital public sphere has enabled.

This section has two seminal essays. Benita Acca Benjamin's 'Television Modernity and Mediated Femininities in Kerala' maps the trajectories of Kerala's televisual modernities and its concomitant ideological articulations of femininity as facilitated by television. Her study sheds light on the ways in which television provided novel terrains for mediating the gendered spatial hierarchies, anxieties and desires prevalent in and around the time when television was introduced in the region. To this end, the essay delves into various domestic and social hierarchies, thus situating an action as mundane as television-viewing within competing power structures. The essay looks at the gendered viewer as a citizen–subject and consumer–citizen whose performative axes are simultaneously contingent on heteropatriarchal assumptions and consumerist aspirations, reifying various gendered cultural ideals that have gained traction in the region.

The compilation concludes with Jobson Joshwa's essay 'Who is Afraid of the Raped Nun?: Discourses, Contestations and Digital Publics', which subjects digital media archives to explore the contraventional digital engagements that arose in retaliation to the affective mobilisation garnered by a group of nuns against a bishop accused of rape. Identifying the nuns' protest as a public assembly of performative bodies that form a continuum with affectively charged digital feminisms, this essay teases out the possibilities of transposing these new medialities into illocutionary assemblages. Even as the essay acknowledges the instituting of new archives of feelings brought about by the affective womanspeak (Pillai 2022), it locates the matrices of gender and modernity within the seemingly projectile trajectories of Kerala's secularisation and Renaissance, enmeshed in the sedimentary fault lines of communalisation of politics and religious pastoralisms, to argue that Kerala's tryst with modernity remains deferred and continues to be haunted by spectres of gender.

## References

Felski, Rita. 1995. *The Gender of Modernity*. Cambridge: Harvard UP.

Fisher, Mark. 2018. *K-punk: The Collected and Unpublished Writings of Mark Fisher (2004–2016)*. London: Repeater. <https://libgen.is/book/index.php?md5=11F9AD944AF6E3217E030B610DD0FAE8>.

Pillai, Meena T. 2022. *Affective Feminisms in Digital India: Intimate Rebels*. London: Taylor and Francis.

Terdiman, Richard. 1993. *Present Past: Modernity and the Memory Crisis*. Ithaca: Cornell UP.

# Confronting Histories

ONE

# Return of the Uncanny *Yakshi*

## *Gendering the 'Spectres' of Kerala's Modernities*

MEENA T. PILLAI

Spectres of gender haunt Kerala's engagements with modernity. Gendered bodies, desires, imaginations, anxieties and repressions, all come to accost the 'new modern' in the innumerable fields of inhabitation that the British colonial empire and native reform projects had sought to institute it in. But then, neither the project of colonial mythmaking nor the zeal for reform can entirely be claimed as the monopoly of the British. This small strip of land had been subjected to different waves of colonisation, which—alongside a rich history of travel and trade, rendered possible by its strategic location at the tip of the Indian subcontinent in a crucial maritime aisle—engendered the possibility of cosmopolitan imaginations within vernacular expressions for millennia. However, that said, one has to concede that encounters with 'other' worlds or trade/travel mobilities need not necessarily translate into structures of cosmopolitan consciousness, or a corporeal, social or religious readiness to engage with the new. Nevertheless, it did create a protracted environment conducive to the condition of being modern in respective epochs of time, without attributing either singularity, superiority or a sense of rupture to such 'new orders of being'.

The new political institutions of nineteenth-century Kerala made it imperative to conceive of a temporal break that could make possible more politically charged imaginations around a progressive ideal, a new subject who violently broke away from the shackles of 'barbarity'. In that sense, the 'pre-modern' was as much an invention of modernity as it was an attempt to debunk the 'farrago of legendary nonsense' (Logan 1887, 244) that constituted the pre-modern and necessitated a conscious breach in time so fundamental to Renaissance refashionings. However, this new relationship with time, new calendars of the self that involved structural redrafting of social contracts, were also characterised by deep ambivalences, the central fault lines of which emerged most crucially on the terrain of gender. Literary archives offer vital clues on how modernity might not have been a rupture in time, but could have constituted continuities and resolutions that both reveal and conceal such paradoxes. It has been argued that the revisionist zeal of the Renaissance did not radically materialise all of a sudden during the nineteenth century, and could be traced back to the early registers of pre-modern subaltern histories of resistance and confrontations with entrenched gendered, caste and feudal structures (Sreekumar 2020, 22).

Kerala's encounter with modernity has historically been cast on the bedrock of male scopic, libidinal and political economies that systematically attempted to manage/tame the sexual agency and desire of other marginalised gender players as cultural signs in need of reform. The 'unreformed' and the 'undead'—those that refused to be written into the intensively oppressive registers of a patriarchal performative modernity, and, in that sense, deflected its benevolent interments—come back as 'hauntological' gender trace, both phobic and erotic, bearing/baring the historic wounds of half or hurriedly buried traumas. Within the multiple modalities of many forgotten folktales, rituals, discourses and practices, one can look for the epistemic gender erasures in Kerala's experiences of modernity. This essay attempts a symptomatic study of some of the temporal slippages that rendered certain social scripts around the representation of feminine agency illegible, in the process institutionalising the region's 'scopic regimes of modernity' (Jay 102), its hegemonic, visual model of the modern era (102). It locates the spectral figure of the *Yakshi* at the intersections of epistemic and semantic violence, in the process attempting to understand the blind spots of gender within the discourses of modernity in the region. The transgressional desires of the spectral feminine form the fault lines that reframe its extant locutions on female bodies and sexualities.

If one goes back in history to look at the Manipravala literature of the thirteenth and fourteenth centuries, born out of the hybrid linguistic engagements of Sanskrit and Malayalam, it is evident that it did evince a high degree of urbanism that Kerala experienced during the mediaeval times and revolved mostly around the *ganikas*, or courtesans, who were educated and refined women. Kesavan Veluthat has pointed out that 'The curriculum seems to have included music, dance, painting, story-telling, versification, kavyas in both Sanskrit and Manipravalam, juggling, chess, different games played during the Onam festival, gambling, and so on. So also, they were adept in the different ways in which they could entertain their patrons (or clients?)' (2013, n.p.). However, the courtesans of the Manipravala *kavyas* were vastly different from those of the Sanskrit *kavyas*.

> While the ganika is generally the female counterpart of the nagaraka in Sanskrit literature, they are the central figures in Manipravalam. This is no contradiction; but it is important that the nagaraka hero's presence is much less visible than that of the ganika heroine who is ubiquitous in the texts. This may be explained against the peculiar social reality in Kerala. Most non-Brahmana upper castes were matrilineal and women had a much stronger presence in Kerala. Marriage as an institution was not very deeply entrenched, with sambandham or a somewhat loose liaison being the accepted practice. It was not just that the Namputiri Brahmanas courted such alliances—members of other castes too entered into such alliances from one's own caste or from other, upper, castes. Women in such a situation had a greater presence than men. (Veluthat 2013, n.p.)

Nevertheless, the fact remains that this greater presence does not translate into agential representations in the literature of that period, which reduced the *ganikas* to mere instruments of pleasure, putting in place a central paradox that would haunt Kerala in the times to come. One sees in later readings of the *ganikas* of Manipravala literature an extreme fear of their sexuality, adopting a Victorian 'moral high ground' that attempts to shrug off the feminine uncanny, which, however, comes to unsettle the neat 'canniness' of modernity whose 'reason' is always already haunted by what it seeks to exclude. For example, many of the *Yakshi* myths and other gendered spectres that were in currency during the mediaeval period are resonant tropes that illustrate the continuities and fluidities in terms of gendered anxieties, between what is marked off as the 'pre-modern' and the 'modern'. There are many *Yakshi* myths around 'Neeli' from Neeliyamman, Pazhayanoor Neeli, Panchavankatu Neeli and Kalliankattu Neeli, among numerous others. There are Neeli stories across South India—in Kerala, Tamil Nadu and Karnataka. Vijaya Ramaswamy has pointed out how Neeli myths are widely variant in nature as they move from one time and space to another, or across genres like ballads, folk tales or dramatic poetic forms Villupattu or Yakshagana (2009, 60–61). What is most interesting, though, is the manner in which Neeli stories 'zigzag between two bi-polarities', where

> she is sometimes the dreaded Neeli pey (the term "pey" can be broadly translated as demoness), sometimes the feared and worshipped goddess Isakki Amman and yet again the revered Karaikkal Peyar of the *Periyapuranam*, a 12th-century Saivite hagiographical text. The versatile Neeli thus goes through a range of imaging from a prostitute to a proselytising Jaina nun to the saintly Shaivite Nayanar "Peyar". (Ramaswamy 2009, 60)

Most of these stories invoke the fear of formidable female sexuality that refuses masculine closures or patriarchal 'caste' laws, coming 'un-dead' to fulfil thwarted desires or pending revenge.

In essence, many of the extant *Yakshi* myths mark the gendered anxieties of a caste-bound and gendered feudal past; if we remember, in a number of the stories, the *Yakshi*'s vengeance is portrayed as the ire against a deceitful or sexually violent upper-caste man (most often a nambuthiri). In the southern ballads of Kerala, too, there are many Neelis, some of which record her origins as a Devadasi in Pazhakaiyoor in Tamil Nadu who is cheated and killed by a brahmin, and her subsequent rebirth in order to avenge the injustice meted out to her by killing the brahmin and the entire village, and thereafter her journey to Venad to be consecrated as a deity (Gangadharan 2005, 17). If the *Yakshi* myths emerged in the first place from the anxieties of such a feudal past and its attempt to 'manage' gendered transgression, or repercussions against gendered violence, it is interesting that the same anxieties and a similar thrust to 'manage' the transgressive feminine operate within the discourses of Victorian morality, and missionary and alternative modernities that emerge in the late-nineteenth and twentieth centuries. Many of them continue into the popular terrains of the culture industry, such as cinema and popular magazines and literature of the twentieth century, and to the new millennial digital mediascapes. Thus, such gendered spectres can be read as revealing the similarities and continuities between 'pre-modern' and 'modern' attempts to manage gender.

If one looks at the folk and subaltern traditions of Kerala, whether it be the *Vadakkan pattukal, Thekkan pattukal, Payyannur pattukal, Chengannoraathi, Pachalloor pathikam*, etc., or ritual art forms like Mudiyattam, there is a discourse of gender that is subversive of hegemonic conceptions (Sreekumar 2020, 23). In an analysis of the women characters who inhabit the sites of oral literatures in Malayalam, K. R. Sajitha refers to figures such as Unniyarcha, Purushadevi Amma and Neelikeshi as 'models who mount a challenge to the roles determined for women' (2012, 33), even as they remain immured within the complex structures of power and representation that mark the literary conventions and the social conditions which gave birth to them. The *Purushadevi ammappattu*, which sings the valour of a valiant woman of the Pennarasunadu, or the *Panchavankadu Neelikadha*, which speaks of a spectral transformation of feminine power, from *Thekkan pattukal* or southern ballads, break the *ganika*-centred representational economies of Manipravala literature, establishing an enchanting, haunting narrative on the enigmas of feminine identity and selfhood. Nevertheless, they engender a trauma that would haunt Kerala's modernities, a crisis of representation foregrounding a fear of the return of the uncanny, creating a disjunct between the desires of a rather shoddily buried past and an uneasy present.

The vernacular *Yakshi* myth can be read as speaking in complex terms to the very paradoxes within Western enlightenment logic. If one looks at early missionary engagements, for instance, it is really interesting to see registers of science seamlessly blending with registers of divinity and superstition. The routes through which modernity's so-called 'rational', instrumental enlightenment logic percolated in Kerala is complex precisely because it came primarily through missionary engagement, which, within itself, was simultaneously unsettled and modified by the debates on reason in the West. When narratives of colonial and missionary modernity, as they emerged in Kerala, sought to 'know' and engage with the gendered spectres, they were trying to know and manage an 'other', both in terms of gender and coloniality, but one that also spoke to the very fractures within their own epistemologies.

The figure of the *Yakshi*, as a spectre of modernity, is a trope that threatens to collapse neat distinctions by returning from time, both as memory and trauma. A symbol of the radical potency of the feminine to disrupt the newfound order and logic of the modern, the *Yakshi* then, is a question that Kerala's modernities—colonial, vernacular, subaltern, among many others—had to grapple with and resolve. The *Yakshi* is a gender trace, as well as a reminder of other subversive traces, an archive that warrants erasure but creates an excess. She is the uncanny in Kerala's traumatic encounter with modernity's gender projects, instilling terror and also possession, threatening the patrifocal and patriarchal heterosexist certitudes of modernity by puncturing it with gendered expressive, threatening, transgressive possibilities. She also unsettles its claimed 'newness' with uncertainties, a fear of the known and the unknown, the familiar and the unfamiliar, the *heimlich* and *unheimlich*, as Freud would call it: an unwanted haunting from the past, where, as uncanny, she is that 'class of the frightening which leads back to what is known of old and long familiar' (Freud 1919, 340).

The many attempts to write gender into the registers of modernity through various processes like refashioning the body, education, and reform, are all thus fraught with a disconnect between a complex present that attempts to make sense and resolve the trauma of an elusive past that itself can never fully be remembered, archived, yet clamouring for forgetfulness. The *Yakshi*, thus, in effect, is a traumatic memory, 'between remembrance and erasure, producing a history that is, in its very events, a kind of inscription of the past; but also a history constituted by the erasure of its traces' (Caruth 2013, 79). The gendered spectres emerge not only as a paradox that defies 'rational' attempts to 'know' the gendered other, but also as part of the vernacular reformist attempt to negotiate with and 'resolve' paradoxes of gender through neat, gendered divisions conceived in its imaginaries, whether between private/public, or homely/unhomely.

There are many complex inscriptions of gendered ideology in Kerala's ballad traditions—the *Vadakkan pattukal* celebrates tales of the valiant Unniyarcha, and the *Thekkan pattukal* or the southern ballads carry references to Pennarasunadu and the valiant queen Purusha Devi—all of which need new gendered acts of archaeology, infusing their archetypes with new politics. The pulaya queen Kotharani ruled Kokothamangalam near Nedumangad, and there are many tales speaking of her bravery. In this context, one can read rituals like *pulappedi*—where on certain days of the year men from 'untouchable' castes had the right to carry off an upper-caste woman seen out of the precincts of her home—as not just a fear of the lower castes polluting the woman found outside her ken, but literally the fear of women's mobility and transgression. It was a ritual that nailed the *Yakshi* who dared step outside the boundaries of her home. Even as such rituals were banned by the late seventeenth century, they lived on in traces, embodied in the fear of the 'unhomely' woman that is central to modernity's imaginations of the 'new home'. The *Yakshi*'s unbound ecstasy, her *jouissance*, in conditions of homelessness, the subversive pleasures and sexual abandon so central to her disruptive energy, and the freedom and rapture that only irreverence can bring her, are all to be tamed and nailed, in the bizarre transformation of her carnivalesque spaces into 'hallowed' homes.

Works like Kottarathil Sankunni's compilation of pre-modern legends in his *Aithihyamala* unfold a spectral geography of gender. The cartographies and logical frameworks of modernity are troubled/tickled by the transgressive potential and tenuous boundaries that stem from its own imaginations/intimidations that hover around the spectral. Gender is the *badha* (an evil spirit) that returns from the past, across the breaches imagined by modernity, one which it failed to exorcise or propitiate with a proper resting place. In fact, it comes to infest Kerala's modernity, a return of the repressed that could never quite be repressed either in the past or in the uneasy present of modernity. Women or gender marginals—in not exactly being the subject of Renaissance reform projects, but as objects in need of such reforms—become both remnants of the past as well as symbols of the uncanny, forced into the peculiar liminalities of social imaginations, poised between desire and fear, extreme fascination and deep-seated abhorrence, fantasy and the real, carrying an archival excess that refuses 'reading'.

The work of compiling the legends and lore of pre-modern Kerala was begun by Kottarathil Sankunni at the turn of the twentieth century and published in 1909. Curiously enough, this is also the year Poykayil Appachan founded his Prathyaksha Raksha Daiva Sabha that mounted a trenchant critique of dominant religions while attempting to reconstruct the histories and mythic pasts of Dalit communities in Kerala. Sanal Mohan's arguments regarding the transformation of Yohannan into a mythical being in the consciousness of Dalits and his exploits being imbued with divinity and miraculousness are especially pertinent here (2005). Udaya Kumar has argued that C. Ayyappan's ghost narrators

> interrupt the enchantment of foundational idioms of the modern social domain. Their autobiographical acts stage the unaccommodation of the social for Dalit subjects, foreground the residue of stigma in its resistance to recompense and its constantly renewed intimacy with life, and respond with idioms of mythical violence. Yet, in the middle of their fierce work of vengeance and destruction, they cry inconsolably, exclaiming why their lives and loves had to smash to

> smithereens like a clay pot thrown on a rock. Their ghost-speech, the litany of rage and lament with its unflinching grip on time, is—to conjure with Poykayil Yohannan's redemptive trope—the letter that Ayyappan insistently brings before contemporary Kerala. (2013, 188–89).

The *Yakshi* stories of *Aithihyamala*, too, demand such symptomatic readings. They need not be considered entirely antithetical to history since they resonate with a cultural power deeper than more transient isolated historical events.

What is to be noted is that while in many parts of the Indian subcontinent, *Yakshis* were rural deities worshipped from the second century BC, later on often absorbed into Jainism and Buddhism, Kerala's ancient folklore seems to transform them into the monstrous feminine, legitimising worshipping them only through a co-option into the pantheon of secondary deities of brahmanical Hinduism. In the grand theatrics of modernity in Kerala, *Aithihyamala*'s *Yakshi* myths can be seen as symptomatic of a deep-seated schizophrenic anxiety around gender. T. K. Ramachandran has argued that the *Yakshis* of Kerala, in being different from their counterparts elsewhere, are projectiles of the fear and aggression in the male psyche, and they might also typify feelings of post-coital rejection and guilt, adding that the fascination/repugnance dyad that is discernible in their portrayals points to the deep-seated schizophrenia of the times (1995, 121). Ramachandran also cites examples of Cherusseri's *Krishnagadha*, which employs highly sensual picturisations to evoke repugnance, which is hardly surprising when we note that the explicitly stated aim of the work is to inculcate ascetic rejection, arguing that the same trope repeats itself in the performance traditions of Kerala where 'the fear of female sexuality and its essential concomitant, the feeling that it has to be curbed lest it become destructive, is the well-spring of the poignant climactic scene of the famous Kathakali piece—Keechakavadham' (121).

Raja Ravi Varma has a famous painting titled *Lady in the Moon Light* (Figure 1, 1889), which has also been called *Yakshi* by many (Varma 1889). Varma's mother incidentally was said to have been possessed by a *Yakshi* when she was pregnant with him, by a *Yakshi* who 'resided' in a temple dedicated solely to her, a little away from other buildings and shrouded by trees, and yet situated within the palace walls (Pai 2011). However, if the lady in the moonlight is a *Yakshi*, her mythic, spectral figurations, and her transgressive potential have been rendered docile and tame in the painting, as though the painter, trained and attuned to the exigencies of imagining the gendered modern, cannot fathom or map the unruly imaginations of gender. The masculinist ideations of mythic narratives that modernity entailed, with the foregrounding of an ideal feminine as a prerequisite for participation in its visual iconography and aesthetics, can help one re-read the painting today as an ideological abstraction of Kerala's modernity.

However, it is in another painting on similar lines by Ravi Varma that the gender paradoxes of the experience of modernity gain a new valence. This is the painting of *Mohini on a Swing* (Figure 2, 1890), where the repressed sexuality of the *Lady in the Moon Light* erupts into a *jouissance*, where the beseeching look for cultural sanction—so implicit in the latter—transforms into a sense of abandon, and irreverence for new social regulations and sanctions, in the former. The 'temptress' painting, however, is the transgressive model, which later on would become part of the stock iconography of the *Yakshi* myth in modernity in its cinematic imaginations in the twentieth century: white-sari-clad, voluptuous, sensual, with feet that are not planted on the ground, gliding, swinging, offering sublime summits of sensuous adventures, rife with scopophilic pleasures but harnessing the potential of danger and death in every flight to fulfilment. It would be interesting to read *Lady in the Moon Light* as an exorcised *Yakshi* or Mohini, embodying modernity's new registers of exorcism or *badha ozhippikkal* as an act of expunging female desire. Such codes make it imperative that the 'hetero-normative' female host body, upon being possessed, has to be physically tortured, caned to conformity and docility, to drive away the *Yakshi*, and, by extension, everything that she symbolises—'unfeminine' vengeance, rational-strategic manoeuvres to hurt the

Figure 1: *Lady in the Moon Light* (courtesy Wikimedia Commons)

Figure 2: *Mohini on a Swing* (courtesy Wikimedia Commons)

hierarchically positioned male enemy and, of course, expressive desire (both libidinal and affective).

Thus, the possessed gendered body becomes a submissive marker—an open call for the scientific-religious male to make the female host body uninhabitable by an act of violence. This tacit permission bestowed on the man—to physically abuse the 'desiring' woman, to kill her 'threatening' inclinations, and to bring her back to the domain of submissive domesticity—has numerous contemporary translations in Kerala, where many women's bodies have been brutalised in the name of *badha ozhippikkal.* This act of exorcism resurfaces and is valorised, especially in Malayalam films and other media texts wherein the exorcised woman is always shown as happy and grateful to her male exorcist (the film *Manichithrathazhu* [1993] being the popular cult classic example) for having 'cured' her of her threatening desires (even though it often comes at the cost of dehumanising acts of physical torture).

This is where attitudes of women towards domestic/spousal violence, as reported by the National Family Health Survey 4 report (2015–16), needs to be historicised as a vestige of the 'taming' that marks modernity's operative logic mounted against gendered transgression. According to the survey, the total percentage of women who 'agree that a husband is justified in hitting or beating his wife for … at least one specific reason' in Kerala is 69.4 per cent (International Institute for Population Sciences 2017, 547). This is also above the national average, which is placed at 51.6 per cent by the same survey (543). The enunciation of contemporary modern 'exorcised' women in favour of husbands possessing the right to resort to domestic violence if the desiring wife transgressed her legitimate boundaries can be read historically as the muted speech of happy exorcised *Yakshis*. The survey can be ironically read as new submissive codes indicating their gratefulness to abusive exorcist *kathanars* (Christian priests, often known to carry out such exorcisms), who nailed them to blissful domestic deity-dom, the myth and mystique of which modernity installed as the 'logic' of being modern gendered subjects in Kerala.

It is in this context that one of the most famous stories of the *Aithihyamala* (2009)—that of Kadamattathu Kathanar, which narrates the tale of a *Yakshi* who becomes a pestilence for east-bound travellers from Thiruvananthapuram—could be placed. She would don the form of a young and beautiful courtesan and waylay travellers, asking for lime to smear on betel leaves, enticing them in the process and luring them into the forest to kill them and suck their blood. Interestingly, Kathanar gives her lime smeared on an iron nail, which, by his magic, is actually pinned to her head, making her docile and his slave. In most Western vampire myths, the vampire can only be killed by driving a stake through the heart. Interestingly, the heart never seems to be the object of containment in the *Yakshi* tales, but the brain is. Here, the transgressive feminine actually solicits the dominant power of the 'scientific' religious man, yielding rich subtexts that offer vital clues on gendered colonial agendas, the ways of colonising the female by sabotaging her reason and thought. *Yakshi* as a gender trace and her graphic death in modernity can therefore be read as symptomatic of the Renaissance logic of the scientific male.

The *Yakshi* also bears testimony to a repressed history of the violence of colonial modernity. Bailey's 1846 dictionary defines a *Yakshan* as 'a demi-god, attendant' on Cubera, while a *Yakshi* is recognised as wife to Cubera or a *Yaksha*, and a *Yakshini* is also defined as 'a sort of female fiend, attached to the service of Durga, and frequently maintaining[,] like a sylph or fairy[,] an intercourse with mortals' (1846, 645). Less than three decades later, Herman Gundert's dictionary records *Yakshan* as a demigod, whereas *Yakshi* is 'a nightmare, also nocturnal pollution … demoniacal possession' (1871, 869). The complete eliding of 'othered' and vernacular strands of meaning, while incorporating the new meaning of 'pollution' is a lexical violence of modernity. The semantic and expressive intent of these lexical inscriptions underscores the gender biases of the discourse of modernity in Kerala. They conscript the manner in which emerging social practices around gender—as well as new ways of constructing systems of gender representations and gender identifications—

align around the axes of power–knowledge–subjectivities, revealing the complex social process by which the concepts of 'social gender' and 'sexuality' are imagined and played out. One can see an erasure of the vernacular/folk inflexions of the word 'Yakshi', coupled with a missionary moralism that degraded/denied native animistic beliefs, rituals and divinations. This inflicts a gendered epistemic violence, carefully crafted under the aegis of a missionary modernity-inflected ethnographic gaze, in the process of attempting to undo the prevalent networks of beliefs, ideologies and social practices that create shared meanings for a people or a community.

Such colonial discourses of modernity render transgressive women's lives and practices unintelligible, forcing upon them the alternative between conjugal self-fashioning or demoniacal nimiety as the only choice available, in the process rendering them increasingly marginalised and vulnerable within changing kinship social patterns. Kathanar's *Yakshi*, in this sense, becomes a public spectacle, the myth so necessary to modernity, which, without installing any juridical procedures in place, can nevertheless engage in disciplining and punishing the transgressive feminine through a political ritual that asserts masculine logos and reason. This is the banned *pulappedi* reborn under the sign of modernity, stabilised by print and propelled by a missionary zeal for Victorian codes of female chastity. The edict of 1696 by Kerala Varma banning *pulappedi* and *mannappedi* proclaims that in the event of such 'pollution' happening to a woman, the pollution shall be considered as removed if the woman bathes in a pond and come out (Yesudas 1975, 54). Nearly two centuries later, Gundert's *Yakshi* is ascribed with 'nocturnal pollution'—with no clause for either divinity or redemption—which, in its sexual overtones might reflect the collective neurosis of the age, but more so the schizophrenia that underlies the gender 'projects' of modernity. Thus, reading the *Yakshi*, her deaths and reincarnations, her wanderings between Eros and Thanatos, her spectral speeches that posit exiles and returns, transformations and translations of her pre-modern archival excess under the aegis of the modern, her sexual transgressions and symbolic castrations, all unfurl a thanatographic testimonial that mixes legend and myth to overcome the limits of non-being in narrating histories of gendered defiance.

The scopic and phobic economies that the Yakshi embodies are spectral requisites that counteract the enervating bindings of the social schema. It necessitates what Kristeva terms an 'identification' with the 'enigmas of the body, the dreams, the secret joys, shames, hatreds of the second sex' (1981, 32). The spectral socii are not mere claimants of an 'imaginary potency' (31); they are illocutionary utterers of 'anterior temporal modalities' that beget an 'antinomy' where the ex-centric discourses of the varied marginalia are re-joined (17). This is not just about counterbalancing the incursions of the 'masculine' time. Rather, it is a concerted attempt to chart a new register of temporality that disjuncts 'a certain conception of time: time as project, teleology, linear and prospective unfolding; time as departure, progression, and arrival' (17). This entails a radical revision of the very idea of modernity being a spatio-temporal rupture and a chronological projectile. Modernity is rethought as an ongoing, performative engagement shaped and reshaped by praxes, paradoxes and possibilities.

The *Yakshi* is both a trope and metaphor for Kerala's modernity and its fraught engagements with gender. It is time to rethink the easy collation of Renaissance ideals with Kerala's modernity and place it within the Foucauldian notion of biopower, where modernity is as much a technology of power as a network of strategies of power complicating the many discourses of culture: 'an explosion of numerous and diverse techniques for achieving the subjugations of bodies and the control of populations' (Foucault 1976, 140). Modernity's promise of rationality, as theorised by Jürgen Habermas and vouched for by contemporary historical events in Kerala, remains largely unfulfilled.

At the same time, amidst competing discourses in a fast-transitioning order, emergent dominant discourses enmesh the female subject in networks of power while simultaneously sabotaging traditional assumptions and meanings. This further necessitates the need to specifically look at it through a gendered lens, as an anatomo-politics of the female body with the purpose of making such gendered bodies docile and manageable, while optimising labour and channelising desire. The threat that the *Yakshi* poses in many of the narratives and incapacitation/incarceration is also very much representative of colonial logic. She is an adequate threat, big enough that her actions warrant a reaction from the religious men of science, but not so threatening that the reason of the time cannot overpower and overcome her. The figure of the *Yakshi* could be seen as a perfect bogeywoman for modernity's gender reform project in Kerala.

Despite multiple historical co-options of the transgressive possibilities of the myth, the *Yakshi* also comes to inhabit new social imaginaries in Kerala, where new generations of women claim her as their political pilgrim mother, one whose 'wayward' travels and 'monstrous feminine' desires inspire their own. The bodies of contemporary non-conforming women, as narratives of the *Yakshi*, trace a continuum with the past as sites of her inhabitations in the future, both as memory and feminist myth. These spectres from the past 'possess' their bodies as a Derridean trace that is also 'the locus of a dissociated self' (Foucault 1978, 263). As the irreducible imprint or mark of the repressed within the feminine, the *Yakshi* as 'trace', as the 'impossible', the 'unthinkable', the 'incomprehensible' or the 'unsayable' within the self, is the 'other' that can never be erased, undermining all logocentric structures of presence (Derrida 1978). Her abjection is redeemed/resurrected in millennial resistances mounted by new generations of women, such as that in Sabarimala around the ascribed pollution of menstruating bodies, an eruption from the past that subverts the present, corrupting and contaminating the contemporary hierarchies of logocentric culture and morality, while sparking new insurrections that defy androcentric disciplinary logic. In that sense, she is a Messianic moment (Walter Benjamin 1999), a proto-feminist index from the past that finds redemption and resurrection in the future, an abject trace of the primal repression that haunts/taunts the certitudes of identity, system and order of Kerala's modernity.

## References

Bailey, Benjamin. 1846. *A Dictionary of High and Colloquial Malayalim and English.* Cottayam: Church Missionary Press.

Benjamin, Walter. 1999. 'Theses on the Philosophy of History'. In *Illuminations*, edited by Hannah Arendt. 253–64. New York: Schoken Books.

Caruth, Cathy. 2013. *Literature in the Ashes of History*. Baltimore: John Hopkins UP.

Derrida, Jacques. 1978. *Writing and Difference*. Chicago: Chicago UP.

Foucault, Michel. 1978. 'Nietzsche, Genealogy, History'. In *Nietzsche,* edited by John Richardson and Brian Leiter. 139–64. Oxford: Oxford UP.

———. 1998 [1976]. *The History of Sexuality Vol. 1: The Will to Knowledge.* London: Penguin.

Freud, Sigmund. 1990 [1919]. 'The Uncanny'. In *Art and Literature,* edited by Angela Richards, trans. James Strachey. New York: Penguin.

Gangadharan, Thikkurushi. 2005. *Thekkankathagaanangal.* Thiruvananthapuram: Vijnanamudranam Press.

Gundert, Hermann. 1992 [1871]. *A Malayalam and English Dictionary.* Kottayam: DC Books.

International Institute for Population Sciences (IIPS). 2017. *National Family Health Survey (NFHS-4), 2015–16: India.* Mumbai: IIPS.

Kristeva, Julia. 1981. 'Women's Time'. *Signs* 7(1). 13–35.

Kumar, Udaya. 2013. 'The Strange Homeliness of the Night: Spectral Speech and the Dalit Present in C. Ayyappan's Stories'. *Journal of Humanities and Social Sciences* XVII(1, 2). 177–91.

Jay, Martin. 2011. 'Scopic Regimes of Modernity Revisited'. In *The Handbook of Visual Culture,* edited by Ian Heywood and Barry Sandywell. London: Bloomsbury. 102–15.

Logan, William. 2010 [1887]. *Malabar Manual.* New Delhi: Asian Educational Services.

Mohan, Sanal. 2005. 'Religion, Social Space and Identity: The Prathyaksha Raksha Daiva Sabha and the Making of Cultural Boundaries in Twentieth Century Kerala'. *South Asian Journal of South Asian Studies* 28(1). 35–63.

Pai, Deepanjana. 2011. *The Painter: A Life of Ravi Varma.* New Delhi: Random House.

Ramachandran, T. K. 1995. 'Notes on the Making of Feminine Identity in Contemporary Kerala Society'. *Social Scientist* 23(1/3). 109–23.

Ramaswamy, Vijaya. 2009. 'Tragic Widows or Cunning Witches: Reflections on Representations of Women in Tamil Myths and Legends'. *Economic & Political Weekly* XLIV(12). 57–67.

Sajitha, K. R. 2012. *Vamozhi Roopangalile Lingapadavi*. In *Dalithamakshara Samyuktham*. Kannur: Paridhi Publishers.

Sankunni, Kotarathil. 2009. *Aithihyamaala*. Kottayam: DC Books.

Sreekumar, T. T. 2020. *Ithrakaalam Ketathalla Navodhanathinte Praarambham*. *Mathrubhumi* (November 29). 22–33.

Varma, Raja Ravi. 1889. *Lady in the Moon Light* (Oil on Canvas). *Wikimedia Commons*. 10 Dec 2022, https://commons.wikimedia.org/wiki/File:Raja_Ravi_Varma,_Lady_in_the_Moon_Light_(1889).jpg. 5 Feb 2023.

———. 1890. *Mohini on a Swing*. *Wikimedia Commons*. 26 Nov 2022, https://commons.wikimedia.org/wiki/File:Mohini_on_a_swing.jpg. 5 Feb 2023.

Veluthat, Keshavan. 2013. 'Of Ubiquitous Heroines and Elusive Heroes: The Cultural Milieu of Medieval Manipravala Kavyas from Kerala'. *Foundation Day Lecture*, Indian Council of Historical Research, New Delhi.

Yesudas, R. N. 1975. 'Pulappedi in Kerala'. *Journal of Kerala Studies* 2(2). 41–54.

TWO

# Imaginations of Pleasure

## *Against a History of Desire in Kerala*[1]

MURALEEDHARAN THARAYIL

Ochira Velukutty (1905–54), an actor specialising in female roles, was one of the stars of Malayalam theatre in the early half of the twentieth century. His most celebrated performance was as Vasavadatta, the courtesan in the stage adaptation of Kumaran Asan's poetic work, *Karuna* (1923). According to reports, the play was performed on over six thousand stages inside and outside Kerala, including some in Sri Lanka. Velukutty continued as the heroine even after women started performing on stage in Kerala. Even in *Karuna*, Velukutty played Vasavadatta while her *sakhis* (companions or attendants) were played by female performers. Historians point out that the early theatre actresses of Kerala were often instructed to follow the body language and style defined by Velukutty.

The stardom enjoyed by Velukutty was not in any way exceptional. Kathryn Hansen, in her detailed study of theatrical performances in South Asia, has traced the long history of men playing women's roles on stage and subsequently setting up the norms of feminine grace (2011). Between 1850 and 1940, there were several such celebrated performers like Naslu Sarkari, Jayshankar Sundari and Bal Gandharva in Parsi, Gujarati and Marathi theatres (Hansen 2002). What appears more significant to our discussion are the stories about the offstage 'performances'

---

[1] An earlier version of this paper appeared as 'Shifting Paradigms: Gender and Sexuality Debates in Kerala' in *EPW*, Vol. XLIX, No. 17, 26 April 2014. pp. 70–78.

of Ochira Velukutty. The only biography of the actor currently available, by K. Sreekumar (2006), narrates numerous stories about the hysterics of male spectators enamoured by Velukutty's 'stage persona'. Some assumed him to be a woman, while others knew well that he was a man and still pursued him with love letters and proposals of marriage. He was even abducted a few times and had to be rescued by other members of his troupe. Renowned Malayalam playwright C. L. Jose once recounted his experience of watching Velukutty as Vasavadatta on stage. By then the actor was closer to middle age, had put on weight and even developed a paunch (which he had to hide wearing a tight belt). Still, according to the playwright, 'the grace and oomph' that distinguished his performance was magical (Muraleedharan 2008). Kodungallur Ammini Amma, a female theatre artist much younger to Velukutty, has also narrated her experience of seeing the famed actor during a journey. She was inside a bus and Velukutty was waiting for another bus on the roadside. Passengers in her bus rushed to the windows to see the star, and, in the ensuing commotion, Ammini Amma could get only a glimpse. 'A fair and voluptuous beauty (*sundari*): that's the only way I can describe him', she recounted later (Sreekumar 2006, 119).

The popularity of Velukutty (and other actors who performed female roles) could be perceived as a striking instance of the performative reiteration of the 'feminine' on the early Malayalam stage and the consequent social imaginary. Since the performer here is a man, one is tempted to read these performances as a patriarchal project to fashion the feminine in public imagination as per male gaze and pleasure. But a more nuanced reading in the light of queer theory could reveal the complex social dynamics of those performances, implicitly inscribed in the responses they elicited from various individuals. Most of the instances cited above are men's responses to a carnivalesque performance of the feminine. When Velukutty had more than one show a day, he used to travel from one stage to another without removing his make-up or changing costumes. He was in this 'female' guise on the few occasions when he was abducted. This could tempt us to assume that the male adulation that pursued Velukutty offstage was still aimed at a persona created on stage.

Yet, psychologists working on body image have consistently argued that a person's body image constitutes a dynamic relationship between the individual, the body, and the social environment (Plummer 2002). This view is amply demonstrated by the account of Ammini Amma as described previously. Apparently, she had never seen Velukutty earlier, and her first meeting with the actor happened on the roadside (an informal space) where he was presumably in 'civil dress'. Yet, she read 'him' as a 'woman', though the object of her perception was a body/person socially classified as male. Without denying the inevitable authority of patriarchy over all these social significations, I wish to highlight the language of desire and pleasure that is complexly inscribed in the various responses to the performance and body of Velukutty. The complicated location of Ochira Velukutty in the social imagination of early-twentieth-century Kerala alerts us to a range of questions about the evolving perceptions of gendered desirability of bodies as well as the complex dialectics of performances and visual pleasures.

## Desire and the Region

Critical Sexuality Studies is a project that has drastically redefined the parameters of academic debates on gender and sexualities in the early decades of the twenty-first century (McArthur et al. 2005). Drawing from feminist and queer insights on sexuality debates, scholars working within this framework assert the need to transcend what they describe as heterosexual privilege, and perceive human sexualities as fluid, multiple and contradictory. They are also keenly concerned of how silences are reproduced in research designs and reinforced by the very questions asked and pursued by researchers. They call it the ignorance project—one where knowledge is constructed, maintained and disseminated while silences are produced (Plummer 1995; Richardson 2000).

Men lured by the performed femininity on/of a 'male' body had a longer tradition in Kerala. Female roles in Kathakali performances were traditionally enacted by men, and the male spectators openly expressing their fascination and sensual desire for these performative femininities (*streeveshangal*) were deemed normal and natural in the early years of the twentieth century. Kathakali and other folk performances of the period were premised on the epic and lyrical traditions, notably associated with the pre-modern, and thereby represented alternative worlds of imagination and pleasure. The lyrical invariably had elements that challenged the fixities of 'realism' and hence I would describe such performances as inherently 'queer'—that is, non-aligned to the normative and the hegemonic. Moreover, Kathakali was appreciated by only a small section of the privileged class/castes, and folk performances also had a very localised viewership. What Velukutty and perhaps other male performers of female roles in the social theatre movement of early twentieth century accomplished, was the elaboration of such traditional and localised patterns of 'desiring' to a wider section of the society, especially other classes and castes.

Incidentally, this was happening in the context of a range of other transformations that are crucial to an understanding of shifting dynamics of desire in the region. In the first half of the twentieth century, 'the Malayalam speaking world' (*Bhoomi-Malayalam* as it was known) was getting ushered into a national modernity premised on post-industrial sensibilities imported through colonial education. Vibrant narratives of modernity were invading the cultural scenario and one of the striking characteristics of the shift was an apparent move towards 'realism', and its attendant ideologies of humanism and logo-centrism. The popularity of Tamil mythological musical plays in the region was in the process of getting replaced by a social theatre movement in Malayalam, promoting 'realistic' narratives and performances. The 'moving pictures', mostly imported from Europe, Mumbai or Madras, were slowly becoming part of the visual culture and pleasure. In literature, the popularity of long poems of the Bhakti tradition was losing out to novels, short stories and secular poems like those of Kumaran Asan and Vallathol Narayana Menon.

In short, one could argue that an indigenous humanism was being forged in the smithy of colonial modernity. Hence, Velukutty could be considered as part of a larger cultural project that was moulding a new national subject. The new perceptions of desire that he embodied were directly feeding into the structure of new genders and sexualities in the making.

## Bodies of Desire and Pleasure

Some of the recent intellectual explorations of the imaginations of body and pleasure could further elucidate the cultural significance of the performance of Velukutty or the other performers of his times and their location in the evolving sensual/sexual sensibilities of early-twentieth-century Kerala (and other parts of India). Feminist thinkers were the forerunners who perceived body as a site of power struggle. In the process, they undermined what had for a long time been a perception based on the organic entity of the body. One of the prime inspirations in this field has been Lacan's observations on human culture as a symbolic order that creates a break from the biological real, capturing and restructuring the experience of life through mediating symbols (Lacan 1977). The body, for example, is conceptualised and organised by labels and categories that, under ordinary circumstances, stand in the way of any direct experience of its existence. As the philosopher Hilary Putnam (1988) has also pointed out, we have no access to such a thing as a language-independent reality. In Lacan's idiom, we would say there is 'no pre-discursive reality' (Lacan 1999, 33). The symbolic order can be briefly defined as a collection of codes and distinctions embodied in language and culture, and Lacan insists that human subjectivity can be sustained only within the limits of this framework. Thus, from Lacan's view, 'reality' as we know it and the 'real' are opposing concepts. What we call reality in describing the world in which we live is dependent entirely on language. It seems almost irrefutable that the capacity to use symbols, including identifying pronouns and proper names, is what makes us human. This is what Lacan means when he underscores in many ways that the subject is an effect of the signifier (Lacan 1977).

The centrality of fantasy in the structure of human desire is also emphasised by Lacan when he points out that if desire were simply a matter of biological drives, one passionate interest might satisfy as well as any other. But objects (of desire) are not readily interchangeable. Hence it seems just as useful to focus on the underlying fantasy structure that selects the object as the key to the problem of desire. Our choices are made on the basis of highly specific unconscious fantasies, which endow our objects with unique promise.

The debate on embodiment is further complicated by Judith Butler (1992) who tried to build a non-dualistic account of the body. Butler conceptualised the body as a system that simultaneously produces and is produced by social meaning and shows how transgressive-body politics can challenge the discursive limits of 'sex'. Judith Butler argues that theories of gender need to return to the most material dimension of sex and sexuality: the body. Butler offers a brilliant reworking of the body, examining how the power of heterosexual hegemony forms the 'matter' of bodies, sex and gender. Butler emphatically states that social power operates to constrain sex from the start, delimiting what counts as a viable sex (Butler 1990; Butler 1992).

Recent feminist scholarship on gender and the body offers new paradigms that recognise the inherent interaction of biological and social systems. For example, Australian philosopher Elizabeth Grosz has illustrated how social meanings external to the body are incorporated into its physiological expression, as well as unconscious and conscious behaviour. In her celebrated work, *Volatile Bodies*, she pursues the lead provided by feminist philosophers like Julia Kristeva and Butler, to criticise the Cartesian line of investigation that refuses to acknowledge the distinctive complexity of organic bodies, and the specific reciprocities of the organic and the psychic that partially constitute that complexity (Grosz 1994, 7–10). She also demonstrates that the sexually specific body is socially constructed: biology or nature is inherently social and has no pure or natural 'origin' outside culture. Being the raw material of social and cultural organisation, it is subject to the endless rewritings and inscriptions that constitute all sign systems (Grosz 1994, 27–113).

Anne Fausto Sterling is another scholar who has argued that sex is more of a continuum and that the body is changeable over the life course rather than fixed at birth. She rejects the framework that views the body and the circumstances in which it reproduces as separable. Instead, she and the other scholars suggest an interactive biosocial model in which internal reproductive structures and external social, historical and environmental factors are inseparable—interacting over time and circumstance (Sterling 2000).

Raewyn Connell, the philosopher who led the debates on masculinity studies in the 1990s, had observed that body-reflexive practices are not internal to the individual. They involve social relations and symbolism; they may well involve large-scale institutions. Particular versions of masculinity and femininity are constituted in their circuits as meaningful bodies and embodied meanings. Through body-reflexive practices, not just individual lives are formed: the social world that frames individual lives is also its product (Connell 1995). David Halperin has also critically evaluated the complicated location of the body within what is described as sexual desires/imaginations: a bio-psycho-social model of sexuality is necessary if we are to understand the various influences on sexual expression across the life-course. Citing instances from Greek mythology and anthropology, Halperin has demonstrated that erotic desires and sexual object-choices in antiquity were generally not determined by a typology of anatomical sexes (male versus female), but rather by the social articulation of power (Halperin 2002).

## History and Anti-history

In the rest of this essay, I shall explore some of the historical incidents that appear to have critically engaged with and, perhaps, restructured the perceptions of sexuality in Kerala. I use the term 'sexuality' here to refer not only to the relational practices but also to the imaginations of desirability and pleasure. I shall begin by trying to revisit some well-known historical conjunctures that appear to have crucially transformed the structures of desire in Kerala.

As I explore the implications of these social texts and their contexts, my objective is not the tracing of a history of the sensual practices/imaginations generated in those conjunctures. The writing of history, especially when it is of a rather complex and unpredictable human exercise like sexuality, cannot camouflage its own reductive enterprise. Writing, invariably, is an attempt to seek inscription within a language, a received mode of communication. As language is one of the sources as well as products of the prevailing structures of power, the visibility it generates reinforces these structures and subsumes the subjectivities in dialogue with them. Moreover, the factors deemed appropriate to be read as expressions of sexuality are invariably identified by hegemonic lifestyles, and that makes it even more difficult to pursue or record the detailed trajectories of sexualities associated with a region. Imaginations about desirability and sensual pleasures do not necessarily evolve following a linear temporal scale. Social formations, patterns of socialisation and cultural frameworks regularly mould conflicting spaces and fantasies that may lead to the co-existence of contradictory imaginations and experiences of desires and pleasures. Hence, my intention is to read the various historical developments and incidents from the recent past of the region as narrative strategies and political projects that not only constructed new 'knowledges' or perspectives, but also constituted the many silences and obscurities that are integral to our prevailing perceptions of bodies, desires and pleasures. Thus, my project is certainly not an exercise in historiography; if at all, it can only be described as an adventure in anti-history.

### *Covering the Upper Body*

Incidentally, a defining characteristic of the female guise on stage, elaborated by Velukutty and other actors who performed female roles, was the blouse: the few rare pictures available of these performers present all of them wearing a blouse and sari. The actors performing female roles in Dadasaheb Phalke's celebrated movie

*Harishchandra* (1913) amply demonstrate this. The location of the blouse in the evolving visual imaginations of body and sexuality in Kerala reveal certain striking contradictions.

Covering the upper part of the female body had been a controversial topic from the early decades of the nineteenth century. The 'breast cloth rebellion' that began in 1828 has already received substantial academic attention and been recognised as one of the earliest revolts against caste hierarchies in the Malayalam-speaking region. Reports indicate that some of the 'upper-caste' women had started covering their breasts with cloth during this period. Much of the discussions on the covering of female breasts have been focused on individuals and communities that claimed and fought for their right to cover female torsos. I consider it important to study the individuals and communities that preferred not to endorse, or were vehemently against, breast-covering. The subjectivities that motivated the anti-breast-cover stance are complex, and are crucial to any examination of the remaking of bodies—male and female—in twentieth-century Kerala. Some of the rare old photographs that pop up on the internet indicate that in the late nineteenth century, many nair women appeared in public functions and even posed for the new technological curiosity called photography, without necessarily covering their breasts. Historians like Manu S. Pillai (2015) have noted that it was customary for nair women to uncover their torsos when visiting members (women) of royal families. Men also used to do the same when meeting people of higher social status. All these indicate that the uncovered torso, irrespective of gender, continued as a sign of humility, till the early years of the twentieth century. Records indicate that even in the early years of the twentieth century, there were many nair women who did not wish to cover their upper body. Some of these women were educated and working as teachers. There were prolonged debates on this issue in the early journals and magazines in Malayalam published around the turn of the century. In 1903, a social reformer and 'feminist' intellectual named K. Chinnamma wrote in the journal *Lakshmibai*:

> They (nair women) do not even know how to cover their bodies properly. During my recent trip to Meenachil Taluk, I happened to see

> some of our nair sisters walking half naked on the public road—which caused me great sorrow and shame. They were on a highway through which all sorts of people, both from within and outside the community, were moving around. Nowadays, when even the illiterate slave caste women who go around cutting grass bother to cover their bodies, the shameless behaviour of these nair women could only be the result of nothing other than gross ignorance. (1903, 122)

For Chinnamma, the dreaded gaze capable of violating the body of nair women is not male, but caste. There were other occasions when nair women willingly uncovered their torsos, mostly during religious functions and when visiting members of royal lineage. The early women's magazines in Malayalam provide ample evidence to prove that attempts to persuade nair women to cover their upper bodies continued even in the 1930s. Evidence of the 'Velur breast-covering protest' (ironically, led by women from 'lower' castes) of 1956 indicates that the practice of not covering breasts in public continued among nair women through the first half of the twentieth century.[2]

If the covering of the breast had different implications for the nadar and nair women, the experience of an ezhava woman from Travancore focuses on the sensuous and pleasurable sensations of covering the upper body. A humorous retelling of an experience of Kunjikavu wearing her first blouse appears in the autobiography of her son-in-law, C. Kesavan, who later became the chief minister of the Kochi–Travancore state. She was fascinated by the idea of wearing a blouse and her partner (never referred to as 'husband' in the narrative) encouraged her when she discussed the idea with him.

[2] The Velur protest happened in a village near Thrissur, where women had been customarily carrying the '*thaalam*' for a three-day festival in the temple. Never before had any of them worn blouses, or covered their breasts. The women performing the rituals were mostly from the dominant nair caste. But in 1956, for the first time, a bunch of women walked towards the temple wearing blouses, and they belonged to different castes—oppressed ones among them. https://www.thenewsminute.com/article/these-kerala-women-changed-history-wearing-blouses-velur-temple-1956-144761 accessed on 8 March 2021.

Later, one of her sisters-in-law from Trivandrum, who had already started wearing this garment, presented her with one. Apparently, Kunjikavu was in a matrilineal household and her mother found her daughter's new fascination abominable. Once, when caught wearing a blouse, she was beaten black and blue by the mother. The highlight of the narrative is Kunjikavu's adamant reaction: 'But nights were for me. Once mother falls asleep, I will take out the blouse and wear it. And (he), like a clandestine celestial lover, would come only late in the night' (Kesavan 1968, 109–11).

The account has been variously interpreted by eminent scholars like J. Devika (2007), Udaya Kumar (1997) and B. Rajeevan (1999), in their discussions on dress reforms in Kerala. In an elaborate and insightful discussion, J. Devika observes that covering of the breasts becomes a seduction technique that transformed the female body into a desirable object. In Udaya Kumar's analysis, the blouse is not seen as a caste marker but an object of personalised enjoyment. He sees the woman who wears a blouse as a desiring subject. Rajeevan has argued that Kunjikavu's narrative records the emergence of a new sense of nudity and the sexualisation of women's breasts.

What I consider striking in Kunjikavu's perception and experience of the breast-cover is its ambiguous signification. Her mother describes it as shameful and degrading, but association with her 'educated sisters-in-law' from Trivandrum makes it a sign of modernity for Kunjikavu. Yet, her experience of the blouse is more strikingly a stimulant of physical pleasure. For Kunjikavu, the blouse appears to be a sensuous experience—it brings in an enjoyable sense of the body. At another part of her narration, she even says that when she wore it for the first time, it tickled her in a very enjoyable way. Apart from pleasantly transforming her own body, it even makes her engagement with her partner more pleasurable. When she wears it, he, too, is transformed in her perception: he becomes a celestial lover on a clandestine visit. Thus, her account elucidates the view later expressed by many embodiment theorists that the body exists through 'intersubjectivity', that is, shared understandings of reality or relationships with other people.

In a sensual encounter, people experience their own bodies and the bodies of other persons simultaneously—as objects and subjects, desiring and being desired (Cahill 2014).

There is a general consensus among academics and historians that the breast cloth rebellion was an anti-caste revolt. The female body invariably is the battleground on which most of these kinds of revolts were/are staged. It is important to examine in detail how such struggles/reforms reconstruct the female body and redefine gender. Colonial modernity, introduced and empowered by English education, certainly must have acted as a new pressure/lure that swayed the educated, middle-class 'upper-caste' women in urban locations into covering their breasts. Yet in the late-nineteenth-century Malayalam-speaking world, the blouse appears to have had contradictory social significations. As it was worn by the educated elite women, it was a sign of culture and progress; but it was also worn by Muslim and Christian women, and hence marked otherness to the 'upper-caste' Hindu women who had been unilaterally claiming the status of 'Malayali women'. Most importantly, it was worn by the performing women (and male performers of female roles) and hence was indicative of 'low moral standards'. It is this third interpretation of the blouse that appears to have direct stakes in the evolving sexual imaginary. The mother of Kunjikavu reacts so violently to her daughter's wearing of the blouse because of the new 'erotically explicit' and seductive status of the blouse that clashed with her own presumed location ('class' status) within the emerging moral fabric (Kesavan 1968). Thus, one could sense the ideology of colonial modernity functioning in contradictory ways in this incident (or its narrative elaboration), both violently marking and striving to remould the 'femaleness' of the body in question.

The complicated dialectics between customs indicative of social status and the dynamics of visual pleasure deserve more nuanced research and debates before we can propose any feasible conclusions. Even the shift from the breast cloth, a very flexible way of covering, to the fixity of the stitched blouse cannot be taken as a natural or smooth transition. The introduction and popularisation of the blouse appear to be a more emphatic redefining of the female body and identity, marking a decisive shift in its location within discourses of desirability and visual pleasure. Perhaps it was also the most emphatic social differentiation of bodies as male and female.

### *Imaginations of Body as Male and Female*

Contemporary patriarchal imaginations of the body appear obsessively concerned with anatomies marked as female. This, in a way, explains why even the term transgender immediately invokes gaudy imaginations of trans women in colourful saris and loud make up. Yet the male body had also been taking turns to feature in the sensual fantasies of Malayalis in manners that did not necessarily contest patriarchal authority. In a striking contrast to contemporary imaginations, some of the folk narratives, especially ballads like *Vadakkan pattus*, frequently featured an eroticised female gaze observing a highly objectified male body. The folk ballads were part of popular culture, and their circulation was through oral traditions. More spiritualised and hence 'de-eroticised' versions of such narratives had appeared in many literary works of the Bhakti period. Classic poetic works like *Krishnagadha* (fifteenth century) or *Narayaneeyam* (sixteenth century) can be seen engaging in detailed 'head-to-feet' descriptions of the worshiped male god, eulogising the corporeality of the divine entity.

In the absence of any significant aisle-painting traditions in South India till Raja Ravi Varma (1848–1906), these poetic works perhaps fulfilled a mission similar to that of Renaissance paintings, by generating a palpable corporeality for the divine or saintly figures. In the process, they also exemplify imaginations of male beauty that prevailed in those times. In the final *shloka* of *Narayaneeyam*,[3] the poet Melpathur Bhattathiri extols not only

---

3 Though *Narayaneeyam* was a poetic work in Sanskrit, it was composed by a poet residing in Kerala to praise the deity of the Guruvayur temple in central Kerala. It was customary at that time to compose 'high literature' only in Sanskrit, as Malayalam still had the status of a 'vulgar' language.

the grace on the face of the worshipped god, but even the beauty of his thighs: 'Thy two handsome thighs, which are solid, soft and charming, stealing Rama's (Lakshmi's) heart' (ऊरू चारू तव-ऊरू घन-मसृण-रुचौ चत्ति्त-चोरौ रमायाः) (*Narayaneeyam*). The printed version of the work appeared only in 1851, published by the government press in Trivandrum and edited by renowned musician Irayimman Thampi (1782–1856) who belonged to the court of His Highness Swati Thirunal (1813–46). The intricacies of the editing process are not available for critical evaluation.

A similar narrative construction of a body marked with male features is available in the description of Madhavan, the chief male character in *Indulekha* (1889), the fictional work celebrated as the first 'full-fledged' novel in Malayalam. But the trend soon disappeared, and a spiritual, asexual version of masculinity started featuring in the mainstream hegemonic literary works of early to mid-twentieth century, especially the novels and secular poetry associated with the era of Kerala Renaissance. Women in the poetic works of Kumaran Asan or Vallathol Narayana Menon continue as corporeal presences while men are transformed as spiritual essences. The theme of an 'embodied' woman interrupting an idealised 'male bond or male world' recurs in many Malayalam literary masterpieces of the early twentieth century (for example, *Ramanan* (1936) by Changampuzha Krishna Pillai; *Nalini* (1911), *Leela* (1914) and *Karuna* (1923) by Kumaran Asan). The revalourising of Buddhist ideals that gathered momentum in the region with the social reform movements of the late nineteenth and early twentieth century—especially the one led by Sri Narayana Guru, and the Gandhian celebration of celibacy that filtered in through the evolving discourse of nationalism—contributed tremendously to the popular assumption that sexuality is a negative energy. '*Mamsa-nibhadham alla ragam*'—True love is not carnal—stated Kumaran Asan in his celebrated poetic work *Leela* (1914). The courtesan, Vasavadatta, in *Karuna* was allowed to meet her 'object of desire', the Buddhist monk named Ananda, only when her body was mutilated and beauty annihilated. The Catholic dogma of 'sexual purity' can be seen conspicuously feeding into this 'modernist' redefining of self and romance. Ironically, the same Vasavadatta, enacted by Velukutty, in the stage adaptation of *Karuna* became a prime component of desirable femininity in the years that followed.

It was this sanitised moral context of mid-twentieth-century Kerala that made a rather docile literary work (in a rather innovative literary genre subsequently known as fictional autobiography), *Ente kadha* (1973; published later in English as *My Story*) by Kamala Das, become controversial so as to generate intense debates about its immorality. The accounts of extramarital affairs in this work might appear naive to contemporary readers, but they provoked a section of the public in the 1970s and resulted in powerful critical attacks against both the work and its author. Rather than the content of *Ente kadha*, the details of the responses it evoked could help us better understand the range of contradictory imaginations of body, sexuality and femaleness in circulation in mid-twentieth-century Kerala. This could also help us understand why another text published around the same time, *Randu penkuttikal* (Two Girls, 1974) by V. T. Nandakumar, a novel based on a 'lesbian' theme, did not provoke any comparable outrage.

The novel by Nandakumar did invite a voyeuristic gaze towards an explicit sexual relationship between two teenaged girls. The afterlife of this novel is far more interesting than its plot. The novel, serialised in a popular weekly, concluded with the apparent heterosexualisation of the two young women, and the subsequent constitution of two new heteronormative nuclear families. But in a preface written for the second edition of the novel, the author chose to talk at length about the many responses he received from his readers, mostly women in same-sex relationships. He concluded the preface by praying for the 'development and spread of lesbianism in Kerala' (qtd. in Muraleedharan 2000, 359). The preface is also indicative of a conjuncture when post-Stonewall Western terminologies like lesbian, gay, etc., were trickling into the local discussions in Kerala. When popular film maker Mohan attempted a screen adaptation of *Randu penkuttikal* in 1978, he instructed the script writer Surasu to steer clear of the 'lesbianism' of the original work, and modify it as the story of a close 'asexual' friendship between two girls. Later, in an interview, Nandakumar observed that the film did not do well because the soul of his novel—that is, the 'lesbian' theme—had not been retained. I would like to read these various cultural productions of the 1960s and 70s as indicative of a renewing debate on sexuality and pleasure.

### *Social Movements and the Sexuality Debate*

Gender and sexuality were central concerns in most of the reform movements initiated in Kerala in the early half of the twentieth century, motivated mainly by colonial education and nationalist fervour. The community-based movements of this period were generally committed to disciplining the diverse conjugal practices in the region, and the consolidation of normative citizenships that could be contained within the moral fold of the nation. As is well known, the evolution of postcolonial national modernity in India was premised on a rigorous disciplining of sexualities, and their rehabilitation into a hetero-patriarchal morality (Arunima 2003; Chatterjee 1993; Menon 2008). Yet oral histories and artistic records seem to indicate that the status of the monogamous (heterosexual) marriage and patriarchal nuclear family had been precarious in Kerala even during the 1950s and early 60s. The intense desire for a normative patriarchal nuclear family and its attendant morality—which serves as the foundation of some of the cult literary productions of this period (for example, M. T. Vasudevan Nair's *Naalukettu*, 1959)—covertly imply this. The eventual consolidation of such a family as the unquestionable social norm seems to have happened only after the much-discussed land reforms of 1963, and the advent of a Gulf-remittance based economy in the state almost a decade later (Osella 2011).

If the early half of the twentieth century turned out to be a period that gave thrust to the establishment of a patriarchal, monogamous moral order across the landscape that extended from 'Kanyakumari to Kasargode' (an old fashioned way of referring to the Malayalam-speaking region) with ample support from the newly hegemonic cultural artefacts like literature and theatre, then occasional dissenting notes can be seen flashing from popular cultural practices. The spread of print media facilitated the popularisation of an indigenous porn culture, in the form of inexpensive books and journals. Increase in the number of public buildings and walls created a space for graffiti. Developments in transportation saw a literal explosion in the popularity of festivals like Kodungallur Bharani and Thrissur Pooram. The lewd songs customarily sung by the devotees attending the Bharani festival in Kodungallur reflect vivid erotic reimaginations of female and male anatomy and sexual potency. Thrissur Pooram, on the other hand, had been evolving as an occasion and venue for explorations beyond the monogamous family and heterosexual morality, leading to vibrant yet muted fantasies of desire and pleasure. The large number of men who visit venues like that of Pooram to seek pleasure from male bodies do not identify themselves as gay or assume that the pleasure they experience is a serious concern in their lives. The anonymity one experiences in the *pooraparambu* (venue of Pooram) is a license for effervescent pleasures that remain unnamed, unreal and hence not disruptive of the hegemonic moral world they inhabit. All these are factors that demand detailed critical evaluations if we are to get a better sense of the complexity of the history of erotic discourses in Kerala.

In spite of its loyalty to the constructed silence around sexualities, the state-sponsored 'family planning' programme of the 1960s found itself under pressure to confront it as a formidable issue if it were to accomplish the mission of birth control. It is now well known that this programme was 'most successfully implemented' (Ramesh and Prajitha) in Kerala, and that it led to the production of a number of publicity documents, including films, which could not evade talking about sexuality. The subsequent option was to talk about sexuality as 'masculine' and 'penis-centred' in a metaphorical and hesitant voice. The most ubiquitous and successful campaign associated with this programme sought to hard sell Nirodh—a brand of condoms produced by the state. While the product was widely advertised, the resulting documents contained absolutely no information about how it was to be used. In the publicity campaigns it featured only as a name.

A prominent vehicle of the birth-control campaign was the feature film *Ollathu mathi* (What You Have is Enough [1967]; dir: K. S. Sethumadhavan) which carried the message of birth control re-designated as 'family planning'. The film unabashedly portrayed sexuality as a male initiative, with women represented as passive receptacles of male desire. It did not mention any possibility of births happening outside the boundaries of the monogamous nuclear family. Although it was an independent venture by a private film producer (Jay Maruthi Films), it was subsequently bought by the state department of public relations and exhibited free of cost all over Kerala, sometimes on roadsides, in public parks and post-harvest fields in villages and towns that had no cinema houses, as part of the propaganda of the 'family planning' programme. Even the dubious naming of a birth-control campaign as a 'family planning' programme helped to nurture the misunderstanding that sex and pregnancy happen or 'should happen' only within the 'family'.

The fledgling feminist movement of the 1970s has been mainly responsible for breaking the silence on sexualities and reopening the debates on gender in India. Historians have pointed out that an organised feminist movement emerged rather late in Kerala, more than a decade after the appearance of its counterpart at the national level (Devika: unpublished). The perceptions about body and sexuality that could be deduced from early deliberations of the feminist movement in Kerala reveal a strikingly heterosexist, and sometimes even puritanical, framework. A great deal of the subsequent feminist debates was on sexual violence, and they rarely engaged with the structure of sensual pleasures in an analytical way. Moreover, they were also rather reluctant, at least during those early days, to engage with controversial issues like sex work or homosexuality (Unni 2011).

## Homo-sociality/sexuality in the 1960s and 70s

In spite of the silence and obscurity that loomed large in Kerala in the 1960s and 70s over issues of same-sex relationships, we encounter certain 'folkloric' dissenting notes. The most prominent is the whispered identification of the Malabar region in general, and the city of Calicut (Kozhikode) in particular, as some kind of a Mecca for homosexual expeditions. Although one is tempted to read this merely as part of a general tendency of the rest of Kerala to see the Muslim-dominated Malabar as its 'uncivilised other', there are other cultural and historical indications that suggest the possibility of greater complexities contributing to this myth. The rich Sufi traditions of Malabar, which continued through the 1960s and 70s as merry, all-male evening get-togethers of music and camaraderie, along with the lesser menace of the 'straightening' (that is, the heterosexist bias) effects of Western education, could have sustained an environment that facilitated freer sensual interactions among men.

In what could perhaps be described as one of the few academic discussions of 'homosociality' and homosexual desire allegedly prevalent in the Calicut region, Filipo Osella prefers to see them as having been produced at the interstices of wider political and economic transformations taking place within the city in the first half of the twentieth century. Observing that an intense homosociality has been central to masculine practices and aesthetics in Kozhikode, Osella adds that they do not belong to an imagined pre-/alternative modern, but to an aesthetic focused on male friendships and the longing for youth, flourishing in an expanding postcolonial bazaar. Osella traces its links to the *mugalil sanghams* (upstairs associations)—that is, male meeting clubs above shops or businesses, which were central to the patterns of male socialisation in Calicut. One of the limitations of Osella's study is its exclusive focus on the koyas, a socially and economically prominent matrilineal Muslim community in Calicut. The study does not pay attention to the participation of men from other religious communities in this culture (Osella 2012). Still, Osella's work is a valuable intervention to a general logic that assumes homosexual practices as a Western or colonial import to the Indian society.

## Suicide Pacts and Sex Work

If what was identified as a population explosion during the 1960s created a context for breaking the silence imposed on the issue of sexuality, the threat of the AIDS pandemic in the later decades of the twentieth century was instrumental in demolishing the obscurity imposed on homosexuality in India. When HIV infections started spreading, international funding and NGO activities flourished in India, initiating programmes that specifically addressed 'sex outside marriage'. Thus MSMs (men who have sex with men) and female sex workers suddenly gained visibility in public debates and programmes. The discussions and activities that followed did also conjure new languages and new identities based on 'sexual preferences' or 'practices'. The trans-women groups that had existed in many parts of India for several decades were suddenly seen through new frameworks moulded on methodologies of Western ethnography and medical knowledge.

A series of suicides, or rather suicide pacts, of young same-sex couples were reported in Kerala during the 1990s. Almost all these youngsters were from the lower economic strata, although many of them were healthy and educated wage earners. A majority of them were women, and included teachers, students, factory hands and government employees. There were also two policemen and a pair of skilled male labourers. Most of the suicides reported were not in the cities, but in villages or small towns. One of the deceased female couples was from a tribal village. The immediate motivation in most cases was the imposition of a heterosexual marriage on one of them by his/her family. Case studies conducted later revealed that many of the female couples, who eventually chose to kill themselves, had initially tried to brave social hostility, attempting either to survive in their immediate society or escape to a more supportive environment in nearby towns (Bharadwaj 2004).

Reports of these deaths, sometimes with photographs of the victims, appeared in all leading newspapers and television channels. This suicide series deserves to be read as a stint of mass 'coming out' in Kerala, even though it involved the unfortunate loss of many valuable young lives. By 'deleting' their existence, these young men and women were forcefully registering their presence in a hostile society. It was a unique way of gaining social visibility—joint suicides involved a powerful statement of protest, as well as the public announcement of new identities. New desires were being inscribed into the social imaginary; a new history was being written.

In spite of the absence of a formal manifesto, these suicides did also signify protests against the institutions of arranged heterosexual marriage and nuclear family that had come to establish themselves as oppressive social institutions in Kerala, more so in the second half of the twentieth century. They occurred at a time when Kerala had already achieved the dubious distinction of being the state with the highest percentage of suicides. Government departments and NGOs had already started analysing the reasons behind group suicides, and identifying the different kinds of familial and economic pressures which figured as prominent factors leading to such unfortunate choices. Yet the issue of sexuality has not been recognised among the possible reasons that motivated people to kill themselves. The suicide pacts did invite international attention and funding to Kerala, and resulted in the setting up of Sahayatrika, a support group that sought to help women with alternate sexual or gender preferences. It also set up a fact-finding team that investigated the many lesbian suicides and prepared detailed reports. It is disheartening to see that similar incidents of female suicide pacts are not covered by newspapers anymore, at least not with the same diligence.

A term that occasionally appeared in newspaper stories of the 1990s is *swavarga sambhogam*, ostensibly referring to homosexual acts, especially among males. The expression highlighted sexual 'consumption' (*sambhogam*) which is indicative of an almost consumerist indulgence in pleasures, thereby blotting out any possibility of mutuality in such a union. Issues of love or companionship, as is evident, remained inconceivable. One could also read here the foundation of a subsequent myth—that a male homosexual is someone who offers his body in a 'feminine/passive' manner for the pleasure of another, presumably a 'masculine/

dominant' male (never identified as homosexual). This helped to keep the imagined penile power of masculinity intact. Surprisingly, even in recent public discussions initiated by the Supreme Court ruling on IPC 377, one could see many 'straight' supporters of gay rights falling back on such a notion, and assuming that a gay man is a male body with a 'female mind' inside.

One can also see that even in 2021, three years after the reading down of IPC 377, most Malayalam newspapers continue to refer to incidents of (male) same-sex rape/seduction as assaults 'against the order of nature' (*prakruthi viruddham*). This is not really surprising, since newspapers in Malayalam continue to talk of heterosexual rape/violence as 'dishonouring' (*manabhangam*)—implying that what a raped woman loses is her 'honour'. Violent rape, gentle seduction, a false promise of marriage leading to sexual union, etc., are all classified as *stree peedanam* (torture of the female), once again defining the role of a woman in a heterosexual encounter as nothing but passive. Moreover, violent physical assault and simple betrayal of trust are not differentiated if it involves a woman and a sexual encounter. Such a stance continues the assumption that women fundamentally have an objective status in sexual interactions and evades any recognition of female subjectivity.

## NGOs and the Sex Workers' Movement

A significant intervention in the patriarchal assumption of the passive and objective status of female subjectivity took place during the 1990s in the form of the politicisation of sex workers, and it derived substantial motivation from the NGO activities in the field of AIDS prevention. During the late 1990s, various initiatives were launched in Kerala to organise the sex workers from lower economic levels, who had hitherto been regular victims of different kinds of exploitation. The sex workers had already formed many informal collectives for mutual support, but the social ostracism and the harsh and insecure conditions under which they survived made it rather difficult for these women to empower themselves or fight social prejudices. There was also gross ignorance regarding the rights of individuals associated with unrecognised labour sectors like sex work that made female sex workers susceptible to police atrocities, torture and extortion. Unlike their counterparts in the metro cities in India, sex workers in Kerala had not been part of brothel systems. This saved them from the exploitation of brothel owners and middlemen, but also predisposed them to work in unhealthy environments and unsafe conditions.

The establishment of the organisation Sex Workers Forum of Kerala (SWFK) in 2000 was one of the initial attempts to generate a support system for the women in sex work. The sex workers' movement generated considerable impact on the social imaginations and even moral frameworks in Kerala. Detailed reports and visual records of the demonstrations and other activities of the movement appeared prominently in newspapers and on television channels. Many 'respectable' men and women came forward to support the movement and it helped break the general assumption that a sex worker is someone who could be ignored, or even shunned, by the mainstream society. Above all, the movement did help to provide a 'voice' to the sex worker who, till then, had been seen as a muted and eroticised body. The various conventions and conferences enabled sex workers to interact with the so-called mainstream society in 'non-sexual' situations, and thus present themselves as individuals with rights and dignity. A striking linguistic innovation of this period is the introduction of the expression 'sex worker'. Nalini Jameela, one of the leaders of the movement, underwent training in filmmaking and produced a short documentary on the lives of sex workers. She later published her autobiography, which went on to become a turning point in the history of Malayalam publishing.

## Interventions by the Judiciary and the State

The initial decades of the twenty-first century witnessed certain landmark interventions, from the state as well as the judiciary, that were vital to the evolving discourse of sexuality and gender in Kerala/India. In 2015, the Government of Kerala declared a Transgender Policy, thereby earning itself the distinction of being the first Indian state to undertake such an initiative. On 6 September 2018, the Supreme Court of India amended Section 377 of the Indian Penal Code (IPC), decriminalising consensual sexual relationships between adults of the same sex. On 27 September 2018, a five-judge Bench unanimously struck down Section 497 of the IPC, thereby decriminalising adultery. In 2019, the central government passed a bill on the protection of the rights of transgender persons.

Perhaps the most surprising of these judgments was the one on Section 497. Most women in India did not even know its implications till the verdict was pronounced. Though popularly known as the adultery law, the section had been misogynist in every sense. It considered any man who had sexual intercourse with a married woman without the consent of her husband as committing a punishable offence. In other words, it upheld a very patriarchal assumption, that a wife is the private property of her husband. As one of the Justices observed, it violated women's fundamental rights to equality, autonomy and dignity. Yet, the public reaction to the verdict, especially those featured on social media, was mostly sardonic, interpreting the verdict as a licence for anarchic sexual explorations 'against family values'. Unfortunately, immediately after the declaration of the verdict on 497, came another one, sanctioning the entry of young women to the Sabarimala temple. Since the temple entry issue kicked up a controversy and led to various protests and agitations, the striking down of Section 497 and its implications were generally ignored and forgotten. The recurring cold-blooded murders of young women and girl students by their 'jilted lovers' or 'rejected admirers' in contemporary Kerala eloquently call for a renewed debate on the relevance of the court verdict on Section 497.

Section 377 of the IPC was part of the legacy of British rule; it was introduced in 1864, modelled on the Buggery Act of 1533 that criminalised sexual activities 'against the order of nature' (IPC 88). A couple of decades after the Second World War, the British Parliament passed the Sexual Offences Act of 1967 that decriminalised private sexual activity between men over the age of 21 in England and Wales. In India, the Section remained in the IPC until the 1990s, when it was challenged by various NGOs and individuals. It is important to note that this section of the IPC did not mention homosexuality. Perhaps the word was not in circulation at the time of its formulation. The section targeted 'whoever voluntarily has carnal intercourse against the order of nature with any man, woman or animal' (IPC 88), with an explanation of what is unnatural: 'Penetration is sufficient to constitute the carnal intercourse necessary to the offence described in this section'. Thus, it was about (male) sexual behaviour possible in engagements with 'man, woman or animal' (IPC 88). The judgement pronounced by the Supreme Court in 2018 also makes no mention of identities; it categorically declares that consensual sexual acts between adults cannot be a crime.

Yet the amendment of Section 377 has generally been interpreted as the legalisation of homosexuality. It endorses a patriarchal stereotype of homosexual relations as fundamentally penetrative. In effect, it results in the identification/construction of a target group/community called 'homosexuals'. Apart from the consolidation of a social identity defined on sexual preference, such an interpretation also leads to a general assumption that those who do not voluntarily identify with that group, that is the so-called majority, have a coherent and uniform sexual imagination/taste that can be described as 'heterosexuality'. Thus, a binary is generated, and a minority created. A similar project can be seen in operation in the efforts to identify trans individuals as a 'third gender'. Such projects camouflage the fluidity of sexual imaginations/preferences and construct neatly perceptible coherent identities based on gendered performances or sexualities, thereby merely enlarging the category of 'others' that define/strengthen 'the normative'.

## Violence, Policing and Criminalising

An expression emphatically etched in the day-to-day interactions of contemporary Kerala is 'moral policing'. It refers to an aggressive intervention, either by the police force or lay persons who become self-appointed moral guardians of culture, to disrupt or limit the freedom and right of citizens who apparently violate patriarchal ethics. Women and youth are the most frequent victims of such assaults. A favourite target of such aggressions are young men and women seen together at locations or times not acceptable to patriarchal morality. There have been instances when married couples were also harassed or humiliated by the 'moral police'. Seekers of homosexual encounters, especially from the 'lower' strata of the society, are frequent victims of public violence and humiliation. Women daring to sit in liquor bars or buying alcohol from legally sanctioned outlets have also been targeted. A few such instances are reported or receive some media coverage, while most go unreported, especially when the victims are vulnerable and lack any strong support system to fall back on.

The high incidence of moral policing in contemporary Kerala needs to be identified as evidence of a moral panic spreading across the state, stimulated by accelerating socio-economic transformations. As Jeffrey Weeks (1985) has observed, sexuality becomes a conveyer belt onto which all kinds of social anxieties are shifted, especially when there are major economic and social restructurings in society. Insecurities about an impending collapse of the prevailing family system and gender hierarchies are among the complex psycho-sexual instincts that motivate such crimes. The recurrence of such instances also reveals a deplorable public ignorance pertaining to some of the fundamental principles of 'democracy'.

The brutal rape and murder of a young woman while travelling in a deserted ladies' coupe of a passenger train, or the suicide of a final-year medical student due to dowry related harassment, sent shock waves through Kerala and generated an unprecedented spate of angry protests and irate debates. Unfortunately, the almost hysterical moral outrage unleashed by such incidents suffer from camouflaged caste, race and class concerns that hinder the ensuing debates from generating any serious investigations of the sociocultural factors that facilitate the alarming incidence of sexual violence in Kerala.

* * *

Rising moral policing, sexual assaults against women and children and circulating misconceptions about alternate sexualities in contemporary Kerala underscore the need for rigorous critical examinations and extensive discussions on the historical evolution and polarisation of gendered and sexual subjectivities in this region. This should be complemented by the creation of new spaces, palpable as well as virtual, to facilitate personal and collective experimentations that seek to construct more fluid and egalitarian bodies and selves. Can gender, a prime component in the construction and conception of modern identities, be completely erased from the social imaginary? Yet, identities are changing, attitudes are transforming, and clashes are inevitable. The unique geographical, political and cultural location of Kerala within the nation, as well as within the global village, is poised to wade through devastating transitions in the years to come. The LGBTQ+ and women's movements in Kerala need to learn from each other's mistakes. The region needs to be retained as a political and critical category, which will be useful in resisting the universalising instincts of political projects. Simultaneously, new coalitions are to be made with race, class and community movements within and across the boundaries of the region, which could both enrich and complicate the imaginations and articulations of gender against the impulses of global comprehensions.

In conclusion, I would like to reiterate that this essay has not been an attempt to map out a history of sexuality or gender in Kerala. I have only revisited some incidents and instances that appear to have engaged with such a history and tried to tease out their multiple implications. Thus, my mission has been fundamentally disruptive, seeking to break coherences and question convenient classifications. Neither do I claim my project to be complete in any sense of that word. In fact, any assumption of completion can only defeat the purpose of such an investigation.

There are also several important historical conjunctures and cultural productions that I could not discuss due to limitations of space and scope. I leave them as fodder for further debates and explorations that will and should take this project forward.

## References

Arunima, G. 2003. *There Comes Papa: Colonialism and the Transformation of Matriliny in Kerala, Malabar c. 1850–1940*. Hyderabad: Orient Longman.

Bharadwaj, Reshma. 2004. *Mithyakalkkappuram: Swavarga Laimgikatha Keralathil*. Kottayam: DC Books.

Butler, Judith. 1990.*Gender Trouble: Feminism and the Subversion of Identity*. New York & London: Routledge.

———. 1992. *Bodies that Matter: On the Discursive Limits of Sex*. New York: Routledge.

Cahill, A. J. 2014. 'Recognition, Desire, and Unjust Sex'. *Hypatia* 29(2): 303–19.

Chatterjee, Partha. 1993. *The Nation and Its Fragments: Colonial and Post-Colonial Histories*. Princeton: Princeton UP.

Chinnamma, K. 1903. 'They Do Not Even'. *Lakshmibai*.

Connell, Raewyn. 1995. *Masculinties*. Cambridge: Polity Press.

Das, Kamala. 1973. *Ente Katha*. Thrissur: Current Books.

Devika, J. 'Feminism and Late Twentieth Century Governmentality in Kerala, India: Towards a Critical History'. Unpublished.

———. 2007. *Engendering Individuals: The Language of Re-Forming in Twentieth-Century Kerala*. New Delhi: Orient Longman.

Evans, D. 1993. *Sexual Citizenship: The Material Construction of Sexualities*. London: Routledge.

Fausto-Sterling, Ann. 2000. *Sexing the Body: Gender Politics and the Construction of Sexuality*. New York: Basic Books.

Foucault, Michel. 1990. *The History of Sexuality: An Introduction, Volume One*. New York: Vintage Books.

Gagnon, John, and William Simon. 1969. 'Psychosexual Development'. *Transaction* 16(5): 17–23.

Gagnon, John, and Edward Laumann, et al. 1994. *The Social Organization of Sexuality*. Chicago: U of Chicago P.

Gardiner, Raleigh M. 2014. *Desire and Fantasy: The Conditions of Reality between the Self and the Other*. Graduate School of Art Theses, Washington University ETD 22. <https://doi.org/10.7936/K74Q7RW4>.

Goodwin, and Jasper, J. 2004. *Rethinking Social Movement: Structure, Meaning, and Emotion*. Lanham: Rowman & Littlefield.

Government of India. 1850. *Indian Penal Code*. <https://legislative.gov.in/sites/default/files/A1860-45.pdf.>

Grosz, Elizabeth. 1990. *Jacques Lacan: A Feminist Introduction*. New York: Routledge.

———. 1994. *Volatile Bodies: Toward a Corporal Feminism*. Bloomington: Indiana UP.

Halperin, David. 1989. 'Is There a History of Sexuality?'. *History and Theory* 28(3): 257–74.

———. 2002. *How to Do the History of Homosexuality*. Chicago: U of Chicago P.

Hansen, Kathryn. 2002. 'A Different Desire, a Different Femininity: Theatrical Transvestism in Parsi, Gujarati and Marathi Theatres, 1850–1940'. In *Queering India: Same Sex Eroticism in Indian Culture and Society*, ed. Ruth Vanita. NY and London: Routledge.

———. 2011. *Stages of Life: Indian Theatre Autobiographies*. New York: Anthem Press.

Jagose, Annamarie. 1996. *Queer Theory: An Introduction*. New York: New York UP.

Kesavan, C. 1968. *Jeevitha Samaram*. National Book Stall.

Kumar, Udaya. 1997. 'Self, Body and Inner Sense: Some Reflections on Sree Narayana Guru and Kumaran Asan'. *Studies in History* 13(2): 247–70.

Lacan, Jacques. 1977. *Écrits: A Selection*. Trans. Alan Sheridan. New York: W.W. Norton & Co.

———. 1977. *The Seminar. Book III. The Psychoses, 1955–1956*. Trans. Russell Grigg. New York: W. W. Norton & Co.

Lacan, Jacques, Jacques-Alain Miller, and Bruce Fink. 1999. *On Feminine Sexuality, the Limits of Love and Knowledge: The Seminar of Jacques Lacan*. New York and London: W. W. Norton & Co.

McArthur, L., Holbert, D., and Peña, M. 2005. 'An Exploration of the Attitudinal and Perceptual Dimensions of Body Image among Male and Female Adolescents from Six Latin American Cities'. *Adolescence* 40: 801–16.

Muraleedharan, T. 2000. 'V. T. Nandakumar: Two Girls (Malayalam)'. In *Same-Sex Love in India*. eds. Vanita R., Kidwai S. New York: Palgrave Macmillan. 358–65.

———. 2008. 'Interview with C. L. Jose' (Unpublished).

Menon, Nivedita. 2008. *Sexualities*. New Delhi: Zed Books.

———. 2012. *Seeing Like a Feminist*. London: Penguin Books.

Osella, Caroline. 2011. 'Desires under Reform: Contemporary Reconfigurations of Family, Marriage, Love and Gender in a Transnational South Indian Matrilineal Muslim Community'. *SOAS Research Online*. <https:// eprints. Soas.ac.uk/12143>.

Osella, Filipo. 2012. 'Malabar Secrets: South Indian Muslim Men's (Homo) sociality across the Indian Ocean'. *Asian Studies Review* 36: 531–49.

Pillai, Manu S. 2015. *The Ivory Throne: Chronicles of the House of Travancore*. New Delhi: Harper Collins India.

Plummer, K. 1995. *Telling Sexual Stories: Power, Change and Social Worlds*. London: Routledge.

———, ed. 2002. *Sexualities: Critical Assessments*. Four Volumes. London: Routledge.

Putnam, Hilary. 1988. *Representation and Reality*. Cambridge: MIT Press.

———. 1975. *Mind, Language and Reality*. Cambridge: Cambridge UP.

Rajeevan, B. 1999. 'From Caste to Sex: A Study on Sexuality and the Formation of Modern Subject in Kerala'. In *Rethinking Development: Kerala's Development Experience*, ed. M. A. Oommen. New Delhi: Concept Publishing Company. 45–59.

Ramesh, Reshma, and Kannamkottapilly Chandrasekharan Prajitha. 2021. 'Family Planning Practices in Kerala: A Critical Appraisal Using National Family Health Survey Data'. *Indian Journal of Clinical Medicine* 10(1–2).

Richardson, D. 2000. *Rethinking Sexuality*. London: SAGE.

Sreekumar, K. 2006. *Ochira Velukutty*. Thrissur: Kerala Sangeetha Nataka Academy.

Unni, R. 2011. *A Snowballing Archive of the National Conference of Women's Movements*. Unpublished narrative contributed to the project carried out by J. Devika for the Indian Association of Women's Studies, Kozhikode.

Wallace, David. 2002. 'Out in the Academy: Heterosexism, Invisibility, and Double Consciousness'. *College English* 65: 53–66.

Weeks, Jeffrey. 1985. *Sexuality and Its Discontents: Meanings, Myths and Modern Sexualities*. London: Routledge.

———. 1998. 'The Sexual Citizen'. *Theory, Culture and Society* 15(3–4): 35–52.

THREE

# Re-reading *Indulekha*

## *Intimate Hierarchies in the Ambiguities of Sanskritised Registers and Domesticated Social Space*

Arya K.

### 1

The structures of power, tradition, caste, faith and gender, consolidated by the local elites were challenged by the rupture created by Westernisation and colonialism as it took root within the Indian subcontinent. While the Western reform endeavours were conceived as a moment of self-critique and introspection by the colonised bodies of these initiatives, the challenges posed by these cultural incursions were resisted by the national enterprises. These national movements, defined and designed via their relation to the colonial interventions, attempted to retrieve traditions and recast them as national symbols. Such symbolic and linguistic restructurings have also described the literary productions in the period. In such a context, colonialism could be identified as a process catalysing the evolution of an elite progressive society, defined via its indigenous sentiments, into cultural 'amphibians' (Menon 1997, 296).

One of the ways in which the cultural elites who were mourning the past evolved into agents who rediscovered the enchantment of the present was through the canonisation of material histories over affective histories. Here, it is pertinent to tease out how the literary sensibilities of the Malayali woman were conceived within these canons. While the literary imaginations found in Malayalam missionary, Dalit and elite prose narratives had more dissimilarities than similarities, the linguistic references (language), national imaginings, imaginative reconstruction of space and subject formation were prescribed by an overtly elitist logic of articulation. To that end, this essay attempts to study the fraught cultural encounter between literariness and feminine affective-scapes in the early stages of modernisation by critically looking at the novel *Indulekha* (1889).

On closely studying the history of Kerala, it may be observed that women did not assume sociocultural agency in the early twentieth century. This could be interpreted in two ways. Firstly, the Malayali public sphere was not conducive to women's sociocultural interactions before the Western reform movements. Secondly, women's cultural negotiations and discursive engagements were left unarchived by the hegemonic narratives that animated this period. As women's discursive engagements were challenged or sidelined from the macrohistories of the period, it is difficult to reflect on this absence of women using documented sources. These unrecorded women's discourses can be retrieved only by tracing the literariness of literature and the historicity of history.

As suggested by the recorded histories of Malayalam literature, while women's literary works can be traced back to the nineteenth century, narrative references that shed light on women's social lives stretch beyond this period. The sensual and affective aspects of prominent women and their heterosexual and domestic engagements have been the subjects of literary discussions in the preceding periods as well. *Sandesha kavyas*, written by men with intense romantic passion and reminiscing about time together with their lover (denoting *vipralambhasringara*); *Acheecharithangal* that sensuously describe women's physical features; and puranic textual descriptions of women denote that women's aesthetic beauty has been the subject of literary narratives before and after the permeation of Western influence in the region.

Though women's creative and literary works have not been recorded within the bound volumes of a literary text or circulated for widespread consumption among reading communities, it could be assumed that they have also flexed their imaginative faculties, as evidenced by the innumerable *Thaaratupattukal* (lullabies),

*Unjalpattukal, Ammanapattukal* and *Kaikottikalipattukal.*[1] These oral narratives, formed within the many quotidian pleasures and interests, captured the 'structures of feeling' (Williams 1985, 184–88) that constituted the everyday, and were lost within the fleeting and non-institutionalised textual registers of familiarity. These gendered cultures of recital that sifted competing versions of oral narratives ceaselessly hinged on memory and women's creative capabilities.

However, these oral traditions that allowed room for subjective inflexions should be distinguished from the more stringent techniques of memorisation and recitation employed in Sanskrit texts like the Vedas, Upanishads and Kavyas, which were preserved as standardised texts. Elite classical art forms like Koodiyaattom and Kathakali rigorously trained the body in ways that could be compared to the uncompromising diligence with which rules were followed in the renditions of Sanskrit texts. Even though these rule-bound art forms considered improvisation as a technique, the sanctity of prescribed formats was asserted by strategically disqualifying random digressions from this standard, reiterating the fidelity to the original prescribed texts through conscientious acts of textual embodiment.

While the cultures of recital associated with women required the repeated studying and memorisation of the text, these oral traditions renounced the text's ascendancy and inflexibility, reifying

[1] *Paatusahithyam* (which refers to poetry that gives emphasis to tune) in Malayalam can be largely divided into two—oral and written. While some oral compositions have been archived within the written literary canons, *Tharattupattukal, Unjalpattukal, Ammanapattukal, Kaikottipattukal, Thiruvathirapattukal* remained as oral art forms outside the rigid formats prescribed by canonical literary standards. *Ammanapattu* refers to songs/oral compositions that accompanied the *ammanakali*, which is a recreational practice in Kerala performed during wedding ceremonies in lower-caste households. *Unjalpattu* denotes a specific kind of folk song. *Kaikottipattukal* refers to oral compositions sung during a traditional *thiruvathira* performance, also called *kaikottikali*, which is usually staged by upper-caste women.

the text's plurality and its interchangeability with textual variants. As a result, a new textual ecosystem premised on the symbiotic complementarity of the creator and the created, and the text and its variants came into being. Through repeated recollections and recitals that challenged the hegemony of monolithic textual formats (Walter 2002, 59), gendered oral cultures were interwoven into the rhythms of everyday life. As the hierarchy between the text and its derivatives was destabilised, text and its constitutive essence were reinterpreted as abstract convictions.

The criterion determining the literariness of Malayalam literature was conceived within the letter-centric modalities of articulation (Williams 1985, 184–88). Since written genres were attributed with literariness as compared to other genres of articulation, these genres were privileged over oral cultures. As a result, palm-leaf manuscripts gained predominance with the introduction of printing in the region. Consequently, gendered cultures of orality and recital were marginalised from the regimes of truth that defined creative literature.

The gendered pedagogic practices in Kerala mandated that male students be provided with Sanskrit-based education (Padmanabha Menon qtd. in Bhaskaranunni 2012, 1054), while Malayalam-centric education was provided to the female students, as Malayalam was considered an inerudite language in the curricula designed for women. Due to this, Malayalam was popularly called '*penmalayalam*' in nineteenth-century Kerala. While men were taught to recite Sanskrit texts rhythmically, women were taught to recite Malayalam texts melodiously. Male subjects educated through a compact and methodical curriculum and embodied ideal modern subjectivities were privileged over the female subjects in the sociocultural spaces of Kerala. On the other hand, the feminine subjectivities that were moulded through the Malayalam-centric curricula premised on the affective and rhythmic rendering of Malayalam texts, had to strive longer to achieve the benefits of modernity.

Since print-based education served as the crux and agenda of modernity in Kerala, informal modalities of education that were presided over by women, and could not be contained within the structure and form of hegemonic pedagogic practices, were not privileged within the normative literary, critical and academic regimes. Instead, women's experiential knowledge gained visibility only within autobiographical and prefatory narratives. As thought was considered preeminent to experience, women's experiential narratives were not attributed materiality within the interpretive frameworks of modernity that privileged the seen and written word.

## 2

Regarding Malayalam, *Indulekha* (1889) assumes a crossway between literature and literary criticism. The imaginative renderings of the novel as a genre and the new plateaus of literariness that Chandu Menon construes in the preface of *Indulekha* coalesced to infuse a new understanding of the novel form in the Malayali consciousness. The novel abounds with temporal bearings, including the concord–discord dyad that marked the Malayali responses towards Western modernisation, new literacy, tradition and modernity. Within the novel, the Malayali woman is identified as a discrete category of subjectivisation. Unlike the male characters in the novel, the unique lifeworlds inhabited by the women characters mark the culturally desired female imaginaries of literariness. These middle-class-Malayali female imaginaries persisted for quite some time in the literary topos.

The different modes of reading inaugurated by *Indulekha* serve as a cultural archive that provides vital clues about Kerala's modernity, its diverse cultures of recital and the criteria that constituted literariness. These new modalities of recital could be evidenced right from O. Chandu Menon's preface (1889) to *Indulekha*. At around the third decade of the twentieth century, the literary critic M. P. Paul canonised *Indulekha*, which was widely regarded as the first quintessentially Malayalam novel, for moulding the affective registers that formed the aesthetic contours of the novel as a literary genre. Later, as the engagements of Cultural

Studies gained traction and visibility, *Indulekha* was subjected to varied kinds of critical scrutiny, revealing the paradoxes and possibilities that the novel embodied and represented. As a result, the historical entanglements between the emergence of the novel as a new literary genre and the multiple trajectories of Kerala's modernity(ies) is a fascinating area of study.

The present essay attempts to build on Udaya Kumar's pivotal study (2007) that examined the new visualities and sensual/affective registers that novels, as a literary genre, inaugurated in the region, and M. V. Narayanan's inquiry (2010) that foregrounds 'genre' in the distinct context of *Indulekha*'s eighteenth chapter. To this end, this study aims to tease out how 'literariness', as a constructed literary–aesthetic attribute of the text, fashioned the affective-scapes of women in the context of the amphibious terrains introduced by *Indulekha*.

Colonial modernity transitioned the savarna middle-class men in Kerala from the loosely-held structures of feudalism to the finitude of clerkship. Meanwhile, savarna women who inhabited the inner domiciles remained rooted, with some privileges to boot. Thus, it is not difficult to see that Indulekha had access to a separate home, collection of books and reading room. Even though she was temporal and deed-bound to the privateness of her house, sans any role in outer discourses, she was granted choices. However, it meant that her English and her embroidering did not transpose into a vocational pursuit, a critique of which can be seen in *Parangodiparinayam* (1892): 'Our women's clothes are barely "*onnarayum mundum*";[2] does that require any embroidering?' (my translation; Menon 2013, 55). The novel ends with the entailing of an Indulekha who lives as a middle-class cosmopolitan woman. The iconic Bangla film *Charulatha* (1964), directed by Satyajit Ray, could be imagined as forming a continuum with *Indulekha*, with the central character who spends her life in idleness after

[2] *Onnarayum mundum*: *Onnara* is a lower garment worn by Malayali women which is tightly wound around the waist, while *mundu* is a thicker fabric that is draped over the *onnara*.

marriage. The literariness in Malayalam interjected the gender consciousness by aestheticising the woman who resides in the interiorities of her house—indulging in writing and reading, idling by embroidering—while the husband with a government job commits himself to the social sphere.

Though progressiveness does not necessarily imply a 'coming out', the choice between the inner and outer spheres is kept beyond the agential-doingness of the woman. The novels of the nineteenth century can be seen addressing the aestheticised fashioning of prototypal women. While 'nation' occupies the conversational node in the eighteenth chapter of *Indulekha,* the fourth chapter in *Meenakshi* (1890), 'A Conversation between Three Sisters', broods on women's conduct, moral rectitude and *sambandham,*[3] affixing the debates on gender consciousness (Nair 1890, 55–56). Unlike in *Indulekha*, here, the figurations happen in the foreroom of the *tharavadu* (a nair house). A foreroom, by virtue of its in-betweenness, conjoins the inner and outer realms of the domicile, even as it projects a vision of the outside. Even though passages in this novel identify masculinist power derivatives as impediments to women's freedom, the commonised readings of literature that locate *Indulekha* within the ambit of its national imaginaries cancel out the literariness of these womanspeaks.

The aesthetic imaginings of Malayalam literature were brought about by an interactive network of varied discourses that operate within an asymmetrical public sphere. These asymmetries form the principal determinant for readers and characters to conceive their ideations of the literary texts as they experience them. The

[3] *Sambandham*: It refers to a conjugal practice that was prevalent throughout the initial decades of the twentieth century among the kshatriya, nair and *ambalavaasi* castes of Hindus. Since only the elder son in a brahmin family was allowed the privilege of marriage, it was customary for the younger sons in the family to engage in sexual relations with women who belonged to the kshatriya, nair and *ambalavaasi* castes. Children from such alliances lived in their maternal homes and could claim matrilineal inheritance. This system was primarily instituted with the aim of gratifying the sexual urges of the younger sons in a brahmin family.

apparency and the normalisation of domestic spaces is one of the most vehement ideations associated with women. It becomes particularly discernible in the scapes of Malayalam literature where the reception of a foreign genus, like the novel, happens within the frameworks of indigenous aesthetics.

*Indulekha* qualifies as an important site of these complex transactions as it portrays the divergent spatial terrains that Madhavan and Indulekha inhabit, despite their equivalent educational status. Madhavan steps outside the house to complete his collegiate education at Madras. Indulekha, on the other hand, is taken along by her uncle Panchumenavan to his workstead, only to be given home-tutoring until she is sixteen. It is only through matrimonial sanctioning that Indulekha finally gets to visit Madras. *Meenakshi* bespeaks a similar narrative, with Meenakshi's education limited to the confines of Puthanmalika, even as her brothers attend college in Madras.

Nevertheless, there is a stark contrast between the lifeworlds of Indulekha—who resides in the upper storey of her mansion—and the other women in the novel, who reel under the domesticities at the bottom tier, thickened by the discursive sphere of the kitchen. The aptitudinal prerogatives of Indulekha, informed by her letterbox, collection of books, jewellery, fondness for dress, English-speaking abilities, love for music and embroidery, and her love life accost the heightened spatial dynamics that the novel imbues to the upper storey. The upper storey is also cast as the transactional space of the complex struggles between the lower tier that Kalyanikutti inhabits and Madras as experienced by Madhavan. Here, the spatial imaginaries are not entirely anchored by a sense of reality or lack thereof. Instead, the moorings are that of pastoral power, duly encapsulated by the way Krishnamenon restrained Indulekha's education within the confines of the home, deploying masculinist soft power.

It could be noted that a specific spatial configuration at work in *Indulekha* forecloses the upper storey from integrating the relational dynamics that a man–woman friendship brings. While Indulekha's conversation with Cherusseri comes to pass at the bottom tier, the bodily acts of Indulekha—including her privacy, love, the discussions on sex within *sambandham* that turns into Madhavan's exhortation on female muliebrity, the refusal of Suri Namboothiripad's proposal, and her interactions with her relatives—happen within the spatial permutations of the upper storey.

This aptitudinal strain of spatial imaginings could also be traced in other discourses, especially in the early paintings of Raja Ravi Varma, with national, regional and contemporary implications. Regional paintings like *Nair Lady Adorning Her Hair* (1873), *There Comes Papa* (1893) and *Reclining Nair Lady* (1902) evince a specific spatial coding of the domestic space. These paintings portray the women engaging in acts like doing their hair or reclining by reading and attending to a child. Interestingly, only in the third painting can one identify the presence of a maid. It is rather unusual for Varma's paintings to have little to no maids, as his early paintings like *Shakuntala* (1870), *Shakuntala Pathralekhan* (1876), *Ashokavaniyile Seetha* (1894) and *Damayanthi* (1895) are distinctive for their profuse presence of accompanying maids. This visible pictorial shift represents an alternative social order that displaces maids from being privy to private space. The women lonesomely retreat to their private spaces, leaving them in the company of objectal experiences, including books. This middle-class spatial imaginary thus becomes an overriding factor that shapes the inner order of the domestic spaces within the novel.

This is true in the case of *Indulekha* as well, as Indulekha is left alone in her privateness with her books, embroidering and listening to music while her maid joins the workforce at the bottom tier. While the space of value in *Indulekha* is constituted by being equally conversant with both tradition and modernity, the emotional nonchalance that readers feel for Kalyanikutti's *sambandham*, and the untoward laughter that Suri Namboothiripad's sexual desire for Lakshmikutty Amma evokes, leaves one with the realisation that specific episodes are kept beyond this space of value. The spaces of value associated with middle-class savarna women determine and control the expressional paradigms of the novel.

In their receptiveness of the novel form, each language creates its own spaces of value to emplace the aptitudinal registers of women within its disciplinary transactions.

Through construing the spaces of value and the encoding of discrete language within the narrative spaces, the Malayali imaginaries interpreted a foreign genus like the novel. The aptitudinal registers instituted by the novel distance and confront the traditional narrative strain, leading to a redefining of aesthetic discernments whereby regional agencies are interpreted and vectors of literariness strengthened.

The narrational worlds of the women characters in *Indulekha* are encumbered with their struggle toward the common language used in the novel, begetting the use of Sanskrit as a discrete language. The body consciousness that is inbred in the very ideations of the novel form hinders the novelist from having a full-fledged description of Indulekha's character. The extravagance on display while describing Suri Namboothiripad is curiously absent in the case of Indulekha. However, the choice of Sanskrit slokas in the love conversations fills in for the limited description of Indulekha, constituting the narrative's discrete language. The Sanskrit slokas within the moralistic narrative codings of the novel bear a gaze on the female body. There is nothing much to separate between the slokas that make for Suri Namboothiripad's objectal gaze towards Indulekha and Madhavan's loving beholding of her. What is at fault is not the betelling of the female body; instead, this description's exclusivity makes it problematic. While Indulekha is reduced to the subject of this gaze, to a state of docile agentiality through the discrete language, Madhavan and Suri Namboothiripad secure a monopolous and visional agency. Sanskrit, unlike Malayalam, eases itself into a particular strain of corporeal writing, satisfying the preceptors competent in the discrete language at that point in time.

Here, one could see the Indian imaginary of a modernised woman. The novels of the nineteenth century curated their modern heroines as housewives who are devout, book-indulging and soft-spoken. Renaissance India modelled their 'ideal woman' after the Western prototypes. The emotional coldness that the readers share for Kalyanikutti's plight in *Indulekha* bespeaks a certain womanliness that does not fit into the conventional frames of femininity. Kalyanikutti is taken along by Namboothiripad by 'locking her up in a palanquin'. At the sight of this, 'women in that house pushed the gentle Kalyanikutti through the western door to the *padinjatta*[4] as if she is an alive swine or something', reads the description of the *sambandham*. This reference to the 'alive swine or something' divulges that Kalyani is yet to attain the descriptive bearing of the 'normal' woman. The sentimental literariness of this novel is enclosed within the women's prototypes devised by the European frameworks of morality.

Through the recurrent practice of reading within the domesticated spaces, women partook in Renaissance endeavours and the national movement. The ones who indulged in the process of writing habituated the specific literary spaces offered by Sanskrit slokas, *Aattakathas, Thirivathirapattu, Thullalpattu,* and drama. Women have taken a considerably long time to transition from the prosodic culture to the everydayness of prose narratives. The same cannot be said about reading, as they read themselves into the imaginary construing the nation. The lifeworlds of middle-class women were reconstituted within the inner logic of nation-building and Renaissance through the curation of various categories of women, including the home-bound reader, the one who leaves dance for music, scriptures for books, and *sambandham* for marriage.

Meenakshi Mukharjee observes that the novel, unlike the modern prose narratives, has succeeded in inscribing definitive spatio-temporal registers (1994, 5). This spatio-temporal enumeration has allowed the curation of a specific kind of vision and agentiality. Here, the narrative preciseness does not impede the exposition of subjectivity. The novel does not restrain the male self to the configurations of spatio-temporal registers; it is imbued

---

[4] *Pandinjatta* refers to a room situated in the Western part of aristocratic homes.

with a nation-transcending spirit. G. P. Pillai's travelogue *London and Paris* (1897) portrays a certain male self that is curious and joyful at the prospect of visiting a distant place. Nevertheless, in certain places, the nation-transcending agency can complicate the nation's experiential paradigms. Only after seeing the tuft on Madhavan's head did Babu Govindasen suspect a possible Malabar connection. Even when the body bears the imprints of nation-bound community rituals, the conscience holds onto the transcendence of the boundaries.

This can be duly referenced in early Malayalam novels, where the pleasure of travelling is derived from the deployment of a nation-transcending agency that operates within the frameworks of a body that bears an imprint of the community rituals within the nation. These spaces of the nation are new urban-scapes that received traction through reforms based on European ideals. The spatial referents of Indulekha, who resides within the ancestral *tharavadu*, are formed amidst the figure of the cosmopolitan hero, who is not disconcerted by the urban social spaces, and that of the parochial *karanavan* (patriarch), who is overwhelmed by regional reforms.

The performative utterances of Indulekha's body, formed within the disciplinary structures at home and in Madras, were articulated through gendered competencies like reading, sewing and singing. Indulekha's spatial signifiers were premised more on reforms than on traditions. While the spatial signifiers of the hero were based on his ability to don/inhabit multiple subjective positions and sartorial practices, the spatial referents of Indulekha were circumscribed within received moral codes. Here, the other characters move towards and inhabit the moral codes upheld by Indulekha. In this context, it is pertinent to delve into the reasons behind construing women's corporeal utterances/performances as self-reflexive agential acts despite being tethered to prescriptive moral codes and patriarchal structures of desires.

In Kalyaniamma's *Vyaazhavattasmaranakal* (Memories of Twelve Years), she reminisces about receiving her ailing husband Swadeshabhimani Ramakrishna Pillai, at the Quilon railway station

(1958, 44–45). Though her brother-in-law warns her that her efforts to meet her husband are futile, she decides to visit him at the station, only to be ignored by her husband who does not even talk to her for about half an hour, after which he starts his journey home. Kalyaniamma remarks that Swadeshabhimani made her acknowledge her mistake through his silence and that she atones for her omission in the same way. Here, it is curious to note that the severity of Swadeshabhimani's premeditated silence assumes the disciplinary language of authority, suggesting that the disciplinary paradigms that mark out women's agential positions need not necessarily be instituted through aggression and violence, as even the affective idiom of love and silence can serve as strategic modes of regulation. Similarly, one could observe that the patriarchal language of affectionate authority is deployed in Indulekha as well. The novel presents Indulekha as a home-schooled woman, suggesting that the patriarchal structures of control and disciplining remain intact though it could be negotiated. Moreover, even Madhavan's quarrels with Indulekha could also be situated within the affectionate language of patriarchal authority. The discourses of savarna middle-class women are aestheticised within domestic imageries through the normalisation and naturalisation of this discrete patriarchal language of affectionate authority. It is this discrete language that (re)configures the educated, self-aware and discerning subject into passive objects of heterosexual conjugality and acculturates mobile bodies into domesticated beings pegged down within everyday monotony.

Here, the narrative strategies deployed by novels to construct feminine subject positions have to be understood. The most important of these is the delineation of naturalised corporeal practices formed at the interstices of past traditions and reformative modernity. Literature that is simultaneously premised on the traditional and modern structures of domesticity was articulated as 'natural'. Another narrative strategy of the novel is its linguistic feature that gives the impression of superficial rejection and discreet espousal. The unfamiliar yet intimate quality of space that unconditionally accepted the discrete essence of language also signifies the crisis of negotiation between tradition and modernity. While articulating this crisis, the emancipatory domestic ideals constructed through such novels only served as mirages that created the impression of choice and freedom. Such received notions of agency defined women's gendered positions not only within novels but also in the plays written/performed during this time. The feminine ideals portrayed within the reconstituted literariness of Malayalam literature simultaneously signified passive objective positions and reformed subjective selves.

* * *

Literariness need not necessarily evolve from within literature. It is constituted by regional aptitudes and crystallises around alternate discourses. Literary genres in Malayalam literature come into being through the aesthetic representation of women's moral codes, Sanskritised sexual awareness and domesticity. Subject formations within asymmetrical public spheres take place by engaging with the crisis between tradition and modernity. The novel, as a genre, moulded its techniques of articulation by strategically reconfiguring the gendered restraints of patriarchal discourses that delimit women into the affective language of love and kinship that fashion the disciplined feminine subject. The methodical cataloguing of generic texts within the disciplinary bounds of library systems excluded books preserved in the dusty and shrouded corners of the home that embodied women's non-canonical creative cultures. Women's literary experiences were naturalised by reinterpreting the aptitudinal structures of novels as literary qualities. Aptitudes of reading were formulated through the naturalisation of value systems. The new literary imaginations formed through various literary forms bear an overwhelming resemblance to women's coffers, carrying an assortment of motley items, the emotional value of which far exceeds their material value. The crises within Malayalam literariness can be delineated only by attempting to re-read the aptitudinal structures and critiquing the disciplinary structures, discrete language, normalisations and spaces of value within the literature.

## References

Bhaskaranunni, P. 2012. *Pathonpathaam Nootandile Keralam* [Nineteenth-century Kerala]. Thrissur: Kerala Sahitya Akademi.

Kalyaniamma, B. 1958. *Vyaazhavattasmaranakal.* Thrissur: Mangalodayam Private Limited.

Kumar, Udaya, 2007. *Kaazhchayum Vaayanayum: Indulekhayum Chihnavyaparangale Sambandhikunna Chila Prasnangalum*. Preface. *Indulekha* by O. Chandu Menon. Kottayam: DC Books. 7–18.

———. 2013. *Abhiruchiyum Achadakkavum: Anthappayiye Innu Vaayikkumbol.* Preface. *Naluperiloruthan Adhava Nadakandyam Kavithvam* by C. Andhapayi. Thiruvananthapuram: Chintha Publishers.

———. 2017. *Writing the First Person: Literature, History, and Autobiography in Modern Kerala.* Ranikhet: Permanent Black.

Menon, O. Chandu. 2007. *Indulekha.* Kottayam: DC Books.

Menon, Dilip N. 1997. 'Caste and Colonial Modernity: Reading *Saraswativijayam*'. *Studies in History* 13: 291–312.

Menon, Kizhackepaattu Ramankutty. 2013. *Parongodi Parinayam.* Thiruvananthapuram: Chintha Publishers.

Mukherjee, Meenakshi. 1994. *Realism and Reality.* New York: Oxford UP.

Nair, Cheruvaalathu Chathu. 1890. *Meenakshi.* Calicut: Spectator Achukudam.

Narayanan, M. V. 2010. *Pathinettaam Aadhyathinte Baakipathrangal. Bhashaposhini.* n.p.

Narendran, K. M. 2001. *Mrigabalikal, Vijayolsavangal.* In *Indulekha: Vaayanayude Disakal*, ed. E. P. Rajagopalan. Thrissur: Kerala Sahitya Akademi. 37–48.

Ong, Walter. 2002. *Orality and Literacy: The Technology of the Word.* New York: Routledge.

Paul, M. P. 1958. *Novel Sahithyam.* Kottayam: SPCS.

Williams, Raymond. 1985. *Keywords: A Vocabulary of Culture and Society.* New York: Oxford UP.

FOUR

# Stree, Purushan, Napumsakan

## *Shaping Femininities and Effeminacies in Early-Nineteenth-Century Kerala*

MAALAVIKA AJAYAKUMAR

This essay revolves around the lexical matrices that structured and tempered terms of gendered references within the discursive contexts of nineteenth-century Kerala and its pre-nascent public sphere. It takes off from two critical premises: (1) that language is an ideational ground detrimental to constituting 'subjects within a hierarchy of relations' (Mills 1997, 38); and (2) that gender is an 'embodied interactional accomplishment' (Charlebois 2011, 9). Anchored on the conceptualisation of language as a potent site of struggle, gendered and otherwise, such an analysis could throw light on the lexical implications of these referential terms while visibilising how, at this juncture, individuals were interpellated to identify themselves as gendered subjects.

Kerala's social reality at this historical juncture (the first half of the nineteenth century) was only partly reflected in the print archives of the pre-nascent sphere, with the number of texts in circulation being largely constrained to instruction manuals, pamphlets and textbooks (with didactic missionary motivations aimed towards children and vernacular schools), a few novels (the readership of which was limited), almanacs, college quarterlies and a limited number of monthlies and periodicals. Out of these materials, this essay subjects to analysis, two crucial archives: Benjamin Bailey's *A Dictionary of High and Colloquial Malayalim and English*, published in 1846, and his later work, *A Dictionary, English and Malayalim*, published in 1849, both of which were printed at the Church Mission Press in Kottayam. These sources could aid an investigation into the vernacular terms of gendered reference that were in use during early-nineteenth-century Kerala and the matrices of colonial, nascent-modern assumptions that structured them.

Bailey's 1846 Malayalam-to-English dictionary [henceforth *1846 Dictionary*] will be posited here as a surface text that evinces a certain *nomos* that positioned gendered social actors within the socio-symbolic terrain of Kerala. Here, I take the gendered social actor as an Althusserian subject, fashioned and conceived through ideological apparati and their interpellations. This analysis would acknowledge that the *1846 Dictionary* allows a textual space that accommodates regional inflections of gendered terms that disturb nineteenth-century missionary pronouncements on ideal modesties and restrictions on heterosexual intimacies. However, if the *1846 Dictionary* evinces the lexicographer's compromise, the 1849 English–Malayalam dictionary [henceforth the *1849 Dictionary*] becomes a textual site of Eurocentric knowledge production and Western ethnographic gaze, that attempts to temper vernacular understandings of gendered terms. An observation by Gayathri Gopinath gains valence against this context. She says, 'An abiding legacy of colonial modernity is its institution of a way of seeing, and hence knowing, that obscures the interrelation of imperial, racial, and settler colonial projects as they produce racial, gendered and sexual subjectivities' (2018, 7).

Bailey's dictionaries, when conceived as a site for mapping ideologically inflected gendered referential items, gain valence in that their analysis can serve as an apt point of departure that allows for a prefatory glance into (1) the gendered referential terms of the nineteenth century that would continue to be prevalent in the Malayali public sphere (even in its retransformed contemporary digital manifestations); (2) the lexical limits and ideological imbrications of the gendered terms as deployed by the nineteenth-century Malayali public; (3) the permissible definitions for non-conforming gender identities that remained conspicuously tacit in Kerala's deliberative terrains; and (4) the moral matrices that were deployed to define womanliness and manliness, as well as to construct desirable and transgressive feminine and masculine categories.

## 1

## The Bailey Dictionaries: Lexicography and Its Gendered Dimensions

Bailey interpreted the 'modern' as that which is 'new' and 'contemporary' (refer to his entry on 'modern' in *A Dictionary, English and Malayalim*, 1849, 303). Thus, it would not be wrong to posit that for Bailey, the historical juncture during which the dictionaries were being penned down was one that was marked at least by 'nascent-modern' tendencies. The definitions articulated within Bailey's dictionaries endeavour to premise the need for a modern cultural totality as 'self-evident'—one that draws the limits of libidinal economies within strict heteronormative, matrimonial frameworks. To solidify and incentivise these curated 'modern' aspirations, the missionary–lexicographer also deploys gender-essentialist fictions to repackage referential terms which evince erotic truth into tacit references of sexual shame, thereby fashioning 'aberrant' and 'transgressive' categories against which idealised gendered subjectivities could gain valence.

A recurring thematic that arises in these definitions is an androcentric emphasis on male virility and female spousal function. This tendency characterises much of Bailey's lexical classification of sexual subjects into ideal, hegemonic and transgressive/perfidious categories of masculinities and femininities. The discursive othering of 'un-modest' feminine categories is further inflected by the caste specificities of the region in the nineteenth century. While the authorial intentions behind the inclusion, selection and curation of these terms do not form the crux of this investigation, these texts often betray a deliberate omission of gender variant categories and records consciously ambiguous definitions of same-sex intimacies. Drawing on Foucauldian formulations of discourse, Mills identifies such exclusions as a preliminary stage in solidifying idealised, delimited practices of discursive interaction (2008, 46).

Secondly, these texts evince more than the linguistic competence or gendered grammar of the nineteenth-century native speaker.

Rather, these gain valence as an 'episteme'—employed here to mean a totality of 'discursive structures which come about as a result of the interaction of the range of discourses circulating and authorised at that particular time' including the 'range of methodologies which a culture draws on as *self-evident* in order to be able to think about certain subjects' (Mills 2008, 51; italics mine). Conversely, it could be posited against this assumption that, while essentialist generalisations of masculinities and femininities are made to seem *self-evident*, a greater 'epistemic violence' (Spivak 2010, 35) can be mapped in the dictionaries' deliberate refusal to allow referential terms for orientations that transgress and cannot be captured within these generalisations.

Thirdly, the dictionaries' presentation of multiple, mutually exclusive meanings of a single entry as 'absolute synonyms' can be premised as a critical lexico-political site of inquiry. The term 'absolute synonyms' is used within this context to mean Igor Burkhanov's elucidation of lexical items that are interchangeably identical with respect to their 'descriptive social and affective meanings' (Burkhanov 1998, 16). While Bailey never succeeds in identifying absolute synonyms, his presentation of various terms has been curated in a way that visually suggests that these meanings have significant overlaps. Yet another seemingly insignificant aspect of these multiple definitions is the unique lexicographic order employed to list them. Such unique curatorial practices of lexical signification would be identified as strategic nodes of understanding the socio-political matrices and androcentric utterances that shaped the social worlds of nineteenth-century Kerala and the lexicographer's incursions into the textual world that attempted to define these utterances. At its core, the publication of Bailey's bilingual dictionaries provides a textual moment—one that allows for an exploration into the linkages between gendered meaning-making and the performative claims that are engendered thus. With a significant number of entries on gender categories alongside trite definitions of their constitutive and assumed 'essentialist' features, Bailey's dictionaries make the rhetorical locus of early gender debates discernible. While

Bailey's definitions (arguably) could have been inflected by familiar Victorian moral matrices, it could also be argued that these entries visibilise the limitations of the semantic terrain within which gendered categories were conceived in early-nineteenth-century Kerala.

## Two Dictionaries: Identifying Colonial Filters and Mapping the Bilingual Malayali

While data on the actual readership of these texts remains sparse, and any investigation into the processes of informant-testing (assuming it was administered at all) that preceded the recording of these entries would, at best, remain a closed corpus, the ingratiation narratives that preface these texts is worth focusing on. Bailey's short prefatory ingratiation narrative to the King attempts to explain the authorial intention as 'a sincere desire to diffuse *real useful knowledge and learning* among your Highness's *subjects*' (Bailey 1849, A2; emphasis mine). This excerpt leads to two critical questions: (1) what is the moral–political load carried by the phrase 'real useful knowledge' as used by Bailey here?, and (2) who are the 'subjects' referred to by the author?

At this juncture, it must be emphasised that any reading of the Bailey dictionaries must be prefaced by a note on a critical distinction between the two texts. While both are bilingual dictionaries, *A Dictionary of High and Colloquial Malayalim and English* (1846) is a text wherein Malayalam words are defined in both English and synonymous Malayalam words. Thus, it is safe to assume that only literate Malayalis of the early nineteenth century (which in itself, would be a minority) could comprehend or intellectually respond to these entries. However, *A Dictionary, English and Malayalim* (1849) has only English entry words which are then largely defined in Malayalam alone. Thus, even the literate monolingual reader would not be able to understand the lexical items against which the Malayalam definitions are given. This further limits the readership to a literate *bilingual* minority. It is possible to argue that constituting the bilingual readers of these entries and in extension the dictionary, would have been educated nairs and certain Christian minorities who, by the late nineteenth century, actively voiced a need for kinship and matrimonial reforms through the institutionalisation of the monogamous family and a shift from matrilineal systems. Therefore, it is this bilingual minority—in effect, an extremely limited audience capable of favouring a move towards the 'modern'—that constitute the *subjects* referred to in Bailey's note of ingratiation to the King.

Secondly, the *1846 Dictionary* attempts to elucidate the meanings of Malayalam words used both in refined and colloquial contexts. It would be apt to suggest that the *1846 Dictionary*'s inclusion of colloquial terms (which includes but is not limited to curse words with sexual connotations), while allowing for a wider textual space, also serves, to an extent, to undergird the lexicographer's claims to reliability. As to whether Bailey's texts do, in fact, evince a faithful record of the unadulterated, on-site, local meanings of these terms is open to interpretation. It is within this space of reasonable doubt that this essay posits its alternate reading of Bailey's definitions as legitimising narratives curated to discursively construct Western ethnocentric notions of modesties and masculinities as desirable categories.

Chattopadhyay notes that an 'obsessive articulation of difference between natives and Europeans, is a mainstay of the colonizer's discourse' (2006, 22). However, considering that the dictionaries were royally sanctioned and released under the patronage of the Rajah, Bailey could not formulate a narrative of explicit critical dis-identification between the ritual-bound, superstitious natives and the 'morally edified' Europeans. At the same time, missionary narratives that fell outside the ambit of the Rajah's control and other regional sanctions corroborate Chattopadhyay's observation. Examples include, but are not limited to, texts like the CMS Missionary Registers released during the early decades of the nineteenth century, the *Church Missionary Gleaner* (1842) and Samuel Mateer's *Native Life in Travancore* (1883)—all of which show instances where the social actors are posited as objects in need of moral-spiritual edification. However, since Bailey could not take such narrative licenses with his dictionaries—the publication of which were contingent on the Rajah's sanction—the missionary-lexicographer instead deploys a lexicographical discourse of respectability that would be favoured by 'interpretive communities' (Fish 1980, 14) of educated, literate, bilingual subjects with modern aspirations. It is this critical tendency that makes these dictionaries anticipate the twentieth-century educated Malayalis' shared aspirations of being 'modern' in a colonial state. The subsequent sections of this essay venture a critical analysis of Bailey's gendered definitions—initiating from hegemonic categories, then proceeding to non-hegemonic, transgressive and gender-variant terms of reference.

## 2

## *Purushakunjaran, Kudumbini, Paurusham, Streelakshanam*: Framing Hegemonic Masculinities and Desirable Femininities in Benjamin Bailey's *A Dictionary of High and Colloquial Malayalim and English* (1846)

The first set of entries subjected to analysis would be those that attempt to define men, women and their assumed characteristic features. It would be possible to argue that a critical-colonial gaze that attempts to place the 'man' as the representative of the larger 'mankind'—in effect, aligning the idealised masculine with the 'universal' and femininities with the 'particular' products of regime and decorum—becomes palpable. The *1846 Dictionary* contains more than twenty entries on men and masculinities, the hegemonic categorisations of which are organised around the ideas of 'virility' and the figure of an imagined householder. This becomes evident even from the basic gendered entries: *purushan* (man) and *stree* (woman).

The Malayalam entry word *purushan* (sans critical affixations) is given six meanings: '1. A man, generally or individually, as male, mankind 2. The soul 3. God, the Supreme Being 4. a name of Vishnu 5. life, the living principle 6. a husband' (Bailey 1846, 510). Here, the order (that is allowed through numbered definitions) followed by the lexicographer gains valence. Bailey allows for the preliminary meanings of *purushan* to be a sexed identity while making sure that it is anchored on the larger collective signified by the last word under the first meaning entry—'mankind'. The gendered meanings of *purushan* are ordered in a way that gives precedence to the universalising claims held by the word 'man' over a heterogenous totality (mankind). A tacit affixation of superiority is also framed, as is evident from the second, third and fourth entries, which link the lexical item *purushan* to 'God' and 'the soul'.

Such entries could be informed by (1) the missionary subscription to a male Creator while drawing a cross-cultural parallel with regional religious male deities (as is evoked through the image of Vishnu in the fourth entry); (2) a tacit ingratiation to the male ruler who sanctioned the dictionary; or (3) the need to create a frame narrative within which subsequent, idealised entries on masculinities (in the *1846 Dictionary*) would gain valence as a dominant, venerable category through which further ideations of a male 'householder' (capable of being a 'protector') can be suggested. To build on this third argument, such a frame narrative would allow the lexical items *purushan* and *purushatha* (defined by Bailey as manliness, virility, manhood and the nature of man) as idealised nodal points around which to hierarchise and arrange other gendered categories. It is also worth mentioning here that the common, on-ground usage of *purushan* (deployed to mean 'husband') is included only as the sixth (the last) entry.

In contrast to this, with only two meanings to its credit, the term *stree* is defined as: '1. A woman, or female in general. 2. a wife' (828), with an emphasis on the spousal function immediately following the first meaning which is given a clear gendered and sexed valence. Thus, a social actor identifying with this gender would be assumed to harbour an intrinsic spousal function. Against the contextual terrain of Kerala's pre-nascent as well as nascent public sphere of the late nineteenth and early twentieth centuries, detailed expositions on women—her education, literacy and behaviour—were all embedded within a larger ideological network that aimed at curating the female social actor as an ideal, literate, regimed wife.

The next set of entries being analysed reveals the features attributed to the construction of hegemonic categories of masculinities and femininities. The referential terms of desirable masculinity are hinted at mainly through five entries—*purushakunjaran, purushanagan, purushapungavan, purushasardulan, purusharshaban*—all of which are roughly defined as referring to a 'superior or excellent man'. It is interesting that Bailey does not elucidate on the elements that are constitutive of this 'superiority'. Rather, the defining feature of ideal masculinity is hinted at through an abundance of entries on 'manhood', which include but is not limited to the entry words *purushatha, paurusham, purushathwam, purushalakshanam, purushadharmam*, etc. Two of the representative entries—*paurusham* and *purushardham*—the definitions of which serve as legitimising idioms, must be subjected to analysis.

The term *paurusham* alone (which literally translates into 'manliness') has been given a total of five seemingly overlapping meanings. Out of these, the second, fourth and fifth meanings read 'the property of manhood, virility, manliness', 'semen virile' and 'strength, power, vigour, bravery', respectively (Bailey 1846, 533). Perhaps the fourth entry, 'semen virile', best captures the unit-idea deployed by Bailey to construct idealised masculinities. The fifth definition, which focuses on the corporeal strength of the male, is arranged in the list of meanings in a way that makes it seem to follow from the preceding meaning entries on the virility and procreative ability of the *purushan*. What is also interesting is a significant recurrence of terms that refer to the 'form' and 'shape' of a man. Examples include (but are not limited to) entries on *purushaakaram* and *purushakrithi* (both of which are defined as the 'form of man') and two more entries—*purushapramanam* and *purushadooyasam*—specifically referring to the height and measure of man (533).

Cora Kaplan and David Glover, in their attempts to map the cultural history and ideations of normative masculinities through history, draw on a significant argument by George Mosse—one that places the locus of the 'manly ideal' on a corporeal fixation. They say, 'At the centre of this ideal lay a renewed emphasis upon the perfectibility of the male body, which became an outward sign of man's moral superiority and inner strength of character' (Glover and Kaplan 2009, 59). While it would be impossible to find a neat corroboration for this argument from Bailey's *1846 Dictionary*, the text does announce, as already noted, an unconcealed focus on virility and the manly form. If *paurusham* provides the discursive framework within which ideal masculinities are placed, the entries under *purushardham* seem to define the desirable features (other than virility) of the husband-householder. Attesting to this theory is the definition for *purushardham* which reads thus: 'Things which beseem a man or are desirable viz. virtue, love, wealth, and final beatitude' (Bailey 1846, 510).

A significant number of entries have also been recorded to define womanliness—*streelakshanam, streethwam, streeswabhavam, streebudhi, sthrainam* (Bailey 1846, 828) being representative examples. If *stree* is defined by Bailey as a woman and/or wife, *streebuddhi* (female intelligence) is deployed as a lexical item denoting 'effeminacy' or 'softness' and *streelakshanam* as the modesty, decorum, decency or propriety of the female sex. Note that manliness—*purushatha* and *purushalakshanam*—explained as virility and manhood, stands in strong contrast to this. It is interesting that the terms referring to woman and womanliness are placed within and in conjunction with frameworks that emphasise a regimed *hexis*—one that extends not merely to the body but also to the mind and behaviours. In strong contrast to this, elucidations on manliness are organised around virility, bearing with it a certain connotation of unrestrained corporeal impulses that attain a dichotomising function when juxtaposed with Bailey's interpretations of 'womanliness' marked by discipline and restraint. In other words, ideal femininities become defined along the terms that would aid the imagined, complementary, monogamous union headed by the virile, potent man whose superiority, by Bailey's own earlier definitions of *purushan,* seem synonymous to 'God' and 'soul'.

The emphasis on the female spousal function when defining femininities is best foregrounded in Bailey's trite definitions of women who are not hierarchically positioned as superior in caste and class. For example, the definition under the entry *pulachi* (an archaic term used to refer to women who belonged to the pulaya caste) reads: 'The *wife of a Pulayan*, a slave woman' (511; italics mine). Such an emphasis is retained in his entries on *ezhathi,* defined by Bailey as '1. The wife of a Chagon (toddy-man) or a *woman of the Chagon tribe*' (92; italics mine), and *paraya* women, defined in the dictionary as '1. *wife* of a *Pariah* 2. A *woman of that class* (432; italics mine)—both being subjects who fall outside privileged caste categories. However, these entries by Bailey reveal yet another discursive site where the lexicographer negotiates with regional rituals and superstitions as well as matrimonial systems that are in conflict with European imaginations of the family.

The first of these arguments is revealed when, in his definition of a *pulachi*, he does not mention its elementary meaning, that is, a woman belonging to the pulaya caste. Rather, it is emphasised that she is the *wife* of a pulaya and thereby a slave woman. It would be possible to argue that such a conspicuous omission of an evident meaning is a lacuna allowed with respect to the idea of *pulappedi*—a custom which dictated that upper-caste women seen outside their home after hours could be claimed by a pulayan, thereby losing her caste privileges and becoming one of the pulayas. Thus, being the *wife* of a pulaya becomes the sole caste marker since, in this case, the woman inherits her husband's caste. Here, again, the onus falls on the woman's spousal role. Yet another absence—in keeping with nineteenth-century Kerala's unique caste-inflected matrimonial specificities—is the omission of any mention of the woman's spousal capacities when defining nair women—perhaps considering the ambivalent, polyamorous spousal positions occupied by women from this caste during this period. Therefore, the sentence under the entry word *achi* simply reads 'a Naiyar woman' (8).

The next set of entries subjected to analysis elicit Bailey's lexical constructions of hegemonic femininities through a coalescence of caste, spousal role and a *maternal* function placed within an imagined monogamous family with a male householder, a chaste wife and a clear unambiguous lineage of inheritance that passes onto the children. It is within these entries on imagined family units and hegemonic feminine categories that Bailey best couches a Eurocentric reading of a male-headed household under the guise of defining colloquial vernacular terms.

An apt point of departure for this analysis would be the entry on family, *kudumbam*. The elucidation on *kudumbam* in the *1846 Dictionary* is wide enough to accommodate multifarious, conflicting, unique systems that are particular to the cultural specificities of Kerala. Split into three, the definitions read: '1. A family, race, household 2. kindred, relationship, connexion by marriage 3. offspring, progeny' (Bailey 1846, 196). Constructing the family unit through marriage is re-emphasised through yet another entry word, *kudumbaprathishta*, defined as '1. Marriage 2. Founding or establishing the family' (196). Here, again, the lexicological order privileges 'marriage' over the literal meaning, which is given the second position.

Against this theme that forces a need to solidify the monogamous family unit, a few of the reverential terms of address denoting the ideal Malayali femininity like *kudumbini, kulastree* and *amma* can be analysed. The zenith of hegemonic femininity is stated using the Malayalam term *kulastree*, defined as the 'chaste wife, *a woman of rank*' or 'a *legitimate wife* whose children have the right to inheritance' (Bailey 1846, 205). By evoking spousal *legitimacy* in the English definition (the moral-colonial sentiments of which are comprehendible only to the educated bilingual Malayali), Bailey effectively writes off those Malayali women whose spousal roles existed outside the institution of monogamous, legal unions. Bailey has also been careful to identify and elucidate chastity as the faithfulness of the wife to the husband (under the entry *pathivrutha*) within the same text (460).

Along similar lines, *kudumbini* evokes the maternal, caste and spousal function (undergirded by marital fidelity) when it is interpreted in English thus: 'the matron, the wife of a householder and mother of the family' (Bailey 1846, 196). However, Bailey also provides a Malayalam definition of the same, which is more inclusive of the upper-caste female members involved in the unique matrimonial systems in Kerala by omitting any reference to the male householder. The Malayalam definition reads: 'wife, a woman with sons and servants' (196; my trans). Here, again, the caste and maternal functions are retained and remain uncompromised, while the evocation of the husband figure as an elementary qualifier is limited to the English definition and would be comprehensible only to a limited audience (who would favour such 'modern' aspirations). It is interesting to note that Bailey has also conferred the idealised English appellation of 'matron' to both *kudumbini* and *amma* (the first definition of which reads 'A mother; matron') (39). The term matron, it could be argued, is loaded in its tacit assumptions. It hints at the role of a domestic administrator, a controller of its members, while also assuming that the matron is propertied enough to have a household to supervise.

These sentiments that deploy the monogamous family as a nodal terrain within which gendered social actors are placed, gain greater valence through idealised masculinist images of the 'husband', 'householder' and 'father' that appear in the text. For example, the masculine counterpart of *kudumbini*, *kudumbi*, is defined as 'The *father* of a family, a *householder*' (Bailey 1846, 196; italics mine). The preferential use of the term 'father', as opposed to 'head' or *karnavar*, must be noted here. The emphasis on the pivotal position that the male spouse must occupy for imagining the family unit is further foregrounded through the many entries on 'widowhood'—*bharthrudukham, bharthrunasam, bharthruviraham* and *bharthruheena* (570), to name a few.

However, no entry best describes the novel, essentialist, spousal roles and the hierarchised frameworks within which the modern conceptions of the family is tacitly pitched by Bailey than the definition of the lexical item *bharthrususrooksha* (literally translating into 'caring for the husband'). The meanings read: 'Faithfulness and *obedience* of a wife towards her husband. To *serve*, or to be faithful and obedient towards a husband' (Bailey 1846, 570; italics mine). The words 'obedience' and 'serve' both explicitly reveal the hierarchy of gender relations that the Western ethnographer's gaze posits as ideal. This is further solidified by packaging the noun *streejithan*—defined by Bailey as 'a hen pecked husband' (828)—as a non-hegemonic, undesirable, masculine category. *Streejithan* embodies the reversal of the ideal modern hierarchy that demands the wife's subservience to her male spouse and protector.

The Western ethnocentric modalities that structured Bailey's mediated, essentialist definitions of regional masculinities and femininities are unsurprising when read against Fleming's observation that 'the historical formation of the European state system was accompanied by images of nurturing mothers and male protectors, and . . . these images sustained a complex system of social roles and gender identities' (1997, 85). One notices the recurrence of similar images—that of the 'virtuous father', 'the virile male' and 'the male protector and householder'—in the dictionaries, even though, at this juncture in history, many of Kerala's dominant kinship systems were yet to allocate these roles to its men. The idioms of maternities are also invoked when these texts attempt to curate desirable feminine categories. Bailey's definitions seem to suggest that women, positioned within the 'new' modern life world, now had to possess a chaste spousal function—in addition to their privileged locations in caste and class—to be the carriers of hierarchical legitimation.

By the early twentieth century, these novel modesties would have solidified, as is attested by the many narratives in the nascent public sphere by nair women. A representative example is the short exposition titled *Ente jeevacharitravum grahinidharmavum* (An Account of my Life and Duties as a Housewife, 1907) that appeared in Volume 2 Issue 12 of the women's magazine *Lakshmibai*. The article was written by a nair woman named Mannattaraveetil Lakshmi Amma. Over the course of the narrative, she explains with pride that her family members—part of her nair *tharavadu*—no longer promote polygamous alliances. She emphasises her unflinching matrimonial fidelity to her husband in spite of his mediocre looks (foregrounding a conscious privileging of the contractual terms of their alliance over subjective libidinal desires) and the respect she has for him (hinting at an explicit acceptance of the man's or male householder's crucial role as the primary caregiver consequent to the new order). She also records a detailed summary, touching upon even the minutest details of her *grahinidharmam* (duties of the homemaker—her 'womanly duties'). Thus, Bailey's novel interpretations of regional gendered terms provided a nascent modern frame for the educated, bilingual reader to conceive of novel femininities and masculinities. The decades that followed would recurrently emphasise these conceptions as ideal.

## 3

## *Koothichi, Pulayadi, Streechauran*: Defining Transgressive Femininities and Salacious Masculinities

While the terms in the preceding sections were deployed to refer to desirable/hegemonic filters of masculinities and femininities, Bailey's dictionary also devoted a rhetorical space to explore transgressive masculine and feminine categories—to define subjectivities that breached matrimonial constraints. Perhaps the complex coalescence and negotiations between the colonial/ Victorian dictums of monogamous matrimonial moralities and Kerala's unique cultural specificities (that sanctioned polyandry within certain castes) is best reflected in the explication of these categories. While, sustaining a vocal, visible distaste for the perfidious female, the text employs lenient descriptions of women from specific castes that do not adhere to these moralities.

Secondly, the use of the cuss words 'whore' and 'harlot' to define colloquial referential terms for the perfidious female, like *koothichi* (Bailey 1846, 215) and *veshya* (741), stand in strong contrast to the lenient positions taken by the lexicographer when defining the salacious male, *streechauran* (828). Some of these definitions—like those that interpret the word *pulayadi*—also bear the load of caste connotations. The term is deployed here as a derogatory, blanket term to refer to adulteresses. The verb form of this caste-inflected term was also deployed to signal the act of adultery—the breach of matrimonial fidelity. These words become critically significant when they reappeared in Bailey's *1849 Dictionary*, wherein the meaning of *pulayadi* was stretched to mean not just a transgressor of the limited libidinal economies allowed by matrimonial sanctions, but also as an overarching term for all acts of fornication, hinting at an absolute lack of libidinal control.

Through the selective exclusion of caste-marked women from the normalising discourse, Bailey's gender-essentialist frameworks for modern ideal femininities and monogamous marriages gather a 'desirable' valence and ideological legitimation. In other words, these excluded female caste-subjects are packaged as signifiers of dis-identification for class-privileged women to fashion themselves in the novel modesties proposed by Bailey. Furthermore, it is this idea of dis-identification that materialises as the locus of consensus between the educated audience of these discursive templates and the missionary–lexicographer.

It is worth noting here that *koothichi* gains a significant contemporary valence when attempting a critique of Kerala's public sphere, since this word of abuse visibly resurfaced in the open deliberative terrains of twenty-first-century Malayali cyberspaces. In the digital public sphere, the *koothichi* (defined by Bailey simply as the harlot) and the *kulastree* (positioned as its dialectical opposite), would be unleashed by both Malayali feminists and anti-feminists alike, as strategic nodes in their discursive engagements with gender debates.

## 4

## *Napumsakan, Streeveshadhari, Streeswabhavan*: Shaping Effeminacies and Coding Gender Variance in Early-Nineteenth-Century Kerala

While most vernacular writings in the pre-nascent public sphere as well as in the early years of the twentieth century were anchored on just two genders (*stree* and *purushan*), Bailey's dictionary evinces that—while severely restricted by orthodox, essentialist readings—there existed in nineteenth-century Kerala, a vocabulary that was deployed to refer to 'gender variant' categories. The *1846 Dictionary* evinces a limited number of both 'refined' and 'colloquial' Malayalam entries deployed to address effeminate males, crossdressers and other non-conforming gender categories. However, it is also interesting to note that the bulk of the terms recorded under this category primarily attempts to map gender non-conforming males and their effeminacies while ignoring gender variance among women. Bailey's entries are thus marked by an absence of referential terms for same-sex intimacies and gender-divergent women as well by the presence of un-nuanced, pithy interpretations of other queer orientations that package these inclinations as aberrant.

While *streeswabhavan* appears in the dictionary as a referential term for a eunuch, *napumsakan* is deployed as a blanket term that signifies: (1) a eunuch, (2) a hermaphrodite and (3) an impotent man; and the term *streeveshadhari* is used to refer to a crossdresser or, in Bailey's words, 'one dressed in female attire' (Bailey 1846, 828). *Streejithan* (referring to a henpecked husband) also belongs under the ambit of non-hegemonic masculinities. Clearly, the focus remains on the male subject who is rendered submissive and undesirable owing either to his (1) impotence or (2) 'unnatural' feminine taste and inclination.

This section on nineteenth-century referential terms on effeminacies gains a novel, critical tenor when placed against the digital public sphere in two overlapping phases. Initially, when using cyber-interactive terrains, the transgressive feminine (*koothichi*) and the effeminate masculine (*paavadadasan*) are both packaged as complementary aberrations constituting the inferior half of a binary that bestowed its desirable half to the hegemonic feminine (*kulastree*) and the hegemonic masculine (*kulapurushan*). The second phase materialised when these referential terms were re-appropriated by feminist counterpublics to subvert this binary.

## 5

## Conspicuous Omissions, Deliberate Additions and the Politics of Silence: A Brief Comparison between Bailey's *Dictionary of High and Colloquial Malayalim and English* (1846) and *A Dictionary, English and Malayalim* (1849)

As mentioned in the third section, the two dictionaries, through their bilingual mode of elucidation and in their very claims to function as textual tools of education, serve to create a native minority as its target audience. The fact that the *1846 Dictionary* could be partly comprehended by monolingual subjects limits the interpretive freedom of the lexicographer owing to a greater accountability with a larger audience. However, the *1849 Dictionary*, also bilingual but with English entry words, further limits its readership to an educated bilingual audience, who at this juncture in Kerala's history were re-evaluating traditional structures that mediated family, kinships, inheritance and matrimonial alliances. Therefore, *A Dictionary, English and Malayalim* (1849), becomes a potent site that evinces the Western, Eurocentric, missionary impetus at (1) deploying the idea of monogamous heteronormativity as a legitimising narrative to undergird gender hierarchies, (2) discursively demonising social actors who posited a threat to the institutionalisation of the male-headed heteronormative family by positing them as 'transgressive' or aberrant categories, and (3) firmly positioning the 'woman' within the domestic sphere and the ideological construct of the monogamous family by positing her as the inferior half of a binary, redeemable through purist notions of chastity.

While the *1846 Dictionary* limits the interpretation of the word *stree* as woman or wife, the *1849 Dictionary* uses 'woman' as an entry term to include the Malayalam word *abala*—meaning 'weak' (Bailey 1849, 540)—as one of its meanings in an attempt to signify 'weakness' as implicit in the condition of being a woman and to premise her as a social subject in need of protection from a complementary, strong, virile male. Similarly, the term 'chastity', which in the earlier dictionary (under the item *pathivrutha*) comprised merely a trite explication to mean faithfulness to one's husband, is explained using plural purist virtues in the new *1849 Dictionary* to bestow added valence to the term. The added definitions under 'chastity' (Bailey 1849, 61) are *nirmalatha* (mildness), *swachatha* (cleanliness, possibly of the mind and body), *suddhi* (purity), *charithryam* (which Bailey himself defines in the *1846 Dictionary* as referring to good conduct and behaviour) and *sareerasudham* (purity of the body, connotatively suggesting that the purity is accrued when the body is free from sexual intercourse outside matrimonial sanctions). To the related item 'chaste', he also adds the meaning *nerayulla*, meaning 'the right way' (61).

What materialises here is the missionary–lexicographer's textual attempt at institutionalising the terms of sexual sanctions by circumscribing libidinal desires through an imagined purist, 'value-intrinsic' notion of the monogamous family. Bailey furthers this legitimising narrative by extending non-hegemonic, gendered, caste categories against whom upper-caste women defined their superiority. The word *pulayadi* gains vigour in this context. While the *1846 Dictionary* interpreted this term to mean 'adulteress', in the *1849 Dictionary pulayadi* recurs under lexical items such as 'whore', 'fornicatress' and 'prostitute'. Furthermore, Bailey adds an item, 'whorish', to mean *adakkamillatha* (that without decorum/ discipline). Thus, by stretching the denotations of the Malayalam word *pulayadi* in contexts outside its original colloquial usages, and by deploying the term 'whorish' (absent under entries in the *1846 Dictionary*) to mean the absence of a regimed *hexis,* Bailey deploys the *pulayadi*—the female occupying a lower position in the caste hierarchy—as a blanket term for all forms of transgression, against whom the chaste *kulastree,* defined by 'her decorum' (the definition given under *streelakshanam*) and her location in the domestic, can rate her own superiority.

Finally, the legitimising narrative is further strengthened by Bailey through the textual acts of either completely omitting or deliberately obscuring nuanced definitions of gender variant categories. For example, the lone entry hinting at same-sex intimacies in this dictionary is the word 'sodomite' against which Bailey provides a mere one-word explanation—*mahadushtan*, meaning an extremely evil man (Bailey 1849, 425). By deflecting the original meaning and providing a negative appellation as its only descriptive meaning, 'sodomite' becomes a lexical space and an open signifier wherein any number of inferior, aberrant and evil significations and assumptions could be written into.

One may also read this omission of same-sex intimacies (especially between women) alongside Holly Williams's study of nineteenth-century England. In her 2017 article titled

'The Victorian View of Same-sex Desire', Williams elucidates on Victorian society's tacit tolerance of same-sex intimacies during the nineteenth century. She says, 'as long as there was a degree of ambiguity … 19th Century society was prepared to turn a blind eye' (Williams 2017, n.p.). It would also be possible to imagine that Bailey transfers this ambiguity into his works, which at times runs the risk of omitting entries on gender variant categories entirely or through unnuanced generalisations, allowing for a certain kind of textual tolerance.

* * *

This essay's synoptic analysis of Bailey's entries evince the patriarchal knowledge systems which were pivotal in shaping the narrative frame within which the gender discourses in the nascent Malayali public sphere of the early twentieth century were conceived. Perhaps it is also worth mentioning here that many of these early definitions retain themselves in contemporary Malayalam dictionaries and even continue to shape the digital social worlds of twenty-first-century Kerala. Interestingly, the twenty-first-century Malayali digital public sphere continue to deploy permutations of the word *streejithan* (like *paavadadasan*)—terms that are misappropriated in contemporary digital registers to refer to men who support Malayali women feminists in their attempts to discursively relegate and construct a non-hegemonic masculinity, as an undesirable and/or aberrant category. This essay was an attempt to uncover the ideational filters through which 'new', 'modern' possibilities of Malayali femininities, masculinities and effeminacies began to be conceived in Kerala, and the ensuing assumptions that continue to inform the state's public-sphere discourses even in its contemporary digital registers.

## References

Amma, Mannattaraveettil Lakshmi. 1907. *Ente Jeevacharitravum Grahinidharmavum. Lakshmibai* 2 (12): n.p.

Bailey, Benjamin. 1846. *A Dictionary of High and Colloquial Malayalim and English.* Kottayam: Church Missionary Press.

———. 1849. *A Dictionary, English and Malayalim*. Kottayam: Church Missionary Press.

Burkhanov, Igor. 1998. *Lexicography: A Dictionary of Basic Terminology*. N.p.: Wydawn.

Charlebois, Justin. 2011. *Gender and the Construction of Dominant, Hegemonic, and Oppositional Femininities*. Plymouth: Lexington Books.

Chattopadhyay, Swati. 2006. *Representing Calcutta: Modernity, Nationalism and the Colonial Uncanny*. Oxon: Routledge.

Fleming, Marie. 1997. *Emancipation and Illusion: Rationality and Gender in Habermas's Theory of Modernity*. Pennsylvania: Pennsylvania State UP.

Fish, Stanley Eugene. 1980. *Is There a Text in This Class?: The Authority of Interpretive Communities*. Cambridge: Harvard UP.

Glover, David, and Cora Kaplan. 2009. *Genders*. New York: Routledge.

Gopinath, Gayatri. 2018. *Unruly Visions: The Aesthetic Practices of Queer Diaspora*. Durham: Duke UP.

Mills, Sara. 2008. *Discourse*. London: Routledge.

Spivak, Gayatri Chakravorty. 2010. 'Can the Subaltern Speak?'. In *Can the Subaltern Speak?: Reflections on the History of an Idea*, ed. Rosalind C. Morris. New York: Columbia UP. 21–80.

Williams, Holly. 2017. 'The Victorian View of Same-Sex Desire'. *BBC Culture*. BBC. 5 Apr. 2017 <www.bbc.com/culture/article/20170405-the-victorian-view-of-same-sex-desire>

# Unsettling Praxes

FIVE

# Fashioning the Reading Woman in Colonial Kerala

## *A Woman Reader's Memoir in Perspective*

MEERA C.

### Introduction: Towards a Cultural History of Women's Reading in Kerala

Reading is a multifaceted act, at once 'affective, performative, material, embodied and sensual' as much as it is 'cognitive and social' (Rothbauer 2016, 3). Since the 1980s, book historians and historians of reading have been increasingly interested in the chequered pasts of reading as a practice as it manifests in particular societies (Darnton 1986; Chartier 1992a, 1992b). William Sherman's concern, expressed in the 1990s, that the predominant theoretical approaches to reading so far are 'peopled with every kind of reader except the real and historical' (1995, 55), seems to be broadly shared by historians of reading, as they explore historically situated modalities of reading and actual readers of the past, effecting a material and historical turn in Reading Studies.

There is a substantial lack of consensus with regard to methods while theorising reading in this manner. The impalpable nature of the phenomenon that reading history seeks to grasp—an act 'too ordinary ... to warrant our attention, and too ubiquitous ... to ignore' (Towheed, Crone and Halsey 2011, 1)—is often complicated by its fleeting nature that 'takes no measures against the erosion of time' (Certeau 1984, 174). Historians of reading hence continue to work with a plurality of methods, conceiving their work as 'an enterprise ... in flux' (Johns 2010). They nevertheless share an interest in the 'historical specificity of the reader as a complex subject' (Beetham, in Colclough 2007, x), seeking to open up the material and cultural pasts of a practice that is both ephemeral and quotidian.

Acts, discourses and practices at the intersections of gender and reading have generated much critical interest (Radway 1984; Flint 1993), pointing towards the possibility of gendering the study of historical reading in specific societies. The present essay analyses reminiscences of reading in the writings of B. Kalyani Amma (1884–1959), whose memoir *Ormayil ninnu* (From Memory, 1964) illustrates an upper-caste woman's distinct engagement with objects, spaces and contexts of reading in late-nineteenth and early-twentieth-century Travancore. *Ormayil ninnu* remains a potent text for a discussion of gender and reading in the region, as it does not just throw light on a subject like reading 'that seldom leaves sources' (Blaak 2009, 37), but uses the act of reading as a discursive site to grapple with questions of gender, subjectivity and modernity.

A key methodological departure in the study, therefore, is to move beyond reading as a noetic engagement of the reader with the text as a 'conveyor of meaning' (Davidson, in Littau 2006, 1), to a material conception of reading as 'a practice embodied in gestures, spaces and habits' (Chartier 1992a, 48). Thus, the essay looks into the material, social and spatial contexts within which the author's reading experiences are forged; and the practices that emerge in relation to reading objects and spaces within the narrative. It also looks at how the identity work involved in the fashioning of a gendered reader-self in the text is tied to the ideations around femininity and propriety central to the conflicting discourses of Kerala's modernity.

## Imagining the Woman Reader: Discourses on Reading and Gender

The late-nineteenth and early-twentieth centuries were significant for the histories of print in Kerala, as printed objects of reading began to be circulated increasingly but asymmetrically among neo-literate and literate readers in Travancore, Cochin and Malabar.[1] On the one hand, these were hitherto unseen cultural artefacts in the material sense, 'shifting assemblages of social relations, which take place and assume form and meaning in time and space' (Mansvelt 2005, 1). On the other hand, these were also carriers of new thought worlds, since Kerala's print culture burgeoned against a context of European missionary interventions. The diffusion of these 'unfamiliar' objects of reading paralleled the rise of new spaces in which acts of reading could take place, such as the modern school and the library.[2] Historical readers' engagement with reading objects and spaces remained structured by their social location, caste and gender being crucial within this.

These decades were also a period of flux for women's histories in the region, as wide-ranging social changes came to refashion notions of gender, under the sway of colonial and missionary encounters on the one hand and vernacular impulse towards reform on the other. A prolific discourse on gender and modernity emerged parallel to this.[3] Figuring closely with this, there emerged discussions on women and reading as well, as commentators contentiously debated the contours of ideal reading practices for women, often prescribed what they envisioned to be the 'modernity' of women's reading, and imagined 'the woman reader' diversely in discursive sites.

On the one hand, the discursive field that prompted these debates was a gendered terrain in its very making. Analysing a popular rhetoric mode of the nineteenth and twentieth centuries that drew parallels between language/literature on the one hand, and the 'woman' on the other, J. Devika has noted how this debate

---

[1] See Priyadarsanan (1982; 1999); Jeffrey (2010).

[2] In Travancore, where Kalyani Amma's childhood was spent, there were 434 government and 1,013 private aided schools during 1902–03 (Vijayan 2000, 142).

[3] For accounts of social transformations across the nineteenth and early-twentieth centuries in Kerala, and its implications for gender, see Kodoth 2001; Arunima 2003; Devika 2006.

reproduced the feminisation of the literature inherent in Sanskrit poetics, resulting in a masculinisation of the implied reader (2013, 37–40). Secondly, even as these debates worked to produce what Kate Flint elsewhere terms the 'topos of the woman reader' (1993, viii), this discourse was not a monolithic one. It figured closely with the ambivalent debates on Kerala's modernity itself and was equally polyphonic. However, anxiety surrounding women's reading acts that might unfold in the changing contexts was never altogether absent from this debate. Cautionary statements thus emerged as a significant strand within the discourse on reading and gender.

N. R. V.'s *Streevidyabhyasam* (Women's Education, in *Vidyavinodini* 1896) is a remarkable example of such cautionary narratives. Written by an author who did not reveal his/her real name, and published in 1896 in a prominent Malayalam magazine from the state of Cochin, the article illustrates the layered nature of gendered anxiety around reading. It also inaugurated a heated debate on women's education, as the arguments put forth by the author were taken up and refuted by several women authors in the subsequent issues. The palpable concern in N. R. V.'s article is linked solely to the idea of women getting educated through the medium of books:

> Around here, women are educated (1) through oral instruction, (2) with the help of books, and (3) in physical skills.... It looks like one can classify education into [oral] instruction, education through letters and physical education. Out of these, education through letters does not seem to be useful to women under any circumstances. (N. R. V. 1896, 74)[4]

In considering book-mediated education improper for women, the text foregrounds the notion of utility, revealing apprehensions regarding women potentially transgressing the social roles deemed appropriate for them within modernity: 'It seems that education

[4] Quotes from Malayalam are translated by the author unless otherwise indicated.

through letters becomes useful only in the administration of political affairs. One cannot say that it is desirable to appoint women for this' (74). Writing about Victorian England, Kate Flint has noted that 'recognizing the potency of the "woman reader" as a subject within cultural discussion is not a self-sufficient end' as it illustrates an 'important network of ideas about the presumed interrelations of mind, body and culture' (1993, 11). Revealing similar ideational interrelations at work, N. R. V. lists biological, social and cultural 'reasons' ranging from women's 'natural' weakness to their lack of 'familiarity with the world' for considering them unsuitable for book-mediated education and the social roles for which it was thought to equip them (74).

In the writings of the time, such a fear of the ideological and political threat posed by the entry of educated, reading women to societal roles deemed 'improper' for them, unfolded in parallel to an emerging moral panic regarding new noetic worlds that may be opened out to reading women within a print-mediated economy of ideas:

> There is no doubt that an education comprising the knowledge of letters would not only deter women from acting morally, but will actively aid in turning them into a breeding ground of vices like adultery and freedom. Since they have a habit of reading, and since they are said to have "hunger two-fold, shyness four-fold, daring six-fold, and lust eight-fold as compared to men,"[5] women may go on reading different kinds of books without distinction. While this could be a matter of either good or evil, as long as we stick to the dictums, it is incontestable that women, having "lust eight-fold," will be most interested in books of that kind. The ill-effects of this need not be explained. None of this will have to be faced, if education remains oral. (N. R. V. 1896, 76)

While many women and men of the time campaigned for female education, others actively joined in this strand of discourse that 'cautioned' women against the ill effects of 'improper' reading.

---

5 The text quotes a Sanskrit dictum from *Chanakya niti-shastra*. The translation used here is by Miles Davis.

The distinction drawn between utility and pleasure often worked to prescribe the propriety of women's reading acts. J. Kunjulakshmi Amma wrote in *Sudharma*: 'Reading is one of the primary ways in which one can properly and happily spend time. We should not be spending time reading prurient books ['*aabhasa granthangal*'] in the place of books that can cultivate intellect and refinement. Although the former may provide temporary pleasure, reading those may have ill-effects' (1903, 18).

Concerns regarding the new thought worlds embodied in the medium of print often came to be entangled with gendered panic regarding the unfamiliar material spaces in which women's education and reading acts may unfold:

> After all, it is from schools that the kind of education mentioned above [book-mediated] can be gained. There is a vast difference between a girl who gains systematic education from schools, and a girl who gains education in one's home without going to the school. Girls who study in schools become capable of speaking without modesty or without fear of an audience. (N. R. V. 1896, 75)

The author adds, 'Even when they are young, it is ideal not to appoint men to teach women' (76). Thus, while ostensibly supporting female education, N. R. V. ends up prescribing the ideal conditions in which it may take place: 'Since education is necessary for women under every circumstance, it is the duty of all of us to orally instruct them and educate them in physical skills, in ways they may find it useful' (77). This narrative's conspicuous apprehension of book-mediated learning can be read against a larger fear of women's encounter with reading objects, noetic worlds and spaces of reading that may spiral outside the familiar, supervised contexts, at a time when the coming of print and the rise of new spaces of reading had started unsettling the insular, caste-bound socio-spatial contexts within which caste women's 'instruction' could have taken place so far.

Acts of reading by historical women unfolded against these contexts. It needs to be stated that at the turn of the twentieth century, those who could read comprised only a fragment of the population, and women constituted only a minority within this.[6] Women's participation within cultures of reading, when at all it was made possible, was largely enabled or bound by their caste and class, which oriented their access to reading material and spaces. This also has to be read alongside the fact that the period between the 1880s and the 1930s witnessed debates on women's education in periodicals, the participation of women in these debates, the rise of periodicals meant for and/or run by women, and the entry of women writers, thus suggesting the possibilities of unrecorded reading acts by women that may have made these engagements possible.[7]

Historical women's relationship with reading in colonial Kerala is thus forged at the intersections of indigenous pre-print traditions, an emergent culture of print-mediated reading spurred by colonial, missionary and indigenous interventions in education and printing, and the shifting educational avenues that were asymmetrically open to men and women in a caste society that was integrating itself into a colonial economy. The historical woman reader in colonial Kerala is also formed at the crossroads of the project of reform and the implications of its discourse for women of different castes, against the contentious debates on the topos of the woman reader sketched above. The complex engagement with gender roles and modernity that pervades *Ormayil ninnu* can only be understood in these contexts.

---

[6] In 1901, Kerala's literacy rate was reported to be 11.4 per cent, and women's literacy rate to be 3.15 per cent (Vijayan 2000, 193). Writing in 1903, Karthyayani Amma quotes Mrs Kannan Nair's comment that 'while the status of female education in Kerala exceeds the rest of India, yet it is only eight out of every hundred women who can read and write' (187). However, it also needs to be noted, as Bhaskaranunni remarks, that literacy rates of the time may not have aptly reflected the numbers of those who could read—those who could read did not necessarily know how to write, and literacy rates could have often reflected the latter (1988, 1043–44).

[7] See for instance, the debates on women and women's education in *Keralisugunabodhini* (1894), *Sarada* (1901), *Lakshmibai* (1906), *Kraistava Mahilamani* (1920) and *Mahila* (1921).

## Self-fashioning and the Gendered Reader in *Ormayil ninnu*

Born in 1884 in Thiruvananthapuram, B. Kalyani Amma was propelled to literary fame by the account of her marriage to the radical journalist Swadesabhimani Ramakrishna Pillai (*Vyazhavatta smaranakal* [Memories of Twelve Years], 1916). She was also an early woman graduate from Travancore, a prolific reader, a writer and one of the editors of the women's magazine *Sarada*. Her *Ormayil ninnu* (1964) contains an account of the contexts and spaces of reading, both extant and emergent, which were open to educated women of nair households in late-nineteenth and early-twentieth-century Travancore. The narrative also offers a fascinating attempt to textualise a distinct 'literary' self, through a recounting of the instances which shaped the author as a lover of literature and a writer (B. K. Amma 1964, 161–77).

Writing about a time when only 3.06 per cent of Travancorean women were literate (Vijayan 2000, 193), Kalyani Amma comes across as an atypical woman reader for the times she lived in. Nevertheless, the text offers vital clues to the contexts in which her aleatory reading acts were forged. Born in a household where women were not introduced to formal schooling until her generation,[8] her narrative is marked by an awareness of herself as a literary consumer who traverses multiple noetic worlds and reader-subjectivities, mediated by objects/spaces of reading in transition. This is evident in her reminiscences of childhood reading, shaped by two reading spaces: (1) the home and the neighbourhood, which are primarily sites of vernacular traditions of 'reading aloud' and the recital of religious/secular literature, and (2) the missionary school, which introduces her to new/emergent modes of reading, premised mainly on the textbook.

---

[8] She comments on her illiterate parents: 'Knowledge gained outside of writing and reading will have to be considered education. Doesn't the non-artificial knowledge gained thus … deserve to be included in the epithet, "education"?' (101).

Kalyani Amma's earliest literary experiences remain moored in the oral culture of songs, prayers and purana recitals to which her grandmother introduced her (162). She remembers the 'reading aloud' of epics that took place in upper-caste homes during evening prayer,[9] and the formally organised public reading sessions of religious literature staged in the neighbourhood (162–64). Critical approaches that privilege incorporeal silent reading as the sole framework to locate the 'modernity' of reading have been problematised by historians who theorise communitarian practices of reading aloud as central to women's reading and female sociality in colonial India (Moitra 2017). In *Ormayil ninnu*, while the practice of reading aloud remains anchored in socially sanctioned contexts of religious reading, it also emerges as the ground for familial bonding and intergenerational transmission of vernacular religious practices:

> I used to wake up listening to my grandmother reciting *Harinamakeertanas*. Gradually, I came to memorise those and learned to recite those alongside her.... She could also sing lullabies, swing songs, *kathakali* verses, *thullal* songs and so on.... I learnt the *puranas* orally from her. It can be said without doubt that the foundation of my literary education was laid by grandmother. (162)

In the narrative, the ritualistic reading aloud of the epics defies being securely placed within the label of the 'non-modern'. In one instance, the young woman reader finds herself responding to this literature subjectively and affectively: 'I felt a special affinity towards learning and reading aloud those portions resonant with the emotions of sorrow and separation, such as Rama's exile to the forest, the lament of Dasaratha and Kausalya, the separation between Rama and Sita and so on' (163). The practice of reading aloud emerges as a site of women readers' subjective, affective

[9] 'In those times, in every home, ... the custom was to read *purana granthas* for long. However, this happened only in those houses where [the members] were literate enough to read *granthas* like the *Ramayana*. In some ancient *taravadus*, youths of the neighbourhood were "borrowed" to perform the *Vrischika* reading' (162).

response to ritually recited religious literature, visibilising the crossovers between reading acts that are often bifurcated as 'modern' and 'non-modern'. Instances like these offer a plane from which to interrogate easy collations between objects, actions and responses, compelling us to rethink the 'modernity' of (upper-caste) reading practices in colonial Kerala from the perspective of gender, in terms of 'an infinity of singular acts' (Chartier 1992a, 47) that straddle multiple noetic and material cultures and produce contingent reader-subjectivities.

*Ormayil ninnu* reveals not only the contingent nature of reading acts performed at the crossovers between traditions in this way, but also exposes the gendered nature of reading spaces, both extant and emergent. As the text notes, the supervised, socially sanctioned contexts where texts were read aloud—whether religious or recreational, within or outside the home—were often accessible to nair women. However, this access came with several conditions: 'Some of my neighbours performed [a play, *Ajnathavasam*] in one of the houses with a large yard. I too could go at night and watch the performance, *because* it was a nearby house and some close friends were involved' (168; my emphasis). Thus, the conditions under which women's recreational acts may take place, and the author's implicit struggle against these conditions, often irrupt in the narrative. Recounting a public reading ceremony, she writes,

> I used to go for these reading sessions in nearby houses. However, having to sit at a distance [from the stage] among other women, and because of their incessant talking and the crying of the children, it was impossible to listen properly to the story or the explanation. [These sessions] were of no benefit, other than the fact that I could vaguely listen to a few new stories. (164)

The author thus marks the experience as non-beneficial in the making of her 'literary self' in a narrative act that at once critiques the gendered segregation that prevents her from enjoying the reading, while also distancing herself from the 'non-literary' women around her.

Other than as a site of socially sanctioned, religious acts of reading, the home rarely emerges in *Ormayil ninnu* as a space that facilitates women's solitary engagement with reading objects. Kalyani Amma remembers her childhood: 'There were one or two newspapers [published during the time], but they were not allowed in my home. The men of my home who held minor government jobs considered reading the newspaper an act of treason' (165–66). The possibility of women's solitary engagement with reading material remained rare within such a context where the choice of reading objects resonated with political and ideological significations beyond the literal reading act, even for men. Exposing women to such 'threats' remained inconceivable in the contexts of nineteenth-century reading described in the childhood reminiscences in *Ormayil ninnu*. Unsurprisingly, Kalyani Amma's only solitary reading experience within her childhood home unfolds as a chance encounter, a clandestine act:

> When I was in the 3rd Form, I was asked to clean my uncle's room.... On the top of the stack [of books] was a pretty, stout English book, bound beautifully in red. It clearly bore the title *Lamb's Tales from Shakespeare* in gilded letters. I brought it out (my uncle was not home for the day). After looking at the pictures, I started reading the stories. I vaguely made sense of the stories, the pictures helped to make out the meaning. I took the book out again several times, whenever my uncle was not home, and finished it in eight to ten days. This is the only good book I got to read from my home. (166)

The home is nevertheless only one of the spaces of reading available to Kalyani Amma: her early reading acts are also shaped within emergent spaces such as the missionary school.[10] The Zenana Mission school that she attended was not a space that could have shaped the reading acts of women across castes,[11] nor

---

[10] The reading material available in the school included biblical literature, textbooks on geography and history, as well as English readers such as *Little Arthur's English History* (B. K. Amma 1964, 64).

[11] 'Because of the circumstances of our school—it stood in the middle of temples, palaces and brahmin mutts—entry was denied to those castes other than brahmins, nairs and Christians, who were censured as the lower castes' (B. K. Amma 1964, 52).

was it potent to satisfy the growing needs of women readers like her.[12] Nevertheless, it acted as a space where alternate reading acts could flourish for the author, introducing her to textbook cultures of reading as a young girl, and to the worlds of Malayalam literature as an older student (64; 167).

Opportunities for solitary reading become available to Kalyani Amma only with time. Entering new academic spaces like the college gives her more agency in terms of reading choices and access to material: 'Once I entered college, I got to read as many library books as I like. I also managed to get magazines and newspapers at home through my friends'[13] (171). She recounts her distinct engagement with the literature that she read during these years:

> I became familiar with prose fiction when I was studying for matriculation. That was when first-rate novels like *Indulekha*, *Akbar* and *Marthanda Varma*, as well as second-rate stories like *Indumathi* and *Vikramadithyan Kathakal* became popular. *Indulekha* and *Marthanda Varma* made their way into every household much like the *Ramayana* and *Mahabharatha*, and their stories became a matter of discussion in the kitchen and the stairwell, the yard and the compound. (169–70)

Thus, crossovers between oral, scribal and printed modes marked the contexts of upper-caste women's literary consumption in late-nineteenth and early-twentieth-century Travancore. In simultaneously articulating reading experiences in domestic and academic spaces as central to the making of her literary self, Kalyani Amma emplaces herself as a reader-subject navigating parallel noetic worlds channelised by media in transition, even

---

[12] 'In my school, there was nothing but textbooks to read. One could not even hear of a library or a book store in those times' (B. K. Amma 1964, 165).

[13] She adds: 'I think it was around this time that newspapers and magazines became popular.... Through my brother, I got to read a few copies of *Vanchibhoopanchika* and *Keraladarpanam* from Thiruvananthapuram, *Keralapanchika...*, *Malayali* published from Kollam, as well as *Manorama* published from Kottayam' (170).

as she remains conscious of the gendered nature of many of the sites where these reading acts unfolded.

From the perspective of gender, the most remarkable aspect of *Ormayil ninnu* remains the attempt to narrativise a distinctly gendered reader-self by the author. Writing on Victorian England, Lyn Pykett notes how the discursive representations of femininity were riven between contending strands of the 'respectable feminine' and the 'improper feminine', in which the notion of proper, respectable femininity figured closely with 'the ideal of the domestic ideology, according to which woman was defined primarily in terms of her reproductive and domestic functions within the developing bourgeois family' (1992, 12). The notion of proper femininity becomes relevant in the context of Kerala as well, in the way it resonates with what has been termed the 'order of gender' that came to be conceived in the discourses on Kerala modernity in the early twentieth century: a proposed social order founded on 'the division of the world into "public" and "private" domains appropriate for men and women respectively', further maintained through 'the complementary exchange of gendered capacities: men as industrious producers in the political, economic and intellectual fields, and women as efficient and active overseers of the domestic domain' (Devika 2005a, xxi).

Kalyani Amma's negotiations of these notions of femininity remain complex, her being both an educated, working woman and a writer, as well as someone who 'appeared to be the very paragon of wifely loyalty, self-discipline and fortitude, [and] was almost universally admired' (Devika 2005b, 12). However, despite the text's implicit tension with the gendered contexts in which women's literary consumption unfolds, *Ormayil ninnu* visibilises curious entanglements between the author's self-fashioning as a reader-subject and the imaginings of feminine propriety within contemporary discourses on gender and reading.

In one instance, a preoccupation with evolving notions of gendered propriety clearly marks the author's remembrance of herself as a reader in one of the ritualistic read-aloud sessions in her home: 'Although I loved it, at times, when neighbours or guests were present, having to read aloud in their presence felt unbearable' (163). In another instance, writing about her encounter with periodicals during her college days, she notes, 'Although I read the political and social articles and news that appeared in *Vidyavinodini* and *Rasikaranjini* with attention and curiosity, my primary focus fell on poetic pieces' (170). While this could be read as the expression of a particular reading sensibility, the remark also resonates with statements on 'appropriate' reading material for women that often appeared in contemporary narratives, an instance being the disclaimer in *Keralisugunabodhini* (1894), an early periodical to identify itself as a women's magazine:

> Nothing political shall be included in this [magazine]. The volume may contain prose or occasionally verse pieces on philosophy, biology, entertaining stories, moral stories, women's duties, cooking, music, histories of great women, regional histories, book reviews and essays on other informative topics. Nor will we be including meaningless debates on religion. (*Prasthavana* 1894, 2)

In another instance, remembering her fascination with stanzas on familial separation and sorrow as a child reader of puranic literature, Kalyani Amma interestingly places this as a premonition of her domestic tribulations in the future: 'I wonder if this was a portent of the fire of sorrow to be caused by widowhood and the loss of children, which found a place in my heart so early' (163–64). She writes about her experience of watching a play: 'When Kunti recited ten *shlokas* reminiscing the plight of those princes and their wife in a forest, … although I was a child, it evoked a motherly affection natural in me. I silently shed tears. I got those *shlokas* in writing the very next day, and memorised them' (169).

The author also prevents herself from using her name as a critical reader, and distances herself from the literary controversies of the time: 'I mostly wrote without signing a name, or under pseudonyms. I also wrote some reviews; however, I had no part in those reviews like "*Sadarama Niroopanam*" and "*Balakaleshavadam*" that created a furore in the periodical world' (171–72). Thus, despite the text's implicit tension with the gendered contexts in which women's reading acts and recreation take place, *Ormayil ninnu* textualises a reader-self that cautiously treads the norms of propriety enshrined in emerging conceptualisations of femininity within the contemporary discourses on gender.

Interestingly, Kalyani Amma's reception as a literary woman can be read in conjunction with these choreographies of the gendered reader-self. A typical instance can be seen in the review of Kalyani Amma's *Mahathikal* (Great Women) in *Sudarshanam* (1909). Despite the author's own position as an educated, working woman, the review praises Kalyani Amma and her literary effort for featuring great Indian women's stories that may be emulated by 'free' women who, among other things, resent reading puranas and take European women as role models (*Mahathikal* 1909, 282–83). The contexts of this reception become clearer when one looks at the scathing critique reserved by the same article for those whom it censures as 'free' women (282).

Thus, the fashioning of a gendered reader-self in *Ormayil ninnu* is intricately tied to what is imagined as 'proper' reading choices/responses for female readers in the cautionary discourses of the time, even as the tensions within the narrative simultaneously belie attempts from the part of the author to engage with gendered material spaces and contexts of reading. These contradictions can be read as the sites at which the non-unitary figure of the historical woman reader is articulated within the gendered material and noetic economies of reading that crystallised around the coming of print and modern education in late-nineteenth and early-twentieth-century Kerala. Women's reading, in terms of the material contexts, spaces and modes in which it takes place, as well as the socio-symbolic valencies it accrues upon itself, emerges in the narrative as a non-unitary social practice that is nevertheless gendered; on to which gets mapped reading acts that are conventionally bifurcated as 'modern' and 'non-modern'. The coming of print and the rise of new spaces of reading produce reading habits and acts that are aleatory in nature, alongside complexly gendered reader-subjects who navigate the 'dialectic between imposition and appropriation, between constraints transgressed and freedoms bridled' (Chartier

1992b, 37). Subsequently, for historical women readers, the practice of reading and the textualisation of the reading experience becomes intricately tied to their conflicted negotiation of gender roles and their fraught inhabitations of modernity.

## References

Amma, B. Kalyani. 1964. *Ormayil Ninnu*. Kottayam: SPCS.

Amma, J. Kunjulakshmi. 1903. *Keraleeya Streekalkkorupadesham*. *Sudharma* 1(1): 16–19.

Amma, Thiruvattattu L. Karthyayani. 1903. *Streevidyabhyasam*. *Sudharma* 1(9): 187–91.

Arunima, G. 2003. *There Comes Papa: Colonialism and the Transformation of Matriliny in Kerala, Malabar, c. 1850–1940*. Hyderabad: Orient Longman.

Bhaskaranunni, P. 1988. *Pathonpatham Noottandile Keralam*. Thrissur: Kerala Sahitya Akademi.

Blaak, Jeroen. 2009. *Literacy in Everyday Life: Reading and Writing in Early Modern Dutch Diaries*. Trans. Beverley Jackson. Leiden: Brill.

Chartier, Roger. 1992a. 'Labourers and Voyagers: From the Text to the Reader'. In *The Book History Reader*, ed. David Finkelstein and Alistair McCleery. London: Routledge. 47–57.

———. 1992b. '*Preface* to The Order of Books'. In *The History of Reading: A Reader*, ed. Katie Halsey, Rosalind Crone, and Shafquat Towheed. New York: Routledge. 36–38.

Certeau, Michel de. 1984. *The Practice of Everyday Life*. Trans. Steven Rendall. London: U of California P.

Colclough, Stephen. 2007. *Consuming Texts: Readers and Reading Communities, 1695–1870*. New York: Palgrave Macmillan.

Darnton, Robert. 1986. 'First Steps toward a History of Reading'. In *The History of Reading: A Reader*, ed. Katie Halsey, Rosalind Crone, and Shafquat Towheed. New York: Routledge. 23–35.

Davis, Miles, trans. *Chanakya Niti-Shastra*. By Chanakya. https://dokumen.pub/chanakya-niti-shastra.html.

Devika, J., ed. 2005a. *Her-Self: Early Writings on Gender by Malayalee Women, 1898–1938*. Kolkata: Stree.

———. 2005b. *Modernity with Democracy?: Gender and Governance in the People's Planning Campaign, Kerala*. Thiruvananthapuram: CDS.

———. 2006. *En-Gendering Individuals: The Language of Re-Forming in Twentieth Century Keralam*. Hyderabad: Orient Blackswan.

———. 2013. *Womanwriting = Manreading?* New Delhi: Penguin India.

Flint, Kate. 1993. *The Woman Reader, 1837–1914*. Oxford: Oxford UP.
Jeffrey, Robin. 2010. *Media and Modernity: Communications, Woman and the State in India*. Ranikhet: Permanent Back.
Johns, Adrian. 2010. 'A History of Reading'. *University of Chicago*.
Kodoth, Praveena. 2001. 'Courting Legitimacy or Delegitimizing Custom: Sexuality, *Sambandham*, and Marriage Reform in Late-Nineteenth-Century Malabar'. *Modern Asian Studies* 35(2): 349–84.
Littau, Karin. 2006. *Theories of Reading: Books, Bodies and Bibliomania*. Cambridge: Polity.
*Mahathikal*. 1909. *Sudarsanam* 1(7–8): 281–83.
Mansvelt, Juliana. 2005. *Geographies of Consumption*. London: SAGE.
Menon, K. Narayana. 1904. *Prastavana*. *Sarada* 1(1): 1–2.
Moitra, Swati. 2017. 'Reading Together: "Communitarian Reading" and Women Readers in Colonial Bengal'. *Hypatia* 32(3): 627–43.
N. R. V. 1896. *Streevidyabhyasam*. *Vidyavinodini* 8(2): 73–77.
*Prasthavana*. 1894. *Keralisugunabodhini* 1(1): 1–2.
Priyadarsanan, G. 1982. *Malayala Pathrapravarthanam: Prarambha Swaroopam*. Thrissur: Kerala Sahitya Akademi.
———. 1999. *Kerala Pathrapravarthanam: Suvarnadhyayangal*. Kottayam: Current Books.
Pykett, Lyn. 1992. *The 'Improper Feminine': The Women's Sensation Novel and the New Woman Writing*. London: Routledge.
Radway, Janice. 1984. *Reading the Romance: Women, Patriarchy and Popular Literature*. Chapel Hill: U of North Carolina P.
Rauternberg, Ursula, and Ute Schneider. 2020. 'Everything but Reading ... : Praxeologies of Book Use'. *Book History Network*.
Rothbauer, Paulette, et al. 2016. *Plotting the Reading Experience: Theory/Practice/Politics*. Waterloo: Wilfred Laurier UP.
Sherman, William Howard. 1995. *John Dee: The Politics of Reading and Writing in the English Renaissance*. Amherst: U of Massachusetts P.
Towheed, Shafquat, Rosalind Crone, and Katie Halsey, eds. 2011. *The History of Reading: A Reader*. New York: Routledge.
Vijayan, M. N., ed. 2000. *Nammude Sahithyam, Nammude Samooham, 1901–2000*. Thrissur: Kerala Sahitya Akademi.

SIX

# Liminal Modernities

## *At the Intersections of Travel Discourses, Gender and Kerala (1880s–1920s)*

SUCHETA SANKAR V.

Writing an epistolary travel poem in 1891, K. C. Narayanan Nambiar arrives, towards the very end, at an unresolved, monstrous encounter: the travelling persona in his *Madirasiyathra* (Travel to Madras) is confronted by a metaphorical 'demoness' whose dark, threatening body, loud shrieks, and billowing strands of hair 'rend the earth' as she thunders into a railway station in erstwhile Kozhikode (qtd. in Chandran 1989, 47).[1] He is, of course, sited in the anxieties and paradoxes of his own travel act, gazing at and reflecting on an approaching steam train. The iconography used in the poem resonates with broader traditions of travel and canonical mobilities that circulated in the nascent publics of Kerala, South India, in the late-nineteenth and early-twentieth centuries. Specifically, it demarcates female/feminine performances of itinerancy as aberrant and culturally transgressive, rhetorically transfiguring the formidable mobility of the train into a gendered, folkloric motif of 'savagery'. In a bid towards edification, the work also implicates and scripts a contrastive hegemonic femininity in

[1] Travel poetry or *yathrakavyangal* is a literary sub-genre in Malayalam, in a canon that includes *Sandesakavyam, Venmani Prasthanam,* and medieval poetry, where travels were deployed as a frame for narration. Unlike other forms, *yathrakavyangal* centralises travel experiences, acting as a precursor of the prose travelogue in many ways. V. Ramesh Chandran, in his work *Sancharasahityam Malayalathil,* details their emergence and evolution (1989, 32–64).

the unnamed *priyathama* (lover/female companion) to whom the travel is related—textually ensconced in an idiom of sessility and *waiting*, she precludes agential stakes in sites of mobility and acts of travel. In effect, the cultural imagination of the woman traveller falls between fears of unrefracted agency and the desirability of apt (im)mobilities.

The current essay seeks to theorise the interstitial terrains in which gendered travel discourses—apropos travelling bodies, mobility experiences and travel practices—are located, specifically in their catalysing of novel formations of self-identity, performativity and spatial hegemonies in the region. It delves into the engendering of tenuous dialogues in emergent 'registers of modernity', throughout the kairotic epoch between the 1880s and 1920s, at the behest of gendered mobilities (corporeal and ideological) (Aguiar 2011, xvii). In doing so, alternative, dynamic possibilities of *being mobile/modern* and *doing mobilities/modernity-work* are coded into social practices, socio-symbolic signifiers, and travel writings through which women's travels are variously articulated and disarticulated, mediated with antipathies and affinities.

The essay submits that such *liminal modernities*, versed in 'a perpetual, though mobile, state of the *in-between* or *entre-deux*', re-frame, pluralise and destabilise the promissory, gendered repertoire of the 'modern' in Kerala (Tally Jr. 2016, ix). It explores this across three interrelated sections, the first of which studies images, conceits and rites that accompany gendered travellers in cultural memory. The second section reviews the ways in which the genre of the novel, a prominent fulcrum of identity formation in the selected timespan, prescribes 'modern/modernising' mobilities for women. The third and final section reads *Oru theerthayathra* (1925), the first travelogue to be written by a woman in Malayalam, as a product of liminal modernity.

## 1

The typologies of travel in Kerala, across the ages, draw on 'power–knowledge' archives populated by figurations of gender. Women and their gendered bodies in transit came to be resolved, albeit ambivalently, as symbolic bearers/markers of immutable, collective identities of *illam/tharavadu/veedu*,[2] kinship hierarchies, conjugal affiliations and communal spatialities. The observance of *pulappedi, mannappedi,* and *parappedi*—'institutionalised form(s) of caste offence'—typically in the months of July and August, are early indicators of the same (Arunima 2003, 67). Under the aegis of these rituals, nair and namboothiri women found outside the bounds of their home could be 'defiled' and kidnapped by men belonging to the subaltern pulaya, mannan, and paraya communities. The women were then deemed to have been displaced from their former caste affiliations and privileges, a social fact announced by way of the performative chant '*Njan kande*' (I saw), or by the flinging of a stone or twig at their bodies by the men. They were ostracised from their families and communities and ordained to be members of 'lower' caste groups. Within the practices' ethos of disciplining the *itinerant feminine,* gendered mobilities beyond the sanctity of the homestead are paralleled with the crossing of caste thresholds, thereby regulating feminine/feminised transactions in fraught economies of mobility. By 1696, these customs had generated enough upper-caste ire/fear to warrant a royal ban by Veera Kerala Varma Chirava Moothavar, before eventually fading into non-practice and taboo.

Yet, the anatomy of these codifications, immuring women in strategic motilities, posited a strategy for negotiating the perceived onslaught of modernity. In other words, the ruling relations through which modern mobilities are acquired/inhabited/practised pinion gendered subjects to disciplinary regimes that (re)produce idealised behaviours, dispositions and self-reflexivity. The lexicons of upper-caste femininity, in particular, drew on truncated agency in modern/modernising spaces to interpellate/hail meanings of controlled, tamed sexuality that operates solely within the confines

---

[2] The word *illam* traditionally refers to the house of a namboothiri brahmin, while the term *tharavadu* connotes an ancestral house, typically of upper-caste or aristocratic families in Kerala. *Veedu* in Malayalam translates to 'home' or 'house', depending on the context.

of the conjugal. For instance, this is epitomised in the fashioning of antharjanams, Malayala-brahmin women, in travel. Steeped in religious routines, domestic chores and moral femininity, antharjanams could not venture out of their houses without the cover of a cadjan umbrella to protect them from 'public' gaze, or without a female chaperone from an intermediary caste to engage with the 'foreign' terrains outside the home. Their exercise of femininity reiterated mythologies of gendered submission and enfranchised caste identities, playing into the fettering of women's mobilities to realms of shared values as opposed to individualistic self-fashioning.

On the other hand, gendered subaltern mobilities signalled a stark departure from these sanitised, 'contained' modes. The bodies of subaltern women predicated on their visibility, labour and agential participation in public spheres were stylised through antithetical travels. Lores such as *Vadakkan pattukal* (northern ballads) document the insurgent desire of its heroine—Unniyarcha, a member of a prominent chekavar/tiyya family, and a skilful warrior—to embark on a pilgrimage across hostile territories, despite the cautioning and objections of the family into which she married. The songs describe her journey to Allimalarkavu, in the reluctant company of her husband, and an attempt by dacoits to ambush them on the path. The image of the vulnerable feminine, often deployed in discourses of mobility, is ultimately subverted here, as Unniyarcha defeats her attackers with her *urumi* (a sword with flexible, whip-like blade) and mastery of the martial arts. Indeed, in frameworks of gendered subaltern agency, this intransigent mobility may be delineated in socio-sexual strategems such as *sambandham*, matrilineal kinship–property contracts, and other relationships of intermediacy. The later cultural and politico-legal deracinating of these institutions, aided by a colonial urgency for regulating hypergamous feminine sexualities, and for instating women's bodies and activities within the 'family', muted their wielding of mobility.

The heightened cultural tensions that surround the unbounded sexualities of women, particularly in socio-public spaces, are enunciated in *Yakshi* mythographies: 'She appears as a beautiful woman who allures unsuspecting men to her dwelling, the dark palm tree, which would be transformed to a palace in the eyes of the spellbound victim. She satisfies the man's desire, but in return takes his life' (Bini 2016, 34). Her malignant, ethereal mobility goes against the patrifocal core of travel, countermanding masculine acts of traversal, male social authority, and tropes of feminine hospitality, ultimately de-feminising/de-humanising her. Fables of Kaliyankattu Neeli and Mangalathu Chiruthevi, for instance, attribute their power to the cognisance of the terrains that are open to them. Later postulations of *Yakshis*, in fact, connote women whose naturalised stations in domesticity were disrupted through sexual violence or the covetousness of men in power. This allows for the cogent mobilities of the Y*akshi* to be politically re-oriented as *prathikaram* (vengeance) for being divested of her status as a 'chaste', normative subject of patriarchy.

One of the most pervasive projects, implied by the intertwining of gender and mobility in Kerala, is to be traced in the vernacular *theendari* which describes the 'impure' status of the menstruating woman. With semantic ties to the cognate *theenduka* (to touch), the term closely associates the female biological cycle to 'ritualistic' pollution, conferring ideations of the profane onto the female body (Devi 2019, Par. 5). It has been used as a hegemonic apparatus to modulate women's access to private/public spaces, and to places of privilege. Alongside its proxemic governing of women's spatial agency, menstrual traditions in Kerala also enforced seclusion from daily affairs. The *thriputtarattu* at the Chenganoor Bhagavathy temple celebrates the goddess's monthly menstruation, ceremonially confining the idol to a separate shrine during the period. She is returned to the main shrine after a 'cleansing' bath in the rivers near the temple.[3] The tokenism of consecrating the

[3] Practices such as *thirandukalyanam,* celebrating menarche, symbolise the travel from girlhood to adolescence and eventual womanhood; young girls are metaphorically bathed, and dressed in finery. Often, such rituals have roots in primordial mother-goddess and fertility cults which faded out or were assimilated into organised systems of religions.

menstruating deity, and by extension, the biopolitical feminine/female body, in a sequestered space, creates a mobility apartheid that is both mystified and normalised, both sacred and taboo. Under its sway, the somatic bodies of women are rendered as illegitimate technologies of travel, or as imbued with an illicit potential for mobility—a conception whose emphatic 'routes/roots' extend into contemporary spatio-temporalities.[4] The semiotic profile of the travelling woman, and her gendered mobilities, is then arrayed within a compromised aesthetic that labours to 'structure at least some parts of social life ... as unchanging and invariant' in the face of the neoteric, transformative 'movements' inscribed by travel, as practice and genre (Hobsbawm 1983, ii).

## 2[5]

In the *Navodhanam* (Renaissance) era, demarcating the late-nineteenth and early-twentieth centuries in erstwhile Malayalam-speaking lands, *sancharaswatantryam* (freedom to travel) emerged as an archetypal thread in various cultural struggles, social transformations and recasting of ideological assemblages.[6] Bearing out an uncanny valency in the region's journey from a fragmented collection of princely and feudal territories, bound loosely by ethnicity, language and customs, towards manifesting a sub-national

---

[4] In *Routes: Travel and Translation in the Twentieth Century,* James Clifford (1997, iii) suggests the dichotomous envisioning of 'routes/roots' as a way of contextualising the relationship between travel and the cultural imperative of being sessile.

[5] Another version of the discussion in this section has appeared in my doctoral thesis tiled *Women's Travel Writings in Kerala: Discourses in Conflict* (2019).

[6] In many of the reform movements that characterised the *Navodhanam* in Kerala, freedom to travel in the caste-mandated public sphere and a vital reformulation of mobilities emerged as key issues; across the 1880s and early 1900s, many movements such as the Villuvandi Yathra (1893), Vaikom Satyagraha (1924–25), Guruvayoor Satyagraha (1931–32), and the Temple Entry Proclamation (1936) contested established norms of travelling/mobility.

identity and the eventual framework of statehood, *travel* appears to transcribe the axiomatics of this 'Renaissance-modernity'. The processes of travelling and modernisation, paralleled with each other, puncture topographies of belonging (identity, space, time). Prefigured in these ruptures is a corresponding slippage towards the *unknown/unseen/unfelt* that fosters chaotic alterations of borders, spatial orders, temporal experiences and reflexivity. This alliance is eminently pronounced and tangible in the widespread reforms that contested social stratifications, discriminatory haptic cultures and the privileged metrics of space through which dominant social groups excluded and governed subaltern bodies in the burgeoning publics of the epoch.

Discourses on gendered mobilities during this period, however, were riven with 'debates on cultural affiliation' (Aguiar 2011, ii). If travel were to be the key to the complex matrices of socio-economic phenomena, modalities of change and liberatory self-fashioning that crystallised in the ambit of Renaissance-modernity in Kerala, then what kind of mobilities would contour appropriate femininities? In the course of a speech made at the Chitoor Balika Sahitya Samajam, Tachattu Devaki Amma intones the possibility that '... [e]ven if women do not enter public life, if they raise able children, is that not in itself adding to the prosperity of the world' (1913, n.p.). The *home* is canonised as a node for idealised feminine mobilities, the inculcation of which altruistically adds value to society.

In contrast, that which is masculine/masculinised came to *be* through behaviours and ideologies that co-opted public spaces in traversals of political, intellectual and civic spheres of life. It was in the exercising of this *purusha* (masculine) mobility that 'modern' social order is instituted. Men were to engage with the public sphere, working towards accumulating capital and power as a tactic for acquiring modernity/progress: a prescription that is, tellingly, mobilised in K. C. Narayanan Nambiar's poem *Sancharam* (Travel) (qtd. in Chandran 1989, 42). On a second level, this capacity for public work/activity individuated men and their contributions to their families, communities and cultural landscapes; their mobilities cast them as celebrated interlocutors between the feminised-private and the male-dominated public, and in turn, modernised their performances of gender.

Women's mobility, on the other hand, was to be rendered through morally sculpting, civilising and binding identities to modern apparatuses of social power, especially the conjugal family within which emotional labour and affectational valence granted modern gendered subjecthood.[7] Glimpses of this nebulous enterprise of gendering may be glimpsed as early as in 1864, through the character of Mariam, the female protagonist of the proto-novel *The Slayer Slain*. She acknowledges an astonishingly 'modern' notion of *selfhood*, declaring to her patriarchal kin, '... but you are mistaken if you think I will submit quietly to what I do not like; my will is as strong as yours, and it can resist' (Collins 2011, 61). Equipped by a 'Christian' education to nurture and persuasively mould an idealised moral familial unit, she voices the principle facet of its circuit of gendering: '... And unless I am married to someone to whom I can look up for guidance and wisdom, someone much cleverer, much wiser, and with more grace and gentleness, in the heart than I have, I shall be, I know, very wicked' (Collins 2011, 71). Women were to *write* the family into terrains already *writ* with masculine authorial power.

Later novels, as one of the dawning literary genres of the period, turn a singularly incisive light onto this paradigm shift. *Indulekha* (1889), the first aesthetically complete novel in Malayalam, posits an equation of '... man for society and woman for home, so in the variegated Universe, the law is not equality but of complementarity' (Aiyar 1916, n.p.). Indeed, the eponymous heroine, Indulekha, and her English-educated lover, Madhavan, carve out terrains of conjugality and spaces for the new, nuclear family, at a historical juncture when marriage reforms were being

---

[7] This observation takes off from the nuanced criticisms on gendered mobilities argued out by G. Arunima in 'Writing Culture: Of modernity and the Malayalam Novel' (1997) and J. Devika in *En-gendering Individuals: The Language of Re-forming in Twentieth-century Keralam* (2007).

fiercely debated, through their *individual* ability/determination to perform and extend sociocultural mobilities deemed natural for man and woman. Within the novel, travel seems to represent a practice that marks modern masculine agency, with Madhavan frequently travelling to improve/better himself (read: education, employment and so on). Indulekha, as intellectually enterprising and resourceful as she proves herself to be, does not engage in travel/travelling activities. In fact, it is only to accompany Madhavan on his appointment to the civil service that Indulekha finally travels: '… [Madhavan] had been taken in the civil service. They went to Madras with Madhavan's father and mother and stayed there comfortably. This story ends here' (Menon 2007, 331).

Other fin-de-siècle Malayalam novels, such as *Meenakshi* (1890) and *Parangodi Parinayam* (1892), show evidence of similar dispositions towards women's social/public agency. For instance, Parangodi, the English-educated heroine of the latter work, is adjudged to possess the wrong versatilities for a Malayali woman. Her prospective suitor, Pangassa Menon, an idealised figurehead of the Malayali masculine within the text, critiques the crafting of her nature and qualities through English education thus:

> … Didn't you say that Parangodikutty's grasp of English is very strong? For us, what purpose does it serve? I am not an Englishman; my mother tongue is Malayalam. *We have no transactions with foreigners.…* But what do women, *especially our women* gain by learning to speak umpteen different tongues? In that time they can very well learn something useful.… (Menon 2013, 30; emphasis mine)

Written as a parody, the novel attacks the apparently 'Westernised' ethos popularised by texts such as *Indulekha.* Interestingly, it chooses to do so by dismantling the sociocultural mobilities and agency accorded to women through modernity, English education and anglophile impulses. In the above passage, Pangassa Menon notes that his family does not partake in transactions with 'foreigners', rendering Parangodi's prowess in English essentially futile as it may no longer aid/abet the prosperity of the familial unit. At a second level, he appears to also be referring to undesirable cultural and symbolic exchanges that are entailed in contact with the outside and the other. The import of his dissent towards English and its possibilities is more directly expressed in his belief that there are other, 'useful' preoccupations/vocations more suited to 'especially our' women. In stark contrast, Korappa Menon Divanji, Parangodi's father, clearly conceives of English education as a means of conferring upon his daughter, precisely the mobilities deemed unsuited to the feminine: 'In England the ruler is a lady now. We also hear that there many English ladies are entering various professions and doing their job as well as any man. Who knows of Parangodikutty's fortune? … Anyhow I must educate her in English' (Menon 2013, 30). Thus, it is clearly conceptions of mobility that become gendered/gendering arenas within such works, coding agency in the entwined contexts of burgeoning modernity and traditional sociocultural/political spheres. By extension, gender also came to inflect spatiality, the inhabitation of spaces, as well as the 'authority' to traverse them.

In tandem, the pervasive category of caste and its manifold implications on hegemonic social mobilities were also being reimagined in the period. In the face of a tradition (brahminical Hinduism) and history that marginalised subaltern identities and experiences, the promises of colonial modernity accentuated the subaltern 'dilemma of belonging' (Menon 1997, 292). *Saraswativijayam* (1892), written by Potheri Kunjambu, grapples with the oscillation between colonial modernity and tradition, crafting a didactic novel that negotiates with and challenges the status quo. The novel—whose epigraph reads, 'Education is the greatest wealth of all'—celebrates English education and Christian values as liberating forces for subaltern castes, as means of accessing cultural resources and social equality. The narrative offers a distinctive counter-discourse to elite-caste domination in the figure of Marathan, a pulayan, whose contention that god exists within all enrages Rathnasekharaillathu Kuberan Nambuthiripad and his overseer, Ramankutty Nambiar. Marathan disputes the established theocracy and caste hierarchy wherein brahmins held a spiritual and religious monopoly. Under Kuberan Nambuthiripad's orders, Nambiar attacks Marathan and leaves him for dead. At this juncture, caste, as a poleaxe of social control, is visible; Nambuthiripad is able to wield his clout further to evict Marathan's family from the village. Spaces and transactions that take place within spaces thus appear to proceed forth from the hegemonic apparatuses of caste.

The colonial law machinery, English education and Christian virtues reify the promises of imperial modernity that interrupt the sway of caste over territories and spatial practices. The colonial legal system disciplines the fugitive Nambuthiripad, deigning to punish him for a homicide that would have been justified under the order of caste. The 'superior' English education that was given to Marathan allows him to ascend to a position of power in society, transforming him into the Christian subject, Jesudasan, a judge who is ironically called upon to rule on his own murder. However, it is the inculcation of the biblical values of forgiveness and compassion in Jesudasan that permits him to show kindness to his once oppressor and acquit him in court. These interventions posit a seemingly 'unproblematic' relationship between the subaltern and missionary colonialism in so-called Malayalam-speaking lands.

The territorial/spatial imaginations that populate such a relationship are often articulated through travel in the novel: 'A procession sets the train of events in motion and ever afterwards the protagonists are on the move experiencing expulsion, ostracism, acceptance and contentment. And it is precisely this movement, from one terrain to another, which generates this qualitative change of state' (Menon 1997, 307). The act of travelling, as opposed to the forced exile of Marathan's family and ritualistic movements choreographed by caste, is initiated by the individual and serves as a trajectory for deliverance. Marathan's travel, for instance, signifies the rhetoric of empowerment put forward by colonial education and Christian missionaries for subaltern castes, positing the transcending of an oppressive brahminical tradition and past. Kuberan Nambuthiripad, in contrast, experiences travel as a fugitive from colonial justice; his movements depose him of caste authority, removing him from geographies of power and privilege.

However, travel attains yet another dimension in the case of Subhadra, Nambuthiripad's daughter, who is excommunicated. Her material/spiritual exile from the folds of her caste and religion is reflected in her disgraced travel to Cannanore, away from the spatial locations that shaped her identity. Like Marathan, she finds her 'true self' through her conversion to Christianity and acceptance of its ideals. Later in the narrative, when she reunites with her husband, who also converts to Christianity, she is conceived of as his equal for the first time. Thus travel, both metaphorically and in experience, allows Subhadra to access gendered modernity, albeit through the aegis of missionary faith. But it is through the arc of Saraswati, Nambuthiripad's granddaughter, that the novel codes gendered mobility. It is revealed that Jesudasan, the transformed Marathan, is married to Saraswati—who embodies a vital cog in the emancipatory journey portended in the text. Her symbolic travel, from being Nambuthiripad's granddaughter to being Jesudasan's wife, echoes a shift in cultural capital; her feminine body, its social journey and 'seamless' transition to a modern, patriarchal institution, demarcated a definitive mode for women's travels that is often replicated in the history of modern Malayalam novels.

The novels of C. V. Raman Pillai, a pioneering writer of the late-nineteenth and early-twentieth-century Kerala, depict the institution of culturally 'sanctified' travel for women. With the ideal feminine gradually inscribed within the family and other privately-owned spaces, the aesthetic of gendered travel was significantly modified to reflect acceptable versions of femininity. Unmediated travel away from the home and other sites of femininity was deemed to be an act of disruption, breaking with the gendering logic of modernity that associates chastity and respectability with the sessile woman. C.V. Raman Pillai's popular female characters, such as Subhadra and Meenakshi, who are touted to be exemplary icons of empowerment, nevertheless are thoroughly enveloped in the master codes of modern travel:

> Most of C.V.'s heroines who venture out of homes invite social stigma like Subhadra or are threatened with it like Meenakshi. Meenakshi, the heroine of *Dharmaraja* who dares to step out into the public domain in search of her lover, has to pay a heavy price in the sequel *Rama Raja Bahadur* for that single act of transgression in being suspected by her own husband for having proven unchaste precisely through that one single act of unfemininity. (Pillai 2012, 24)

In the legacy of these mobility portrayals, entrenched diversely throughout the history of modern Malayalam literature, the *female/feminine* contravenes the purpose, perspectives and attitudes demanded of modernised/modernising travel and travelling subjectivities.

## 3

The earliest known Malayalam travelogue written by a woman, *Oru theerthayathra* (A Pilgrimage; henceforth referred to as *OT*), opens with an enumerative, anodyne description of a *contact zone*: 'On the 31st of June, 1921, we embarked on our journey to Jagannatham from Madras. The railway station there is called "Puri". It is located at a distance of 776 *nazhika*s from Madras. We purchased a direct ticket to "Puri", and boarded the Kolkata Mail that departs at 7 pm' (Ammalu Amma 1925, 1). The scene documents the travelling/writing *I*, situated in an amalgam of ideas and practices that surround gender, 'meeting, clashing, grappling' with vectors of mobility and modernity. Far from the arcane, demonic vision that was embossed onto K. C. Narayanan Nambiar's encounter at the beginning of this essay, through the course of Tharavathu Ammalu Amma's religious tour from Palakkad to various pilgrimage centres in India, published in 1925, discourses on oppositional mobilities assume a disinterested, explicatory tone. Turning away from narratives of the 'marvellous', the text produces 'an ordered survey of spaces' through which the novel, strange *topoi* of travel could be negotiated (Nayar 2005, 214–15).

In part, the aesthetic corroborates lattices of 'modern' gender, as they occur in cultural imaginaries and literary representations, in spatialising highly specific performances of travelling and writing. It transliterates the traveller out of the rhetoric of domesticity and the emotional labours (care, love, nurturing) entailed in sustaining it, curating a public authorial voice that explores, analyses and records. Such reflexive self-fashioning reveals an ongoing conversation with a schismatic, oscillating condition that, at once, foregrounds the modernity of *being enroute*, and the margins of mobility allotted to the gendered body. In other words, the travels inscribed in *OT*, while characterising the charter to enlighten and modernise by travel, also threatened the hierarchy of conscious values that administers gender.

The chassis of the pilgrimage, a contradictory travel form that harkens to the tenet that '*self* and *place* are integrated realities, and that the self may be changed with a change of place', engages directly with the textual conflicts that impel *OT* (Leed 1991, x). As a practitioner of mobility, the pilgrim is a curious addition to the early landscape of travel. Contrary to the rhetoric of epic narratives, wherein the journeys were always divinely ordained acts of destiny, pilgrimages revolve around the individual desire to transform. Interweaving personal zeal, and a voluntary setting out from home territories, its framework disrupts a key tenet of theocratic ideology—the effacement of the self. Interestingly, the mediating consciousness of the traveller/writer is diffused within the collective pronoun: *njangal* (we) in *OT*, reconciling in a sense with the spiritual dictates of the form. Significantly, this narratorial voice posits an aggregate of travelling identities, as opposed to travel being a singular act by Ammalu Amma. Indeed, her journeying occupies the gamut of altruism, with its stated purpose being to hallow the mortal remains of her brother in holy places. Thus, having erased the scope for individualised pleasure, and the language of its gendered desiring subject, *OT* seeks to redeem the dominant ideals, realities and social aspirations that augur hegemonic performances of identity.

Yet, by its very nature, *OT* problematises neat categories that set pilgrimages apart from 'secular' travel forms (trade, tourism), exploration and demotic mobilities. Though spawned by the intention of travelling to and experiencing sacred/ritualistic spaces, pilgrimages invite the intervention of other projects vis-à-vis 'adventure, escape, economic advancement, political gain; and the pilgrimage site was often ... linked to an evolving set of objectives' (Brummett 2009, ii). In this sense, traversing across Jaganathapuri, Kasi and the banks of the River Ganga, among other destinations, the lineaments of Ammalu Amma's mobilities cannot be limited to those of a pilgrim alone. Her travelling gaze, expansively chronicling lived experiences of transit, people, cultures, etiquette and travel trivia for her readers, is textualised in a pastiche of life writing, history lesson, itinerary and travel guide. It emplaces the narrative in a regimen of authenticity, saturating it with signs of *witness* such as railway imagery, names of towns in-between destinations, or edifices of newness such as bridges. This is illustrated, for instance, by the meticulous reproduction, running into multiple pages, of the Sanskrit *slokas* chanted by Hindu priests by the side of the Ganga, or the fees exacted at temples for various rituals (Ammalu Amma 1925, 60–69, 149).

The objective, then, is to extend *OT* past traditional conceptions of 'unverifiable records of private experience taking place in profoundly unfamiliar surroundings' in the masculinised, modernised backdrop of Malayalam travel discourses (Campbell 1988, ii). Peripherality, even in the most perfunctory sense of *seeing* spaces/places for the first time, is resisted through vivid discursive complexes: '... The *Shonibhadhra* bridge ... is the longest in India.... Once the train is on it, the sight of the gushing waters of the river, as far as the eyes can see on either side, is enough to *make anyone* marvel ... to fill *most people* with fear' (Ammalu Amma 1925, 41; italics mine). The sway of novelty, even as it percolates the very optics of the text, is tempered as a universal, quotidian response, a *rational* acknowledgement of spectacular difference. Translating the exotic into usable, witnessed epistemologies, maintaining the fiction of voiding biases of personality/fascination in conveying this knowledge, grants authority to the travelling/writing self, an agency that is historically, expressly, denied to gendered subjects in the knowledge–power muniments of travel in fin-de-siècle Kerala.

The acute liminality of *OT*, bordered in/out by gender, genre and practice, signifies peculiar discontents of modernity in Kerala. Carrying architextual echoes of travel discourses in Malayalam, linking distant cultural heritages and accelerated transformations, with 'uncertain future(s), *the liminal* imprints structured enclosures, creative transgressions, and spaces-in-flux' (Fryxell 2019, 290; brackets mine). It represents the imbrication of the unique modernity mythos in Kerala (rife with narratives of emancipation, development and progress) with mobilities pertinent to idealised, hegemonic subjects. In the historical, accidental making of Kerala, it is this striated self-identity and its ideological modus operandi that closes infinite thresholds, annexing and territorialising subjectivities, bodies, meanings and actions onto each other. Gender, penetrating the constitutive dichotomies of temporal/spatial, regional/'global', home/away and self/other, offers an intrinsic frame for the manifestations of these powers. It offers, through technologies of gendering, or being gendered, an arrest of that which is *in medias res,* transient.

The performance of travel, imbued with movement, motilities and transmutations as a discursive necessity, draws out the vacillations of modernity internally divided along trajectories of gender. Positioned in liminality, the gendered travelling/writing subject wields 'conditions characterized by the dislocation of established structures, the reversal of hierarchies, and uncertainty about the continuity of tradition and future outcomes' (Horvarth et al. 2015, ii). The roaring, speeding 'demoness' of a steam train, the nearly-catatonic mobilities of the antharjanam and Tharavathu Ammalu Amma's pilgrimage (sanctioned through caste/religion, but made atypical through gender), cleave 'the modern' originated in the *Navodhanam*/Renaissance. It can no longer, cognitively and experientially, be a single space. The modernities of travel/mobility, at the intersection of gender across its tropes of Malayali-ness, standardised femininities and insidious cultural moorings, are liminal, conflicted spaces, at the heart of which lie the regressions that render the trajectory of modernity in Kerala oxymoronic.

## REFERENCES

Aguiar, Marian. 2011. *Tracking Modernity: India's Railway and the Culture of Mobility*. Minneapolis: Minnesota UP.

Ammalu Amma, Tharavathu. 1925. *Oru Theerthayathra*. Kottayam: Norman Printing Bureau.

Aiyar, Subrahmanya N. 1916. 'Onam Day Speech'. *Subhodini*, n.p.

Arunima, G. 2003. *There Comes Papa: Colonisation and The Transformation of Matriliny in Kerala, Malabar, c. 1850–1940*. New Delhi: Orient Longman.

———. 1997. 'Writing Culture: Of Modernity and the Malayalam Novel'. *Studies in History* 13(2): 271–90.

Bini. S. 2016. 'The Divine and the Diabolic Feminine: Dynamics of Caste and Gender in the Narratives about the Goddesses and the Yakshi in *Aithihyamala* Texts'. *Journal of Arts* 5(1): 29–44.

Brummet, Palmira Johnson. 2009. *The 'Book' of Travels: Genre, Ethnology, and Pilgrimage, 1250 to 1700*. London: Brill.

Campbell, Mary Baine. 1988. *The Witness and the Other World: Exotic European Travel Writing, 400–1600*. Ithaca: Cornell UP.

Chandran, Ramesh V. 1989. *Sancharasahithyam Malayalathil*. Thiruvananthapuram: Kerala Bhasha Institute.

Clifford, James. 1997. *Routes: Travel and Translation in the Late Twentieth Century*. Cambridge: Harvard UP.

Collins, Mary Frances. 2011. *The Slayer Slain*. 1864. Kottayam: CMS.

Devaki Amma, Tachattu. 1913–14. *Sthreevidyabhyasathinte Uddesam*. *Lakshmibai* 20(1): n.p.

Devi, Gayatri. 'Has Kerala Always Considered Menstruating Women Impure?'. *Feminism in India* Jan. 15, 2019. <https://feminisminindia.com/2019/01/15/kerala-menstruating-women-impure/>.

Devika, J. 2007. *En-gendering Individuals: The Language of Reforming in Twentieth-century Keralam*. Hyderabad: Orient Blackswan.

Fryxell, A. R. P. 2019. 'Time and the Modern: Current Trends in the History of Modern Temporalities'. *Past & Present* 243(1): 285–98.

Gluck, Carol. 2011. 'The End of Elsewhere: Writing Modernity Now'. *The American Historical Review* 116(3): 676–87.

Hannerz, Ulf. 1986. 'Theory in Anthropology: Small is Beautiful, the Problem of Complex Cultures'. *Comparative Studies in Society and History* 28(2): 362–67.

Hobsbawn, Eric. 1983. 'Introduction: Inventing Traditions'. In *The Invention of Tradition*. eds. Eric Hobsbawn and Terrence Ranger. London: Cambridge UP.

Horvath, Agnes, et al. 2015. *Breaking Boundaries: Varieties of Liminality*. London: Berghann.

Leed, Eric J. 1991. *The Mind of the Traveller*. New York: Harper Collins.

Menon, O. Chandu. 2007. *Indulekha*. Kottayam: DC Books.

Menon, Dileep. 1997. 'Caste and Colonial modernity: Reading *Saraswativijayam*'. *Studies in History* 13(2): 291–312.

Menon, K. R. 2013. *Parangodi Parinayam*. 1892. Thiruvananthapuram: Chintha.

Nayar, Pramod. 2005. 'Marvelous Excesses: English Travel Writing and India, 1608–1727'. *Journal of British Studies* 44(2): 213–38.

Pillai, Meena T. 2012. 'Modernity and the Fetishising of Female Chastity: C. V. Raman Pillai and the Anxieties of the Early Malayalam Novel'. *South Asian Review* 33(1): 53–75.

Tally Jr., Robert T. 2016. 'Foreword: "A Utopia of the In-Between", or, Limning the Liminal'. In *Landscapes of Liminality: Between Space and Place*. Eds. Dara Downey, Ian Kinane, and Elizabeth Parker. Rowman and Littlefield: ix–xv.

SEVEN

# Sewing Malayali Christian Women

## *Missionary Makings of Sartorial Morality and 'Modern' Domesticity in Travancore*

Arya A.

> Whereas the distinction of the faithful from unbelievers, even by outward signs and habits, is a thing which has always been endeavoured, that so the one may be known and divided from the other; therefore the Synod having observed that there is no distinction either in their habits or in their hair, or in anything else, betwixt the Christians of this diocese and the heathen Naires, doth command, that henceforward no Christian do presume to bore their ears, or to do anything to make them large, except women, among whom it is a universal ornament; and whosoever shall transgress herein, shall be punished at the pleasure of the prelate, who shall not suffer them to wear an ornament of gold or of anything else in their ears; and whosoever shall presume to wear any such ornament shall be thrown out of the church neither shall the *casture* be given them until such time as they are brought to yield effectual obedience, and to leave off all such ornaments ... [Decree XVII, 'Christians to be Distinguished From Heathen By their Dress, & c.', *The Acts and Decrees of the Synod of Diamper 1599*] (qtd. in Zacharia 1994, 210)

This essay is prefaced by the conscious curation of vernacular Christian subjects through both apposition and opposition of indigenous symbolic markers in Travancore by the Christian Diocese and the relatively new faction of Protestant missionaries. Over the years, as the Christian community grew dynamically, owing to the shifting socio-religious economies of the nineteenth century, the missionaries grew equally anxious of the caste-signifying appurtenances on the bodies of their new converts.

Their bare bodies adorned in coarse unstitched *mundu*, inflected by amulets and other insignia—which were markers of regional sacred belief conventions—was a location of colonial Christian anxiety. As J. Devika notes, even from the Synod of Udayamperoor (The Synod of Diamper) convoked in 1599, particular emphasis is laid on the need to differentiate between '*Nazranis* and *Malayalees* ... expressed externally through the dress and ornamentation' (2005, 465). The resultant project of insulating converts in Travancore was effectively negotiated through sumptuary regulations like that of sartorial codes predicated by discourses on civility, modesty, respectability, hygiene and cleanliness.

Proselytising projects coloured by such apprehensions often demanded both visible and corporeal embodiments of the effects of 'Christianisation' among their converts. Evidently the mission's soteriology in the region that employed the idiom of respectability and modesty often conflated their impulse to convert with the imperial logic of rendering the natives 'modern' and 'civilised' (Kent 2004). As the large corpus of robust literature on the intersections of Christian missionary conversions in colonial South India suggest, at the epicentre of the mission's civilising gaze was the initiative to re-sartorialise 'lower-caste' women's 'heathen bodies', and to reorganise their labour from the public spaces to the interiority of their homes. This essay furthers such explorations by arguing that crucial to this 'civilising' project was the integration of converted women into a quintessentially feminine labour economy, that protected their 'virtues' from the unsolicited gaze of the 'indigenous', 'licentious', 'godless' men. The mission laid precedence on the family and the role of women as mothers, responsible for their health, cleanliness, modesty and respectability. And for the mission, respectability was enmeshed in sartorial morality, making it exigent that the woman knew how to sew and clothe her family, embodying modesty that the 'light of salvation' bestowed on them.

Permeating the paradigm of reform straddled by the Christian missionaries is the nebulous presence of sewing and needlework initiated among the converted native women. This is a shared legacy that one may observe across cultures and regions where the mission engaged with similar projects of subject/identity production among its converts. Sewing/needlework as a performative endeavour that traverses multiple economies often functions as a metaphor for women's domesticated location, dictating the range of women's mobility, confining women's labour and contracting the range of their permissible activities. The space of Travancore inhabited by bodies, inflected by caste markers, unfolded as a potent ground to receive and refract the modalities of demarcation written onto the sartorial practices of converted Christian bodies.

The essay operates with the hypothesis that Christian missionaries in nineteenth-century Travancore deployed sartorial 'reforms' and sewing practices among converted women as a mechanism to produce a uniquely vernacular strain of Christian female subjects. The analysis attempted here engages with fictional accounts written during the time by borrowing from Dilip Menon's frame of categorising the nineteenth-century Malayalam novel as an 'amphibious artefact', which continues the 'reform agenda' of the time, enclosing the native 'in a form that is European' (1997, 296, 299). Against an archival enquiry into the various missionary records, the essay places the proto-novels of Mrs Frances Collins' *The Slayer Slain*[1] (hereafter *TSS*) (1864–66), and Variyath Chori Peter's *Parishkaravijayam*[2] (Triumph of Reform; my trans.; 1906), to situate emergent sartorial habits in Travancore engendered by the Christian missionaries and the ensuant performative productions of 'modern' domesticities, anxieties and reform, and the concomitant consolidations of converted Christian womanhood in Travancore.

---

[1] Mrs Collins' 'novel' *The Slayer Slain was* serialised in *Vidyasamgraham* from 1864 to 1865 and was later translated and published in Malayalam by her husband Richard Collins in 1877 as *Ghatakavadham*. The plot reveals the reformation of Koshy Curien, presented within the cultural rubric of caste system in Travancore, and is an interesting tract on the 'superiority of Protestantism over the indigenous Syrian Christianity' (Menon 2002, 1665).

[2] It is commonly recognised as the first novel written by a Latin Catholic, in Malayalam.

Christianity in Travancore was by no means a monolithic commune. C. J. Fuller's study on Christianity in central Travancore identifies that there were three major categories of individuals who professed Christian faith in the region: the 'Syrian Christians, Latin Christians and New Christians' (1976, 54). Though these denominations straddle schismatic tensions contingent on their origin, liturgical traditions and caste affiliations, inciting assemblages of 'Christianised' pollution conventions appropriated from the region, their core principles are structured around a shared theology. While acknowledging the methodological inadequacies inherent in academic practices that conflate different Christian/Catholic/Protestant populations in Travancore, as the current essay locates itself within a shared economy of orthopraxy among these denominations, it employs the term 'Christian' as a protean interchangeable label for them.

## Sartorial Labour, Prohibitions and 'Modern' Domesticities

Studies on nineteenth-century 'mass conversions' to Christianity in Travancore reveal an idiom of ruptures and reinscriptions. It emerges in the annals of history as a continuous jousting between adaptation and improvisations amongst the natives and the mission. Robert Caldwell's accounts of improvising biblical liturgies to suit the demands of nadar converts, who wanted Christianised rites akin to the regional ritual of *ayudha pooja*, calls forth such engagements with vernacularisation of conventions (Hardgrave 1969, 48). Discernibly the missionaries were rather sceptical of their converts' polytheist adherence to such regional rituals and practices. The interior locations of these practices/ performances/habits, often carried out in private caste-segregated spaces, away from the moralistic 'edifying' gaze of the missionaries, impregnated these indigenous domestic-familial spaces with Christian-apprehension. The sex-segregational practices of the region cordoned off male missionaries from accessing most private dwellings, which further mystified the angst-ridden appeal of the Malayali domestic home.

In missionary writings, vernacular homes often emerge as the site of transgressive undoing of their careful Christian 'teachings'. The *Report of the Second Decennial Missionary Conference: Held in Calcutta, 1882–83*, records such uneasy panics: 'the heart of Hinduism is ... but enshrined in its homes, in the family life and hereditary customs of the people; fed, preserved and perpetuated by the wives and mothers of the region' (Greenfield 1883, 210–11). In addition, informed by the gendered logic of the Metropole, where the quality of 'homelife' remained the responsibility of women, the missionaries began to regard women in the region as 'formidable obstacles to progress', capable of unravelling 'Christian understanding painstakingly created by Christian churchmen and their male students, converts, and inquirers' (Kent 1999, 118). The fact that the women they addressed were bearers of caste symbols considered 'heathen', as opposed to the markers of 'civilising' effects of the gospel, further contributed to their moral panic. For the missionaries, these conditions required an immediate recourse, one that would open up multiple loci and modalities of interactions, allowing penetration into these gendered spatial boundaries.

Since the earliest arrival of the Protestant missionaries in Travancore in 1806, 'lower-caste' women's bare bodies were of particular interest to their discourse. Early mission narratives and colonial administrative reports on Travancore chronicle diatribes of varying degrees, addressing moral outrage on behalf of Malayali women's supposedly compromised sense of modesty. By 1812, the mission was able to extract sanctions from the Resident of Travancore that allowed shannar women converts to cover their bosom. This re-sartorialisation was part of their 'civilising' project, an undertaking punctured by a 'discourse on modesty' and sartorial morality of their women converts. The ensuing Breast Cloth revolts in 1828–29 and again in 1858–59, and women's engagement with the Christian jackets/*ravukkay* and their appropriation of upper-caste *melmundu* are events that are well documented. While the missionaries fought to erase visible markers of converted women's pre-Christian excesses, obscuring regional grammars of their femininity, caste order and social status, the converted women, rendered nameless in history, reduced to a typology to predicate the missionary discourse of modesty, found their own infringements. In fact, for a considerable time, the *ravukkay* designed for them were vehemently resisted in favour of a *melmundu*. Charles Mault wrote that the converted women often looked upon the *ravukkay* as 'an invidious badge ... from which the people turned away with ... abhorrence' (qtd. in Kooiman 1980, 158). Women's resistances to such social and sartorial morality desired by the missionaries furthered the chasm between the missionaries and their unyielding Malayali women converts.

As refashioning of the community was peculiarly central to the religious imagination amongst the Christian factions in the region, it is generative to locate agents that facilitated such tacit possibilities. Interesting to this concern is Stephen Greenblatt's theorisations in *Renaissance Self-Fashioning* where he argues that for new ideologies to have some palpable impressions in a region/culture, it should have some bearings in pre-existing systems. 'An ideology', he writes, 'that is perceived as perfectly alien would permit no point of histrionic entry' (1980, 227). Read along this logic, Eliza Kent's work on Bible women in South India postulates that *zenana* missions that came into existence around the mid-nineteenth century were in part a 'response to the urgent need' felt by missionaries 'to contain what were seen as subversive capabilities' of the converted women (1999, 118). Consequently, among converted Christian communities in Travancore, it can be argued that the *zenana* missions and the presence of missionary families acted as familiarising agents of 'histrionic entry'. They opened up locations of deferential interactions, which were crucial to the demarcation of a vernacular Christian womanhood. While indigenous homes were inaccessible to the predominantly male missionary population, the influx of women missionaries created new spatial porosities and possibilities (Hunter 1984; Haggis 1998; Kent 1999).

The boarding schools that mushroomed in the region further assisted the project, providing insulated environments where women could be trained and moulded without the undoing interference of their homes and native habits. Malathi de Alwis' study on Christian boarding schools in Ceylon records that 'the "careless" and "restless" bodies of ... native girls were disciplined and moulded ... via a "gospel of gentility" that sought to produce "respectable" ladies who were both pious and industrious, restrained and gentle' (2005, 181). The projects intended to carry out the re-sartorialisation of converted women were also made possible by the industrious training of girls in these boarding schools, who were instructed to manufacture hundreds of stitched *ravukkay* that could be distributed among the communes.

Equipping these women in the 'craft' of stitching and the ensuant sartorial labour economy had a dual function. Primarily, it provided material embodiments for their re-sartorialisation projects across the region. The sartorial labour of native young girls and converted women 'besides supplying the Boy's school with jackets and trousers, ... [also] prepared a large number of women's jackets which are sold to the people as soon as they are ready, at full cost' (1861, 16), records *Annual Report of the Travancore District Committee in Connection with London Missionary Society, South of Travancore, for the Year Ending December 31, 1860.* Secondly, as de Alwis observed, 'sewing played a crucial role in the very moulding of Christian Women, in the construction of a particular moral demeanour ... insist[ing] on neatness, orderliness, concentration, patience and precision' (qtd. in Kent 2005, 81). John A. Jacob's *History of the London Missionary Society in South Travancore 1806–1959* reiterates the above sentiment. He notes that '... the constant handling of fine and delicate materials, and the necessity of keeping them spotless [and] clean tend to refine the character and habits of the women' (1990, 69).

The nebulous presence of sewing and needlework that plague the 'moral' Christian training of women by missionaries are also made visible in the proto-novels by Mrs Collins and Variath Chori Peter. Mariam in Mrs Collin's *TSS* is often conceived in the text as doing embroidery on upper-body garments that could be fashioned as a blouse. In similar lines, to depict

Monica, who could be considered his central female character, as an industrious, 'virtuous', 'desirable' woman, Variath Chori Peter flourishes the narrative with accounts of her engaging in sewing and 'reformed'/'modern' dressing practices. The literary imaginations of 'ideal' Christian femininities in Travancore consciously replicate the domesticated regulation of women's quotidian practices, as institutionalised and structured within missionary environments.

Christian missionaries predicated their imperative of 'respectability', 'modesty' and 'reform' amongst its Malayali converts through systematic reorganisation of women's social order. The regulation of the sartorial practices is hence, by and large, a regulation of the moral social order. Draping the Malayali Christian women's bodies in sartorial conventions deemed appropriate by the mission is an unequivocal mechanism of prohibition. The radical privatisation and sartorialisation/coercive dressing of Malayali women's bodies reveal the mission's anxieties of its unruly potential. In her discussions on the reconstitution of the *bhadramahila* in Bengal, Himani Bannerji argues that the distinctions of morality and immorality written onto the naked and/or clothed body of women engenders a regressive differentiated constitution of 'the sexual and the social [posed as asexual and therefore virtuous]' (2001, 105). The symbolic schemes of reforming sartorial practices of women was indicative of the critical 'moral' significance of their role in the Christianisation of conjugality and domesticity in Travancore. There is a significant de-emphasis of the erotic and the desiring, closing off regional permutations of sexualities and femininities and masculinities. The engagement with sartorialisation and re-sartorialisation of converted women's 'heathen' bodies in Travancore radically reoriented indigenous locations of spatio-socio-libidinal economies.

Central to the fulcrum of domestication of femininities in Travancore was the realisation of a conjugal reform and resultant establishment of the 'Malayali Christian family'. Ann Laura Stoler argues that 'family, as Foucault warns us, should not be seen as a haven from the sexualities of a dangerous outside world, but as the site of their production. Colonial authorities knew it only too well' (1995, 112). To this end, it became imperative that Christian missionary families be deployed at various mission centres. Rufus Anderson's 'Introductory Essay on the Marriage of Missionaries' (1836) which served as an introduction to the memoir of Mary Ellis, an Anglo-American LMS missionary wife, voices the importance of such strategic deployments: 'The heathen should have an opportunity of seeing Christian families. The domestic constitution among them is dreadfully disordered . . . the character of society is formed in the family. To rectify it requires example as well as precept' (Anderson 1836, xi). Subsequently, the mission's vernacularisation of the Christian family evolved from a Victorian heteropatriarchal ideal of the 'modern' domestic front, where women's social responsibility was to create a gentle, moral and benevolent influence on the family—an ideal that conflated domesticity with subservience to the patriarch of the family. The resultant conjugal resocialisation was predicated on quotidian practices of women limited to and regulated from and/or within the interior of their homes.

Peter's *Parishkaravijayam* is a text that abounds in descriptions of what qualifies as an ideal Christian woman. He insists on chastity (*pathivrathyam)* and '*adakkam, lajja, elima*' ('discipline/modesty, shame, humility'; my trans.; 1907, 83) as characteristics of 'good' Christian women. Education of women is a pronounced discourse in the text and the author makes a conscious attempt to dramatically differentiate women of 'learning' from others via reductionist characterisations. His heroine could sew and was proficient in needlework. She is versed in English, educated and well-read. She reads books and also performs sartorial reforms amongst members of her family. Designed as Peter's mouthpiece for reform in the text, Mathu gives long litanies of the virtues of this new conjugal order, where women educated in the Christian convents 'ran' the domestic familial space. Mathu's long monologues insisting on the importance of women's education in Christian homes (1907, 92–95) share its uncanny diction with what may be categorised as sentiments that are unapologetically 'Victorian'. The author precociously warns the readers that education advocated for women is to be entertained to ensure her role as a successful domesticated wife responsible for training children and inculcating 'good' Christian habits in the family (1907, 93).

The missionary spectre of 'domesticity' and 'reform' looms large in characterisations of women and social spaces in the proto-novel. Upon marriage, Monica's betrothed gifts her a sewing machine and a book titled *Grihabharanam* ('Regulation of the Home'; my trans.; 1907, 103). The book is supposed to provide 'the heroine of the house with necessary qualities' (1907, 104), so that she can be a '*yuvatiratnam*' ('a gem of a woman'; my trans.; 1907, 89) that may 'shine in her husband's crown' (1907, 90). In Mrs Collins' *TSS*, we see the beginnings of such literary reiterations, where women educated in boarding schools come back to domestic environments as reformed and relatively 'modern', situated as sites of reason and ideal behaviour. This kind of ideation is reciprocal of the very Christian logic, where Christ, as the Son of God, evolves as the embodiment of the finest qualities imaginable by mankind. In a similar fashion, missionaries sought to reorganise converted women in ideals of domestication imbued with patience, subservience, gentility and a virginal virtue indicated by the neatly stitched, often meticulously embroidered, white clothes they are instructed to wear.

The reformed domestic spaces reiterated in these proto-novels reveal fraught terrains of 'modern' refashionings, that is if the condition of being 'modern' is to be determined by a series of productions or affectations. If indeed that is the assumption, Timothy Mitchell's location of 'the production of modernity' as involving 'the staging of differences' and the performance of 'distinction between modern and non-modern' is of interest to this analysis (2000, 26). In such sites of productive engagements, there is a 'double difference', writes Mitchell, a register of 'indeterminacy and ambivalence' as well as the 'enormous power of replication' (26). If the 'modern domesticities' produced by Christian missionaries in Travancore are subjected to this framework, the refashioned sartorial body of Christian women becomes the site of the staged performative 'double difference'. Their bodies, sartorial labours and acts of dressing and undressing, emerge as slippery points of contamination, where the differences between the Christianised and non-Christianised/'non-modern' vernacular womanhood are embodied.

It also facilitates and organises multiple strains of subversive aspirations, reordering femininities in the region through denouncements and simulations. For instance, the operative logic of this productive replication can be evidenced in Monica's instructions to her widowed godmother on the benefits of wearing loose fitting clothes and its supposed benefits for the female form (Peter 1907, 95–96). Mariam, in *TSS*, desperately tries to performatively differentiate herself from the betel-chewing, loudly adorned Syrian Christian figure of the potential mother-in-law (Collins 1865c, 238).

Modernity, as Steven Smith argues, is a site of anxiety and pride, essentially characterised by ambivalence and self-criticism that instructs political progress (2000, ix–xiv). In the proto-novels under consideration, education and reading, even when championed as desirable, also figure as sites imbued with ambivalence. On the other hand, sewing and the sartorial imaginations emerge from these dialectical locations as the performative loci of missionary 'modernisation' of Malayali women. The ability to read, if not the very act of being educated itself, is identified as a leisurely afterthought by caricatures of 'non-modern' figurations in these proto-novels. But the valency of the 'craft' of stitching and sewing remains unchallenged, validated and reinforced by both 'modern' and 'non-modern' mouthpieces in these fictional realms. Monica is chastised by her mother for reading books (Peter 1907, 92), whereas her sartorial engagements never warranted such scrutiny. Mariam is certain that if she fails to marry into an educated family of 'Christian' belief, she will be forced to relinquish her reading habits, as evidenced in her rumination: '… I shall never have any time for reading, but she will call me idle and hide my books' (Collins 1865c, 238). Interestingly the narrative does not shadow similar anxieties of prohibition with respect to her expressed interests in needlework and other sewing practices.

In the two texts in consideration, education of Christian women is treated with suspicion, developing alongside a disincentive economy among Malayali factions, as reciprocated in the words of the prospective mother-in-law from Collins' narrative: 'I have never a very high opinion of girls that can read. They never make good wives' (1865c, 238). Sewing, in both fictional and historical grounds, evolved as a coveted capital. Mary Elanor Anabel Chamberlain or Mrs W. I. Chamberlain's account of *zenana* mission's engagements in South India attest to the fact that 'crocheting, needlework and embroidery worked their charm' (1925, 28) among native women. Sewing practices hence became incentivised by the mission in their conversion endeavours, where native women were enticed to engage with the gospel in exchange for sewing lessons.

## Sewing 'Modern' Christian Malayali Women

Sewing, as a performative act, has been embroiled in the contentious gendered dialectics of discourses on the hierarchies of art and craft. Rozsika Parker in *The Subversive Stitch: Embroidery and the Making of the Feminine*, clarifies that the distinction between the craft of sewing and the art of painting is in 'terms of *where* they are made and *who* makes them. Embroidery ... was made in the domestic sphere, usually by women ... Painting was produced predominantly ... by men, in the public sphere, for money' (1984, 5). The parallels drawn between women and embroidery, craft and femininity, have often engaged in 'the stereotype of the virgin in opposition to the whore, an infantilising representation of women's sexuality' (Parker 1984, 2). The image of Penelope weaving has long captured the Western imaginary, where a certain strand of domestication is bred in conjunction with the act of weaving and virginal morality.

This form of a private domestication infringed by the very nature of sewing and its resultant labour that produces material effects, had crucial ramifications for missionary endeavours around the globe. Stephen R. Riggs' 1869 account of missionary projects in Dakota, *Tah-Koo Wah-Em Or, The Gospel Among The Dakotas,* makes an interesting reference to converted women as 'willing scholar[s]' who 'spun and knit and wove garments for herself and household' (1869, 180). Scholarship into Christian missionary projects in different parts of the world reveal distinctive re-sartorialisation endeavours carried out by them.[3] Cultures of sewing emerging from these discourses may be a crucial point of reference in contextualising the strategies of producing vernacular tangents of Christian subjects. It reveals a sociology of the body, where restraint of desire and regulation of sexuality, key to the project of missionary 'reform' and discourse of 'modesty', are maintained through the 'control of female sexuality' (Turner 1984, 114) by policing their bodies and marking them with heteropatriarchal modalities.

Christian boarding schools were sites capable of inflecting both heterogenetic and orthogenetic assemblages of respectability among the vernacular women of Travancore, 'transforming their "heathen bodies" into "respectable" ones' (de Alwis 2005, 181). Malathi de Alwis argues that 'the plying of the needle involved the very embodiment of Christian virtues of piety, industry and docility' (2005, 181). The project of re-sartorialisation of women in the region was also closely negotiated by careful strategic deployment of the skills of young native girls in the convents. Their proficiency in the craft is something that the missionaries incentivised. Samuel Mateer writes in *The Land of Charity: A Descriptive Account of Travancore and Its People:*

> Lace-making, introduced by Mrs. Mault in her boarding school at Nagercoil, and by Mrs. Lewis at Santhapuram, has succeeded to perfection. Admirable specimens of fine pillow lace, in cotton and gold and silver thread, manufactured at the Mission school, were shown at Madras, and in the great London and Paris Exhibitions, in all of which they gained prize medals. Being sold for the benefit of the female schools, the profits have greatly assisted this department of our work. The employment has also spread to Tinnevelly. A suggestion

[3] See Hunter (1984); Davidoff and Hall (1987); Choi and Jolly (2014).

> has recently been made that it might be more profitable, instead of merely copying and repeating, as has hitherto been done, the old standard English patterns and styles, to get up real Indian designs in accordance with the purest national taste and styles of art, so as to establish the Nagercoil lace as a purely indigenous production. The suggestion seems important, and worthy of being carried into effect. (1870, 108)

Inferring from Mateer, it is evident that sewing traversed multiple registers; it is engendered by and within an imperial logic of capitalist economy and production. There is also a moralistic dimension as it allows for a prohibition of mobilities of the converted Christian women, who once were part of the active labour force inhabiting unique spaces of casted-gendering and labour cultures in Travancore. The conversion of their 'heathen' bodies was also dictated by freeing them from a form of casted public labour and entrapping them instead, in a chaste Christianised economy of sewing and ensuant practices.

Converted women's co-option as 'working women', moderately educated, entrenched in a moneyed economy, producing materialities of cultural embodiments and an affective trajectory monopolised by Christian learning, affixes them within a framework of middle-class eclecticism. They are women who are evidently demarcated from the tangents of their 'missionary sisters'. They no longer hold significations of their native caste and gendered history. They are subjects of continued disseminations, inseminations and improvisations. Though Monica and Mariam, tailored by Peter and Mrs Collins respectively, are placed within a jarring optimism central to colonial missionary rhetoric, their apparent liminality and alienation is appallingly visible. They are sites of ambivalence and anxieties, difference and deference, imitations and dissonance. They embody the energies of an anachronic space and continuing time, occupying the paradigm of the desired, desirable and the deterrent.

It can be said that the boarding schools were responsible for producing primarily three distinct categories of womanhood significant for the missionaries: the 'educated', trained women who could potentially marry missionary men and then continue the 'civilising' process; the 'Bible women' who are characterised by Eliza Kent as 'paid assistants' within *zenana* missions: 'though sorely neglected in the official accounts ... [they] were crucial mediators between the culture of mission stations and that of Indian villages' (1999, 119); and the convent-educated women, who were the products of peculiar interactions between the mission and the indigenous emerging middle class that straddled reform. Both Monica and Mariam are products of this lineage. They harbinger potential for multiple infringements to the categories of vernacular feminine across castes, class and religious boundaries. They are the prototypes of domesticated 'modern' selves, re-ordering bodily practices and sartorial imaginations.

The Christian discourses on modesty required converted women to dress with 'piety'. The sartorialisation in the region, besides being indicative of rigid systems of caste and its pollution conventions, was also contingent on Travancore's geographical disposition and its climate. In *Parishkaravijayam*—a proto-novel written about five decades after shannar women protested against dominant (nair) castes for their right to cover their breasts as well as wear the *melmundu*—the heroine is affronted by the inadequacy of thinly woven, possibly cotton, single-layered *kuppayam*/blouse. In a tone of authority, Monica prescribes the use of an '*ulkuppayam*' ('camisole'; my trans.) (Peter 1907, 96) underneath the *chatta*, which must definitely be of a loose fitting. This marks a decided shift of Christian subjectivities oriented around a 'discourse of modesty' to a 'discourse of regulation', from covering/clothing to layering and being pinned in place, predicated on women's '*shareera-adakkam*' (bodily discipline/bodily modesty; my trans.) (1907, 95). *Parishkaravijayam* juggled anxieties of social reform and the role of women and their education in society. The sartorial instructions made to women in the text is evidently reciprocal of the theorisations on the 'omnipresent male gaze that women's bodies' were subject to in conditions of social 'reform' (Bannerji 2001; Gupta 2014; Devika 2015).

While Mathu in Peter's text is a lynchpin for late-nineteenth-century and early-twentieth-century ideas of 'reform' that circulated in Travancore, and author's own public voice of *reason*, descriptions of and by Monica fascinatingly reveal slippages of a certain crisis in 'middle-class' Christian subjectivity, owing to rapidly reorganising systems in the region. Her voice is used to emphasise not just the role of women and by extension the wife, but also as a means to deploy as well as conflate characteristics like respectability, subservience and marriageability. As the male voices in the text engaged in discussions of reform, social mobility and status, and debated encroachments and violence of *parishkaram* (reform) on tradition, the author used the voice of the 'educated' Monica, of around twenty years of age, to restrict and reorient the mobilities and planes of interaction among women. Mathu pronounces this domesticated purpose with much clarity; women, he asserts, must be educated, so that children could be dressed in clothes that reflect hygiene, cleanliness, their age and importantly, their '*vargam*' (category of caste/community/gender) (Peter 1907, 93). Their education does not and should not necessarily warrant employability, but their skills are welcome in the household, to be of assistance to their husbands (Peter 1907, 92, 95). The author is specifically engaging with the Christian project of delineating spaces, based on the 'doctrines of separate spheres', differentiating between the feminine domestic and the masculine public (Haggis 1998; Kent 1999; Bauman 2008).

While the domestic and private spheres are inhabited by women who stitch and micromanage the biomedical bodies of the members of the family, without dissent or strife, the men traverse the publics, engaging in public discourse, participating in the growing nascent civic society of the time. The injunction regarding how women of respectability must adorn themselves is essentially a conceited effort to produce managed and manageable typologies of femininities that are virtuous, moral and desirable extensions of heteropatriarchal imaginations. The 'sewing body' of women, ordered by Christianity, performs and produces systemic infringements to traditional economies, spatial mobilities and labour of women, creating domestic typologies of womanhood—'civilised', 'modern', middle-class/bourgeoisie and in flux, emblematic of Foucault's genealogy pertaining to modern modalities of production of power/knowledge and the self (Mitchell 2000, 5).

## Paradoxical Missions of Domesticity

The mission of domesticity and re-sartorialisation in Travancore was not without resistances. It was an assemblage of a series of processes—dynamic, contenting and complimenting, and informed by impulses and agents of action and inaction. The delineation of the domestic by missionaries was one of the many ways in which they tried to homogenise the region's vernacular modalities of caste organisations, gendered histories, aspirations, concerns and violences. While sewing ensured a re-socialisation of women and their labour in Travancore from the outside to the inside, the modalities of sewing institutionalised by the mission reoriented missionary women from the interiority of their 'homes' to the very visible publics of the mission stations. Mrs Mault, one of the first generation of missionary wives who moved to Travancore in 1819, is recorded in archives as having 'establish[ed] a school for converts and a "lace industry" to employ the converted women' (Haggis 2000, 108). While the native women were secluded in their homes and their mobility redrawn and limited, the missionary women who refigured the role of native wives as a dispensable appendage to the patriarchal logic, increasingly held more demonstrative and authoritative roles of considerable traction in these missionary projects. Hyaeweol Choi and Margaret Jolly, responding to this apparent avowal and disavowal of the domestic, write: 'Christian Mission was often spoken of as domestic duties and housework, a paradoxical metaphor' since this removed them far and beyond the imaginations of a 'sphere of home' (2014, 4). But then again, their large-scale deployment and evangelising missions is recorded in the male-dominated missionary archives as 'Women's Work' (Davidoff and Hall 1987, 117), subordinate to the mainstream missionary organisation, beneficial only for various economic mobilisation (Haggis 2000, 111). The peculiar categorisation of a 'private sphere' and domestic within the economy of sewing and lace-making is a rather neat and easy paradigm. Upon consulting various editions of the *Annual Report of the Travancore District Committee* from 1828 to 1922, especially the ledger for receipts on 'Sale of Lace' from respective boarding schools in Travancore, it can be concluded that sewing cultures engendered by the mission were a complex interaction between means of production, marketing, circulation and dispersion of ensuant profit. Lace production is an organised network, employing the labour of indigenous 'working women', that is situated within shifting modalities of the global economy and the rise of the moneyed intermediary class in Travancore and the bourgeoisie middle class in the Metropole.

The mission also shared the colonial preoccupation with the 'body as an object of hygienic regulation and medical intervention' (Mitchell 2000, 25). They trained the women in the boarding schools to assist with medical regulation of the body. In *TSS,* Mariam, who returned from the convent school, is portrayed as being capable of assisting/resuscitating an unconscious man, Paulosa (Collins 1864b, 84). Along similar trajectories, *Parishkaravijayam* also provides multiple references on how convent education would help organise the health and hygiene of the newly formed cis-gendered heteropatriarchal family unit. Missionary literature also places much emphasis on the role of women as mothers and their responsibility in maintaining a clean, healthy environment and a pious, religious household. An interesting tangent of inquiry is the question of a different site of domesticity, viz the (predominantly) white missionary households. While the missionary women were instructing 'domestic ideals' to the converted indigenous women, it is imperative to scrutinise who laboured in the missionary homes. Who cleaned and sewed their corsets and skirts? Who washed their sartorial adornments and who raised their children while they went on projects of civilising indigenous women, their homes and vernacular kinship patterns? Accounting for this double standard in regulating women's mobilities as trafficked by missionary engagements in colonial regions, Susan Thorne writes, 'Part of the transformative power of the missionary project was its sanctioning of transgressive behaviour as religious exceptions to gender rules' (1999, 50).

* * *

One may conclude that introduction of sewing and needlework among Malayali women as a strategy of 'reform' and means of subject production by Christian missionaries resulted in new consolidations in the social order. However, domestication and the production of a certain category of Malayali women was a project not unique to Christian missionaries. The last decades of the nineteenth century and early twentieth century witnessed ruptures and fissures in 'traditional' social formations of Travancore with visible resistances written onto women's bodies. *Achipudava samaram, Kallumala samaram* and *Mukkuthi samaram* were some of such infringements that had specific ramifications contingent on casted-gendered re-socialisations and 'reformation' of the Malayali woman. Through a consolidation of print and public discourse and sometimes legal litigations, women in the region were drastically *reformed* and *re-formed*, forming multiple legacies and consolidations of femininities and womanhood. The 'mission of domesticity' and its engagement by Christian writers of the age can essentially be located as an early and localised point of entry to reveal the dynamic economies of neo-impulses that infiltrated Travancore, which left lasting ripples in the sociocultural, gendered fabric of the region.

## References

Anderson, Rufus. 1836. 'Introductory Essay on Marriage of Missionaries'. In *Memoir of Mrs. Mary Marcy Ellis: Wife of Rev. William Ellis Missionary in the South Seas, and Foreign Secretary of the London Missionary Society* by William Ellis, vii–xxii. Boston: Crocker & Brewster.

Anon. 1861. *Annual Report of the Travancore District Committee in Connection with London Missionary Society, South of Travancore, for the Year Ending December 31, 1860*. Madras.

Bannerji, Himani. 2001. *Inventing Subjects: Studies in Hegemony, Patriarchy and Colonialism*. New Delhi: Tulika Books.

Bauman, Chad. 2008. 'Redeeming Indian "Christian" Womanhood?'. *Journal of Feminist Studies in Religion* 24(2): 5–27.

Collins, Mrs. Richard. 1864. *The Slayer Slain. Vidyasamgraham* 1(1): 35–40.

———. 1864b. no. 2, Oct, pp. 80–88.

———. 1865a. no. 3, Jan, pp. 134–36.

———. 1865b. no. 4, April, pp. 183–87.

———. 1865c. no. 5, July, pp. 231–40.

———. 1865d. no. 6, Oct, pp. 284–88.

———. 1866. no. 8, April pp. 369–73.

———. 1877. *Ghatakavadham [The Slayer Slain]*. trans. Richard Collins, Kindle ed.

Chamberlain, W. I. 1925. *Fifty Years in Foreign Fields, China, Japan, India, Arabia: A History of Five Decades of the Woman's Board of Foreign Missions Reformed Church in America*. New York: Women's Board of Foreign Missions.

Choi, Hyaeweol, and Margaret Jolly. 2014. 'Paradoxes of Domesticity: Missionary Encounters in the Making of Christian Homes in Asia and the Pacific'. In *Divine Domesticities: Christian Paradoxes in Asia and the Pacific*, 1–26. Canberra: Australian National UP.

Davidoff, Lenore, and Catherine Hall. 1987. *Family Fortunes: Men and Women of the English Middle Class 1780–1850*. Chicago: U of Chicago P.

de Alwis, Malathi, 2005. '"Respectability", "Modernity" and the Policing of "Culture" in Colonial Ceylon'. In *Gender, Sexuality and Colonial Modernities*, edited by Antoinette Burton, 179–94. London: Routledge.

Devika, J. 2015. 'The Aesthetic Woman: Re-Forming Female Bodies and Minds in Early-Twentieth-Century Kerala'. *Modern Asian Studies* 39(2): 461–87.

Fuller, C. J. 1976. 'Kerala Christians and The Caste System'. *New Series* 11(1): 53–70.

Gupta, Charu. 2014. 'Intimate Desires: Dalit Women and Religious Conversions in Colonial India'. *The Journal of Asian Studies* 73(3): 661–87.

Greenblatt, Stephen. 1980. *Renaissance Self-Fashioning: From More to Shakespeare*. Chicago: U of Chicago P.

Greenfield, Miss. 1883. 'Women's Work in the Indian Mission Field'. *Report of the Second Decennial Missionary Conference Held in Calcutta, 1882–83*, 210–211. Calcutta: J. W. Thomas, Baptist Mission Press.

Haggis, Jane. 1998. '"Good Wives and Mothers" or "Dedicated Workers"? Contradictions of Domesticity in the "Mission of Sisterhood", Travancore,

South India'. In *Maternities and Modernities: Colonial and Postcolonial Experiences in Asia and the Pacific*, edited by Kalpana Ram and Margaret Jolly, 81–113. Cambridge UP.

———. 2000. 'Ironies of Emancipation: Changing Configurations of "Women's Work" in the "Mission of Sisterhood" to Indian Women'. *Feminist review* 65: 108–26.

Hardgrave, R. L. 1968. 'The Breast-Cloth Controversy: Caste Consciousness and Social Change in Southern Travancore'. *The Indian Economic & Social History Review* 5(2): 171–87.

———. 1969. *The Nadars of Tamilnad: The Political Culture of a Community in Change*. Berkeley: U of California P.

Hunter, Jane. 1984. *The Gospel of Gentility: American Women Missionaries in Turn-of-the-Century China*. Connecticut: Yale UP.

Jacob, John A. 1990. *A History of the London Missionary Society in South Travancore, 1806–1959*. Nagercoil: Diocesan Press.

Kent, Eliza. 1999. 'Tamil Bible Women and the Zenana Missions of Colonial South India'. *History of Religions* 39(2): 117–49.

———. 2004. *Converting Women: Gender and Protestant Christianity in Colonial South India*. New York: Oxford UP.

———. 2005. 'Books and Bodices: Material Culture and Protestant Missions in Colonial South India'. In *Mixed Messages: Materiality, Textuality, Missions*, edited by Jamie S. Scott and Gareth Griffiths, 67–88. New York: Macmillan.

Kooiman, Dick. 1980. *Conversion and Social Equality in India: The London Missionary Society in South Travancore in the Nineteenth Century*. New Delhi: Manohar Publishers.

Mateer, Samuel. 1870. *The Land of Charity: A Descriptive Account of Travancore and Its People*. London: John Snow and Co.

Menon, Dilip. 1997. 'Caste and Colonial Modernity: Reading *Saraswathyvijayam*'. *Studies in History* 13(2): 291–312.

Mies, Maria. 1982. *The Lace Makers of Narsapur, Indian Housewives Produce for the World Market*. London: Zed Press.

Mitchell, Timothy. 2000. 'The Stage of Modernity'. In *Questions of Modernity*, edited by Timothy Mitchell,1–34. Minneapolis: U of Minnesota P.

Parker, Rozsika. 1984. *The Subversive Stitch: Embroidery and the Making of the Feminine*. London: The Women's Press Ltd.

Peter, Variath Chori. 2012. *Parishkaravijayam* [Triumph of Reform]. 1906. Kannur: Sahithi/Sree Shankaracharya University.

Pitman, E. R. 1903. *Indian Zenana Missions: Their Need, Origin, Object, Agents, Modes of Working and Results*. London: John Snow and Co.

Riggs, Steven R. 1869. *Tah-Koo Wah-Em Or, The Gospel Among the Dakotas.* Boston: Sabath School and Publishing Society.

Smith, Steven. 2016. *Modernity and Its Discontents: Making and Unmaking the Bourgeoise from Machiavelli to Below.* New Haven: Yale UP.

Stoler, Ann Laura. 1995. *Race and the Education of Desire: Foucault's History of Sexuality and the Colonial Order of Things.* Durham & London: Duke UP.

Thorne, Susan, 1999. 'Missionary Imperial Feminism'. In *Gendered Missions: Women and Men in Missionary Discourse and Practice*, edited by M. T. Hubert and Nancy Lutkehaus, 39–65. Ann Arbor: U of Michigan P.

Turner, Brian S. 1984. *The Body and Society.* Oxford: Blackwell.

Yesudas, R. N. 1975. *A People's Revolt in Travancore: A Backward Class Movement for Social Freedom.* Thiruvananthapuram: Kerala Historical Society.

Zacharia, Scaria. 1994. *The Acts and Decrees of the Synod of Diamper 1599.* Edamattam: Indian Institute of Christian Studies.

EIGHT

# Cookbooks from Kerala

## *Creative Adaptations and Inscriptions of Alternative Modernities*

Gigy J. Alex

Across history, many scholars of culture have positioned food and practices of cooking as exercises of power, reflected in recipes (literacy), choice of ingredients (class/caste/religion) and mode of cooking (Barthes 2013; Levi-Strauss 1957; and Mintz 1986). While Levi-Strauss maintains that the culinary denotes 'a language in which it unconsciously translates its structure—or else resigns itself, still unconsciously, to revealing its contradictions' (47), Barthes observes that 'elitist' food practices manifest 'the bourgeois domination of culture' (79). It is this structuring of power, transmitted through cookbooks, that allows for 'what people eat' to express 'who and what they are, to themselves and to others' (Mintz 1986, 13). In this sense, cookbooks as tangents of modernity discourse, become vital indicators in contextualising the milieu and sociocultural history.

Food and food writing, as constituted by cultural, socio-public discourses, demarcate certain conditions of cohabitation of the aesthetic with the 'modern'. Of the many gastronomic agents that are mobilised in this context, the 'cookbook' signifies the stabilisation of 'the ephemeral culinary product within a network of non-culinary discourse' and thus refines the 'culinary' (Ferguson 1998, 600). Against the critical backgrounds of neo-postcolonialism and cultural studies, the cookbook genre may be located as 'disseminators' of a specific *modernity of taste* that is closely tied to the circulation of feminine identity, efficiency and gender expectations in Kerala. The micro-narratives that permeate food writing are crucial to this endeavour, as food cultures, gastronomic principles and genealogies of food mark a significant area where 'recipes and cookbooks used food to familiarise housewives with the new logic of the modern household' (Berger 2013, 1632). This essay studies the rhetorical strategies of the cookbook, and its transformations of the architectural spaces of the kitchen, discourses on mechanisation and new technologies, and its reification of 'legitimate' worldviews about social behaviour, family management and gendered roles in contemporary Kerala.

## Western Culinary Modernities

The culinary aesthetics borne out by cookbooks in contemporary Kerala can be historicised and analysed anew through an exploration of the culinary programmes of the imperialist/neo-imperialist West. Throughout the twentieth century, it is possible to delineate the prevalence of kitchen manuals as a key element of modernisation, particularly in gendered domestic spaces, as noted by Laura Shapiro in her seminal work, *Perfection Salad: Women and Cooking in the Turn of the Century* (1986). These manuals helped the elite and rich women to instruct their servants, manage their homes and perform domestic chores. In due course, as expenses increased, technological advances, the influx of processed and pre-packaged food and kitchen gadgets allowed the housewives to dispense with domestic help. To accommodate this change, kitchen manuals were redesigned to educate upper-middle-class white women on home management and on how to run their houses without domestic help. In this fashion, domestic spaces became agencies promoting efficiency, planning and financial management, and cookbooks came to be aimed at restructuring the perfect Western home into an efficient financial hub which would indirectly help women to participate in nation-building: 'If the home were made a more businesslike place, if husbands were fed and children raised according to scientific principles, if purity and fresh air reached every corner of the house—then, at last, the nation's homes would be adequate to nurture its greatness' (Shapiro 2001, 4).

Thus, the process of modernisation in the Western world transformed cooking into a patriotic act (beset by scientific temperament) and the mother–housewife into a driver of social transformation. If the space of the kitchen would enable the construction of nationhood, it was also capable, as popularised in the West, of sculpting and mobilising the ideal woman. Cooking, the central sphere of activity within this space, became depicted as an enjoyable act that prepares a 'happy homemaker, a wife and mother whose unpaid labour is done for loved ones because of natural, altruistic, and maternal instincts' (Swenson 2013, 139). Thus, the feminine ideal that centres around the kitchen and cooking is a patriarchal product constructed within the public–national and private–domestic binary, with the cookbooks legitimising and propagating food habits, kitchen practices, and modes of consumption associated with social capital and cultural privilege. The genealogy of the cookbook genre in Kerala followed a not-so-dissimilar trajectory, deepening the fault lines of modernity through the curation of new culinary-scapes.

## Appropriating Modernity

The circulation of cookbooks in Kerala, in their introductory stages, was meant for the rich, middle-class women who had the leisure time to read and experiment with recipes. Thus, mostly circulating among the elite, affluent women who had access to power structures, cookbooks ignored the popular dietary habits and food practices of the masses by stressing on hygiene and cleanliness inside the kitchen, rearticulating the hegemony of colonials dishes and encouraging social divides. The modernisation strategy adopted by the gastronomes of that period structured a modernity that was consistent with Western aesthetic standards and disseminated through Western cookbooks. Often, newly-wed women were gifted cookbooks by their families so that they could consult the cookbooks to please and surprise their marital family with delicacies. These strategies stress the hegemonic control of patriarchy, which romanticises and celebrates women in the roles of wife and homemaker and institutes knowledge of cooking as a prerequisite for the modern Kerala woman. These stipulations emplace the cookbook as 'a work of social history' through which parameters of gender in 'modern' conjugality may be traced (Storace 1986, 56).

The cookbook genre in Kerala thus achieved a gendered circulation in spaces earmarked as feminised/feminising: familial terrains, fields of domesticity and private spheres. Evidence for the same could be seen in the earliest artefacts of print modernity in Kerala: popular magazines. Recipe sharing was a regular column in popular magazines such as *Kraistava Mahilamani* (1920) and *Vanitha Kusumam* (1926). They were also keen on instructing women readers on housekeeping and home-management. A long array of popular magazines that tiptoed in adopted the mission to modernise Kerala women in the pattern of their Western counterparts. They, by earmarking regular columns, focused on modernising them through Western modernist strategies related to the crucial areas of (1) cleanliness and hygiene, which led to the feminisation of cooking, (2) mechanisation of the kitchen, and (3) adoption of cuisines from across the world.

*Pachaka deepam* (1963), one of the earliest cookbooks, addressed the significance of cleanliness in its preface. It instructed that kitchens were to be plastered and cleared of cobwebs while promoting the importance of cow dung plastering for plain floors. Manjeri N. G. Seetaramayyar, one of the early cookbook authors, also dedicated a page exclusively for discussing cleanliness. Many popular magazines advised modern women to take care of their personal hygiene and also insisted on the relevance of considering the kitchen as a space of honour. They were also instructed to keep a dustbin in the kitchen and to clean the utensils using tamarind and ash. Concerns over cleanliness and hygiene percolated into the Malayali imaginations through the idealisation of *parishkaram* and *adhunikata*, which allowed hegemonic femininity in Kerala to be sculpted in accordance with imperial tastes. This is most apparent in the colonial sensibility that pervaded the instructions handed down to women regarding the organisation of their kitchens, the popularisation of words like 'pantry', and the introduction of aprons and other Westernised kitchen behaviours. This structured a propaganda to modernise women in keeping with certain traditional values attributed to established femininities in Kerala. Ideal modern women were the memsahibs (an 'urban lady' of colonial and modern India). An analysis of the titles of the books by Mrs K. M. Mathew clearly depicts how the route paved by patriarchal imperialism prescribed the responsibility of homemaking and kitchen-management as woman's business and responsibility. To name a few titles: *Pachakakala, Pachakamaduri, Nadan pachakarema, Adhunikapachakam, Pachakapanchami, Veettammamarkoru koottukari, Adukkalajolikku eluppavazhikal, Pachakeswari, Pachakanavami, Pachakadasami*, and the posthumously published *Ruchi ragam*, *ruchi thalam*, *ruchi pallavi*.

The titles of these cookbooks give the impression that the emancipated modern woman should be ready to assimilate the patriarchal temperament of the time and understand the scientific nuances of cooking. Along with feminisation, the artistic temperament attributed to cooking is interesting. The modernity that these cookbooks articulated tried to conceptualise the ideal woman as someone who is well-versed in traditional and modern cuisines so as to serve as the architect of the gendered space of the kitchen. The titles hint at the projection of a 'feminine' figure constructed in the network between imperialism, patriarchies and proto-capitalism. The meticulousness with which the household chores are performed and cleanliness within the home is ensured, suggests the way in which these recipe books envisage ideal femininity. An ideal housewife is expected to consider cooking as an art and understand the nuances involved in cooking. She is the epitome of culinary brilliance. This has moulded a new pattern of taste among the middle class, who can afford to buy a cookbook and test the samples—'Taste, a class culture turned into nature, that is, embodied, helps to shape the class body' (Bourdieu 2013 [1979], 34).

Mrs K. M. Mathew urged men and women to distinguish between need and luxury and instructed elders to gift their daughters with modern technical utensils rather than jewellery or expensive costumes. She also suggested the keeping of a clock or timepiece in the kitchen for effective management of time. In a sense, this also meant a cultural displacement of traditional food preparations and lifestyle. Gulf remittance and foreign exchange aggravated the same. People from abroad started bringing various electronic gadgets like the toaster, microwave, eggbeater, juicer, oven toaster grill, etc., which transfigured traditional ways of cooking. This led to the transfer of work from humans to machines and technology, and paved the way for the introduction of scientific specifications in food preparation, making use of standardisation and measurement. Another aspect of this development, later on in the domain, is the emphasis on budget—specifically, the trope of women managing the kitchen and domestic resources within a stipulated capital. These cookbooks, in the context of Kerala, emphasised the problematic of 'the modern' where women were portrayed as providers and caretakers of all at home. This cultural dilemma can be seen in the cookbooks from Kerala, where 'the mobile and shifting meanings of the modern as a category of cultural consciousness' looked at the varied and disparate aspects of modernity imbibed by the gastronomes from Kerala (Felski 1995, 8). And that is why, for a long time, cookbooks tended more to reflect the tastes, habits and preferences of the affluent household.

The cultural processes of modernity led to the advent of a large array of tastes and preparatory styles. The tendency to symbolically perform modernity is evident in the ingredients that came to be popularised through cooking. Towards the mid-sixties, the gastronomic sensibility of Kerala was dominated by ingredient items like maida, which was described in recipe columns of that period as the '*American Maavu*', as it was imported from America. The popularity of the *American Maavu* was widely accepted, and it was an essential ingredient for most of the popular snacks of that period. Rather than endorsing its health benefits, maida's rising currency in culinary circles hinged on the opportunity it presented for the adoption of modernised food habits. This harks back to a phenomenon noted by Osella and Osella (2000), reflected in the consumption practices of the affluent populations in Kerala. They preferred 'packet food' (mass-produced, branded food) instead of locally available, home-cooked food materials: 'A small packet of Pomsy brand fried potato snacks, ready-to-eat and available at village bakeries for Rs 5, carries more cachet than a plate of the same potato snacks fried at home …' (Osella and Osella 2000, 127).

Yet, this was also a period that saw drastic modulations of culinary spaces. Kerala, being an agrarian society, used to have an orchard in the backyard of every home, and a kitchen garden to grow the basic ingredients for food preparation. The idea of three meals a day was alien to the everyday Kerala household menu, which concentrated more on the idea of a brunch and an early dinner. Purely from an academic and anthropological perspective, works like *Nammude nattarivukalum pazhamchollukalum kadamkkathakalum* (2012) have discussed various kinds of *kanji* (gruel) that were popular in different parts of Kerala. They discussed the health benefits and medicinal significance of food on the body, as this was consistent with the dietary practices of most Malayalis at that time.

Despite acquiring the veneer of critical enquiry, the cookbooks were primarily used to shape the discourse on women and family. Societal expectations regarding gender roles and performances were reflected in the prefaces of these popular cookbooks as they conceived women as superwomen, effectively planning all the meals and managing the home. Though this idyllic picture of colonial modernity was depicted in elite houses, the reality was quite different, which was never recorded in any of the cookbooks of that period. Though the socio-political and cultural transformations that geared our attention include the unexciting everyday life and practices, culinary maestros who advocated the Kerala model of modernity never addressed the significance of domestics and their role in the kitchen. In an urge to discard the traditional as clichéd and uncouth, these cookbooks never tried to not only deconstruct the dichotomy between the sacred and the profane, but also to discuss the significance of sharing the same dining space: 'The Indian experience of modernity thereby appears incomplete and defective: blocked or still in transition—clinging to the ruminants of a feudal past, or somehow fundamentally "other" and beyond the scope of modernization theory' (Osella and Osella 2000, 257). By adopting scientific cookery and by signifying aspects related to nutrition and home-management, these cookbook authors became victims of the ideologies undergirding women's domesticity. While looking at culinary modernity, one could read the apprehensions that lie between the self-representation of modernity in public discourses and the practices generated by the same. One of the key issues of the project of modernity was establishing and defining itself, which in turn would produce otherness and ambivalence as most of the colonies within the European discourse remained unexplored, especially in matters regarding food habits and food cultures, and the colonies were considered as laboratories for developing modern forms of knowledge. Research and work done by anthropologists like Colleen Taylor Sen are exceptions in this regard.

Unlike in the history of the American cookbook—a history where we could come across a clear-cut transformation in the development of mainstream culinary narrative, including cookbooks of Native American, Latino, Asian and African American cuisines and recipes—Kerala cookbooks started attempting the regional and religious variations quite later. Even then, none of the cookbook authors or foodoirs attempted to document tribal cuisines or yesteryear popular cuisines of their own state. We come across this gap while investigating the strictures of Kerala modernity.

Food being a text, meanings attributed to it are constantly defined, redefined and transformed through various food practices and representations: 'Every ingredient, each dish, the meal structure, and all the elements forming a culinary culture are connected. They are influenced not only by the past, frequently interpreted and practised as tradition, but also by new occurrences resulting from both internal dynamics and the incorporation of external elements' (Parasecoli 2014, 416). Cookbooks from Kerala are significant agents to represent Kerala's complex engagement with modernity. At this juncture, we could think about the argument made by J. Devika when she looks at Kerala women as 'Cinderellas of social development' (2014, 208). She discusses how the Malayali woman became famous in the 1970s when they identified themselves with the developmentalist ideas of women's liberation based on the international model of social development. While going through the cookbooks, and their generic properties and the modes through which they discursively construct their readers, it is quite evident that 'when men radicalised and democratised the domain of politics, women rationalised and sanitised the domestic domain' (Devika 2014, 208). Thus, we can substantiate that the authors of early cookbooks, while conceiving a Kerala model of modernity, were also reinforcing 'Malayalee Patriarchy' (Devika 2014, 208).

## Hybrid Modernity

A typical Kerala cookbook will be an assortment of dishes that are purely traditional, dishes that arrived from other shores, and dishes that were assimilated and incorporated. It is this assimilation and incorporation into the native cuisine that is instrumental in creating a hybrid alternative modernity to Kerala's food narratives and food history. Bill Ashcroft, while elucidating 'alternative modernity', makes it clear that 'alternative' refers to an alternative to Western modernity. In such a situation, the renewed modernity becomes 'transformed and multiplied' (Ashcroft 2009, 84). This alternative modernity becomes hybrid by popularising the international and the regional, the ethnic and the continental. The role played by Christian missionaries and publishing houses in this regard cannot be ignored. *Veetamakkoru kaithozhi* (Handmaid to the Housewife), written by Sr. Dolores Kannampuzha, first published in 1973, could be considered as 'an Encyclopaedia for Women' (Kizhakkemuri 2011). With the aim of providing complete healthcare and value education, the book is structured as a compilation of recipes and wellness guides. It considers the needs and expectations of people belonging to different social classes and economic statuses. The readers are introduced to meal planning, planning feasts, serving, standard measurements, the significance of family and communication, counselling, health benefits of different varieties of food, etc. The new crop of Indian cookbooks was fuelled by the spread of print media and the cultural rise of the new middle class. Through cookbooks and recipe sharing, food emerged from its traditional and moral social matrix into the public domain and evolved as a social text.

The alternative modernities initiated by print modernity is visible when we investigate the role played by various publishing houses in Kerala, like *Malayala Manorama* and *Grihalekshmi*, in representing the modern woman who has evolved and transformed her domestic space through adaption and acculturation. Mrs K. M. Mathew led the recipe columns in the popular magazines *Malayala Manorama* and *Vanitha*, while Dr P. B. Lalkar, who wrote *Veettammamarkku oru guide* (1990) and several other popular cookbooks, served as the head of the publication division of *Grihalekshmi*. This tie between the publishing industry and the cookbook genre is evident in the case of cookbook authors such as Ummi Abdulla (who published with Orient Longman), Toshma Biju (who writes for *Kanyaka* magazine) and Swapna Thomas (Indulekha.com). Their cookbooks deal with regional dishes as well as recipes from interstate and international platforms. The hybrid variety of recipes popularised by these culinary aficionados gave thrust to ethnic, regional, intra-national and international cuisines. The gradual transformation in the titles of the cookbooks justifies the fact that 'while authenticity, attractiveness, and nutritional value remain the dominant values of the new cookbooks, efficiency, economy, and utility are becoming increasingly respectable themes' (Appadurai 1988, 8).

In the initial and introductory stages in Kerala modernity, cookbooks were emblematic of a period when women were encouraged to come out of the kitchen and actively participate in nation-building and empowerment campaigns. Progressive thinkers and restaurateurs like Devaki Narikkatiri Antarjanam, who wrote *Sthreekal adukkala upekshikkarathu* (Women Should Not Abandon the Kitchen), encouraged women to participate in public and political spaces and at the same time, establish their expertise in the culinary space too: 'From cottage to palace, everyone can partake in reforming the kitchen. Indeed, reform that does not root itself in the kitchen cannot be long-lived' (Antarjanam, translated by Devika 2005, 157). This hints at the gradual transformations in culinary spaces which spread to its participants, and at their ramifications, both within and outside the domestic space.

## Culinary Constructs of Kerala

As food and culinary practices are a powerful cultural statement, contemporary foodoirs have re-appropriated and redefined their roles to accommodate the changing socio-political scenario. The contemporary cookbooks include local food practices and ethnic culinary habits, asserting Sherrie Inness' argument that cookbooks are not inert but speak about society's expectations about men and women as 'they evolve with the times, reflecting larger culinary and cultural changes in the society' (Innes 2006, 121). The significant contributions of publishing houses and the propinquity between authors and publishing agencies became a pertinent factor in the circulation and popularity of cookbooks. Flourishing new media (like Facebook, blogs and YouTube channels) to share recipes and discuss food narratives—thereby shifting domestic spaces into the public domain—also have to be considered in this regard. The fluidity of the cookbook genre—to stress the significance of micro-histories, its liberty to accommodate other genres, particularly memoirs, and the inclusion of detailed food histories—enhanced the scope of cookbook discourses.

Cookbooks from Kerala weave memories and family histories into the culinary descriptions and recipes, thus encompassing tendencies beyond imperial modernity. While ancestral memories and anecdotes of culinary culture serve as socio-political texts, sharing recipes could be considered as an alternative modernist strategy by the foodoirs from Kerala. This trend evolved after a series of attempts to imitate the Western model of recipe sharing and exchange of culinary narratives. Writing recipes is 'a much more complex and gendered performance' (Ray 2012, 710). But when gastronomes from different parts of Kerala, from disparate backgrounds, started publishing their cookbooks, the image of the ideal housewife began to be questioned and a plethora of cookbooks emerged which eventually assimilated the essence of a period of transformation.

One of the prominent gastronomes of Kerala, Suma Sivadasan's works—including *Kanjeem kareem kalikkam* (2017), where children are introduced to the world of culinary secrets, which was the first of its kind in Malayalam; *Nammude nadan currykal: Malayalathinte manamulla currykal* (2016), where ethnic cuisines related to folk and local culture are discussed; *Upperikal paaneeyangal payasangal* (2013); *Madhurapalaharangal pazhapalaharangal kekkukal* (2013), where the author concentrated on specific themes and effectively categorised the culinary range so that readers can find and consult the relevant text without losing time—have adopted certain novel schemes to re-present the region's food choices and preferences to the younger generation. This could be an attempt to manifest a renewed modernity against the institutional narrative of the West. Thus the 'other' cannot be treated as external to modernity just as modernity cannot be seen as a discrete Western project totally external to the 'other' (Osella and Osella 2000, 261).

The influence of religions and regions in naming a cookbook is yet another model where the authors concentrate more on popularising intrastate cuisines and cuisines based on festivals. This could be considered as an instance of culinary confidence and gastronomic consciousness that has evolved in due course. Moreover, the period also witnessed the attempts to glocalise the regional by discussing/sharing recipes popular in *thattu kadakal* (roadside eateries) and toddy shops, so as to popularise the ethnic and indigenous cuisines in a global scenario.

A varied description and representation of the food narrative is introduced into the gastronomic food history of Kerala by Vijayan Kannampilly. His *The Essential Kerala Cookbook* (2003), which could be studied from an anthropological perspective to understand the culinary history of Kerala and the role of religious and caste distinctions in the culinary tradition, gives a historical understanding of recipes, cooking utensils, etc. It could be considered as a reference text of the kitchen, and also as a text that has extensively consulted anthropological and food texts from multiple perspectives from the regional, national and international levels. *The Suriani Kitchen* (2009) by Lathika George, who refers to herself as an 'accidental cookbook writer', also adopts such a perspective, where a greater thrust has been given to the traditional recipes of Kerala. This cookbook familiarises the Kerala kitchen space by giving a glossary of different modes of cooking, and familiarising the spices and herbs commonly used in Kerala cuisines. This book sets the Suriani category as a standard upon which the various recipes are explained. An interesting feature of this cookbook, comparable to Ummi Abdulla's *A Kitchen Full of Stories*, is the incorporation of beautiful photographs. Though this strategy also imitates contemporary foreign cookbooks, these books make themselves stand out by incorporating personal memories as mediums that connect people to their own land.

In the current socio-political scenario, where microhistories mould the identities of a place and its people, cookbooks are not mere recipe collections; they are also sociocultural texts that speak about its people and their histories. This is evident in the memoirs and essays titled *Adukkalayil ninnum kitchenilekku* (2013), *Kaipunyam athava chila adukkalakaryangal* (2006), *A Kitchen Full of Stories* (2018), *Kalladuppukal: Malayaliyude marunna adukkala* (2017), *Menusmruthi* (2016) and *Aavi parunna pathram* (2018). In these texts, recipes, histories, visual images and literary texts are infused with memories, histories and food stories. This wide range of food texts are agents of cultural mapping as they give a comprehensive understanding regarding the place and its people.

* * *

This essay through its genealogy of food histories looked at how the Kerala modernity differs from that of other parts of India in its treatment of the genre, and also the epistemic strategies it adopted in connection with the publishing industry in Kerala. Gastronomes from Kerala looked at the aspect of alternative modernity as a 'site where people "make" themselves modern, as opposed to being "made" modern by alien and impersonal forces, where they give themselves an identity and a destiny' (Gaonkar 2001, 18). Cookbooks, as products of cultural modernity, are representations of 'structures of production and distribution' and habitual practices brought before political spaces (Goody 1982, 37). Cookbooks or modes of recipe-sharing that had evolved in the West were assimilated by the colonial counterpart, and they were used as a platform for acculturation; and print modernity helped in adapting them into the changing demands of contemporary social transformation. With the emergence of several micro-histories associated with cooking, culinary acts moulded the culinary confidence and culinary consciousness of the Malayali.

Though the cookbook genre evolved as an act of appropriation, it has used print modernity to mark its identity from the nodal agencies of various regions, religions and castes. In its evolved alternative modernity, though cookbooks agreed with the traditional formula of depicting the woman as a cooking diva in its initial phases, it has moved out of the domestic space and kitchen cupboard to public spaces, libraries and coffee tables as agents of socio-political and cultural deliberations. Being a twentieth-century commodity, cookbooks from Kerala have become progressive by imbibing a hybrid culture, and are anthropological evidences for a place and its people.

## References

Antarjanam, Devaki Narikkatiri. 2005. 'Women Should Not Abandon the Kitchen'. In *Her-self: Early Writings on Gender by Malayalee Women (1898–1938)*, edited by J. Devika, 151–57. Kolkata: STREE.

Appadurai, Arjun. 1988. 'How to Make a National Cuisine: Cookbooks in Contemporary India'. *Comparative Studies in Society and History* 30(1): 3–24.

Ashcroft, Bill. 2020. 'Alternative Modernities: Globalization and the Post-colonial'. *ARIEL* 40(1): 81–105.

Banerjee-Dube, Ishita. 2018. 'Modern Mixes: The Hybrid and the Authentic in Indian Cuisine'. In *Exploring Indian Modernities: Ideas and Practices*, edited by Leïla Choukroune, Parul Bhandari, 169–87. Singapore: Springer.

Barthes, Roland. 1957. *Mythologies*. New York: The Noonday Press.

———. 2013. 'Toward a Psychosociology of Contemporary Food Consumption'. In *Food and Culture. A Reader*, edited by Carole Counihan and Penny Van Esterik, 23–30. New York: Routledge.

Berger, Rachel. 2013. 'Between Digestion and Desire: Genealogies of Food in Nationalist North India'. *Modern Asian Studies* 47(5): 1622–43.

Bourdieu, Pierre. 2013. 'A Social Critique of the Judgement of Taste'. In *Food and Culture. A Reader*, edited by Carole Counihan and Penny Van Esterik, 31–39. New York: Routledge.

Civitello, Linda. 2007. *Cuisine and Culture: A History of Food and People*. New Jersey: John Wiley & Sons.

Devika, J. 2014. 'Women in Contemporary Kerala'. In *Indian Women—Revisited*, edited by Devaki Jain and C. P. Sujaya, 208–18. New Delhi: Ministry of Information and Broadcasting.

———, ed. 2005. *Her-Self: Early Writings on Gender by Malayalee Women, 1898–1938*. Kolkata: Stree.

Felski, Rita. 1995. *The Gender of Modernity*. Cambridge: Harvard UP.

Ferguson, Priscilla Parkhurst. 1998. 'A Cultural Field in the Making: Gastronomy in 19th-Century France'. *American Journal of Sociology* 104(3): 597–641.

Gaonkar, Dilip Parameshwar. 2001. 'On Alternative Modernities'. In *Alternative Modernities*, edited by Dilip Parameshwar Gaonkar, 1–23. Durham and London: Duke UP.

George, Lathika. 2003. *The Suriani Kitchen. Recipes and Recollections from the Syrian Christians of Kerala*. London: Penguin Books.

Gilbert, Sandra M. 2014. *The Culinary Imagination: From Myth to Modernity*. London: Norton.

Goody, Jack. 1982. *Cooking, Cuisine and Class: A Study in Comparative Sociology*. Cambridge: Cambridge UP.

Innes, Sherrie A. 2006. *Secret Ingredients: Race, Gender, and Class at the Dinner Table*. New York: Palgrave Macmillan.

Jyothish, V. R. 2017. *Kalladuppukal: Malayaliyude Marunna Adukkala*. Kerala: DC Books.

Kannampilly, Vijayan. 2003. *The Essential Kerala Cookbook*. New Delhi: Penguin Books.

Kannampuzha, Dolores. 1975. *Handmaid to the Housewife*. The Medical Mission Sisters. https://www.youtube.com/watch?v=hEwmk0FyWJc

Kizhekkemuri, D. C. 2011. 'Preface'. In *Veetamakkoru Kaithozhi*, Sr. Dolores Kannamuzha, N.A.; N.A.

Levi-Strauss, Claude. 2013. 'The Culinary Triangle'. In *Food and Culture. A Reader*, edited by Carole Counihan and Penny Van Esterik, 40–47. New York and London: Routledge.

Mintz, Sydney M. 1986. *Sweetness and Power: The Place of Sugar in Modern History*. New York: Penguin Books.

Nair, Bhaskaran Cheppatu. 2011. *Malayalisadyayum Arogyavum*. SPCS.

Neuhaus, Jessamyn. 1999. 'The Way to a Man's Heart: Gender Roles, Domestic Ideology, and Cookbooks in the 1950s'. *Journal of Social History* 32.3 (Spring): 529–55. JSTOR. https://www.jstor.org/stable/pdf/3789341.pdf

Osella, Filippo, and Caroline Osella. 2000. *Social Mobility in Kerala: Modernity and Identity in Conflict*. Pluto Press. JSTOR www.jstor.org/stable/pdf/26549625.pdf.

Parasecoli, Fabio. 2014. 'Food, Identity and Cultural Reproduction in Immigrant Communities'. *Food and Immigrant Life* 81(2): 415–39.

Ray, Utsa. 2012. 'Eating "Modernity": Changing Dietary Practices in Colonial Bengal'. *Modern Asian Studies* 46.3 (May). *JSTOR* www.jstor.org/stable/41478327.

Rombauer, Marion. 1969. *Abridged from Little Acorn: The Story Behind the Joy of Cooking 1931–1966*. Bobbs-Merrill. https://www.harvardsquarelibrary.org/biographies/irma- rombauer/.

Sen, Colleen Taylor. 2016. *Feasts and Fasts. A History of Food in India*. London: Reaktion Books.

Shapiro, Laura. 2001. *Perfection Salad: Women and Food at the Turn of the Century*. New York: The Modern Library.

Storace, Patricia. 1986. 'Repasts Past: Delicious Memories from Antique Cookbooks'. *House and Garden* (June): 62.

Swenson, Rebecca. 2013. 'Domestic Diva: Televised Treatments of Masculinity, Femininity and Food'. In *Food and Culture. A Reader*, edited by Carole Counihan and Penny Van Esterik, 137–53. New York and London: Routledge.

Theophano, Janet. 2003. *Eat My Words: Reading Women's Lives through the Cookbooks They Wrote*. New York: Palgrave Macmillan.

Vester, Katharina. 2015. *A Taste of Power: Food and American Identities*. California; U of California P.

# Disquieting Continuities

NINE

# Television Modernity and Mediated Femininities in Kerala

Benita Acca Benjamin

Oskar Negt observed that 'media should not constitute the core of a critical media theory' (1978, 64). Instead, it should be emplaced within the history of the region, the politico-public discourses, competing hierarchies and socio-economic tensions that mediate and constitute the dynamics of the medium. Likewise, the introduction of television in Kerala is intertwined with national and regional histories. Since the cultural representations prevalent in any region reflect the techniques of subject formation (Mokkil 2010, 3), a study aimed at reading the nature of televised images would in turn reflect the political economy and dominant ideologies that inform these representations. When television was first introduced in 1959 in India, its major concern was to ensure 'community development and formal education' (Kumar 2012, 296). The state-sponsored television service revealed the aspirations of a newly-independent postcolonial country and stayed closer to the social reality of India. Programmes like *Bharat ek khoj* tried to introduce the viewers to Indian history. Some of the other programmes that were telecast included *Malgudi Days*, which depicted the life of young Swamy, and *Wagle ki duniya*, a sitcom which depicted the affairs of a middle-class civil servant named Srinivas Wagle. These programmes tried to constitute a cultural imaginary among a diverse audience through the representation of the struggles and anxieties of the common man. Thus, the programmes tried to fashion a pan-Indian identity (Mankekar 1999, 106).

As a national network instituted for the welfare of the public, Doordarshan served as an infotainment platform that aimed to connect the heterogeneous population of the country (Mathai 2015, 258). Therefore, it becomes impossible to gloss over the 'national interest' behind the discourses subscribed and validated by Doordarshan. Through the programmes that were initially telecast, Doordarshan tried to reaffirm Kerala's identity as a sub-national entity. Almost all the programmes telecast by Doordarshan tried to fashion a civil society that was unequivocally dedicated to national development and modernity. Consequently, it served to capture the 'private life of the nation state' (Ellis 1982, 5). The national network tried to strategically fashion the most intimate space of the nation—the family. This reiterated the importance of aligning the family to the interests of the larger society as 'home ... was not a complementary but rather the original site on which the project of nationalism was launched' (Chatterjee 1993, 147). Thus, the programmes that were telecast tried to co-opt women into the project of patriarchal nationalism.

Though television was introduced in India in 1959, Kerala had to wait for over two more decades before being introduced to television. Though Malayalam programmes were telecast from August 1975, it remained largely inaccessible to the Malayali public as it was broadcast from Madras. Later, the then prime minister Indira Gandhi decided that the Asian Games, which were held in India in 1982, should be telecast all over the country (Santhoshkumar 2014, 38). As part of this, Doordarshan was introduced in 1982 in Kerala. Nevertheless, Malayalam Doordarshan that telecast Malayalam programmes was introduced only in 1985. Kerala's first encounter with television was part of the larger project of national development and social integration, as in most other non-Western countries (Rajagopal 2014, 84). The nationalist propaganda tool was received with excitement, though the discourses disseminated by television changed over time to assimilate into the sociocultural conditions of Kerala. As a result, in the national and regional context, television escaped the narrow bounds of a communication tool as it also assumed several social functions. This evolution in television's role suggests its potential in facilitating the 'hypodermic injections of modernity'

(Vilanilam 1996, 70). In the next section, this essay attempts to understand the ways in which the new media spaces inaugurated by television mediated gendered spatial relations, gendered anxiety and gendered desire in response to the changing cultural economy of the region.

## Mediating Gendered Anxiety and Desire

The introduction of television served to inaugurate, and address the lack of, 'modern publics' (Rajagopal 2014, 84). The huge crowds that thronged to watch the Asian Games that were telecast through the public television sets installed in a few places in Kerala suggests the ways in which television constituted the changing dynamics of the Malayali public sphere. Robin Jeffrey's observation about printing and its progression from being a rare and scarce medium to a mass medium in Kerala is relevant in the evolution of television as well (2010, 259). As television traversed from teleclubs and community halls to the intimate space of domesticity (Chandran 2014, 18), it also amplified its power to reconfigure and reinscribe spaces and social roles. As a result, the modernity into which Kerala was ushered into through television sought to influence the spatial dynamics through new technologies of subject formation.

When television was a rare medium, not every family could afford the luxury of having a television set. Hence, it was a ubiquitous sight to see many families, even a whole neighbourhood in some cases, huddled together in front of a television set owned by any family in the locality (Chandran 9). This would inevitably lead to the commingling of the private and the public (9). In a way, this led to the transformation of the domestic space into a miniature and transient public space. By constituting alternate terrains for the creation of new publics within the private sphere, the introduction of television refrained from destabilising the hegemonic spatial organisation either through the feminisation or domestication of the public sphere. As a result, the spatial reconfigurations initiated through the introduction of television did not lead to the demystification of the male-dominated public sphere. Thus, even in the initial phase, when television was primarily an instrument for social development, it deferred the task of challenging the masculine public sphere. Despite the configuration of familial spaces by television through discourses of national development and the consequent co-optation of the private sphere for mediating modernity, the modern publics forged by the medium in its initial days were the consequence of an increased socialisation in the domestic space and not the supplanting of the exclusivity that characterised the public sphere.

The 'publics' constituted by the narratives and discourses circulated by television was inadequate in compensating the exclusivity of the actual public sphere. Just as the audience who gathered in a shared space to view television failed to challenge the public sphere, the virtual network of heterogeneous viewers also fell short of replicating the dynamics of the public sphere. While Doordarshan tried to superimpose a uniformity that would potentially construct a 'community from above' with citizen–subjects who are devoted to the nation state (Mattelart 1980, 20), this affectively and discursively constituted community cannot be equated to the actual public sphere. Though television functions as a site for various deliberations, the sociality and mobility that characterises the public sphere cannot be reproduced by the vicarious and distant publics forged by television. Hence, it constitutes only a 'pseudo-public sphere' that allows 'para-social interactions' (Robins and Webster 1993, 33).

In its initial days as state-sponsored television, Doordarshan did not have the technological acumen to facilitate deliberative democracy. Though live telecasting of news or debates on socio-political issues would later consolidate television's position as an inevitable constituent of participatory politics, such dialogic attributes could not be conceived by Doordarshan as it could only telecast pre-recorded programmes at this point in time. As a result, the modern publics constituted by television is not synonymous to a counter-public space as the exclusivity of the public sphere was not compensated by television, though it effectively disrupted and mediated the boundaries between the public and private spheres.

As observed by Uma Chakravarty, television is a domesticated medium (2000, 13). Television not only mediates the discourses between the public sphere and the private sphere but also ensconces the domestic sphere as a primary site in the formation of feminine subjectivities. When television was introduced, Kerala was undergoing rigorous transformations in the familial space. The disintegration of the matrilineal family and the burgeoning of small families entailed the rise of new anxieties in the latter half of the twentieth century (Devika 2002, 7). Social, material and moral norms were realigned to complement the small-family norm. As a struggling postcolony which was gearing towards development, and as a state with an overwhelmingly large literate population, the Family Planning Programme aspired to facilitate progress in the national as well as regional levels. This accentuated the family as an 'individualizing' and 'domesticating' space that would redesign the 'modern family' as a site where the citizen–subjects are appropriately fashioned (11). The anxieties of the small family that had to maintain its efficiency against the legacy of the traditional matrilineal household and the gendered responsibilities that ensued from the modernisation of the domestic sphere, resulted in the redefinition of women's role in the household as the primary caregiver and spouse. As a result, the ideal Malayali woman was expected to embody the 'natural disposition' and 'socially acquired ability' to care for the family (Devika 2009, 81). Moreover, reconfiguring the modern family as a small family where the affective care of the mother could be appropriately utilised suggests attempts at 'disciplining the intimate' (Pillai 2014, 11).

Thus, the shifting ideas and practices that had direct bearings on the family were also instrumental in the cultural reconstitution of subjectivities. One of the programmes that was telecast by Malayalam Doordarshan was *Sindooram*. (The title refers to the red-coloured smear on the forehead of married woman.) As observed by Santhoshkumar, the programme not only aimed at bolstering the mental and physical health and well-being of its women viewers but also tried to develop the employable skills of women (2014, 52). On emplacing the images and discourses circulated by the medium in the specific social, cultural and political conditions of the region, it assumes a significance which was hitherto not ascribed to it. While it remains that *Sindooram* sought to facilitate the empowerment of women, the fact that it referred to a specific category of women, i.e., married women, through its title, suggests the gendered matrices around which normative gender identities are performed. Later programmes like *Veetuvishesham* (Household Affairs) and *Koottukari* (Female Friend), intended for a female audience, also hints at the unstipulated gender expectations that determine and circumscribe the sociality of women.

These programmes hint at the subtle reorientation of feminine affective labour into the domestic sphere. These programmes that construct a virtual and gendered sociality for women aim at alleviating the anxieties of the small-family norm by initiating discussions and prescribing remedies that address the concerns of the heterosexual women audience. The moral economy associated with idealised femininity and the cultural economy linked to the changing ideas, practices and discourses in the region, converge at the realm of the domestic in validating and prescribing certain models of femininities. This, in turn, alludes to the way in which modernity and femininity are discreetly mediated through television.

The shift to the small-family norm was also accompanied by the proliferation of discourses that normalised women's salaried employment (Devika 2002, 41). Though women's participation in income-generating jobs outside their homes might have altered the domestic political economies, it cannot be assumed that it led to substantial changes in the gender equations within the domestic or public spaces. Women's status as secondary income generators solidified certain feminine virtues as a prerequisite in defining and circumscribing the scope of women's employability. The 'womanly qualities' that define feminine domestic roles were also transcribed onto their socio-public roles to inaugurate new gendered mobility regimes that are congruent with normative performances of gender (Devika and Sukumar 2006, 4470). In this context, programmes like *Sindooram* consolidated non-disruptive feminine skills that would assist their navigation across spatial hegemonies.

The domestic space underwent another radical transformation in the 1970s and eighties due to the migration of a considerable number of Malayali men, following the Gulf boom towards the beginning of the last quarter of the twentieth century. As a result of this large-scale migration, women started to helm many domesticities due to the absence of their male counterparts (Gulati 1983, 2222). Nevertheless, the drastic rise in the number of female-centred households cannot be considered as an indicator of the emotional wellbeing of women. While women acquired control over the economic affairs of the family, many studies suggest that the mental health of a number of young brides who were married to the Gulf migrants deteriorated (2225). The new responsibilities that ought to be managed single-handedly, in most households, coupled with the loneliness and conflicts of being uprooted and transplanted into a new household without the presence of one's husband, accounted for the psychological issues encountered by many young wives in Kerala (2225, 2226). Thus, new domestic and gendered anxieties burgeoned during the time. Programmes like *Sindooram,* which sought to address the emotional and psychological dilemmas underwent by many women, not only tried to address the issues related to the all-round wellbeing of women but also helped them adapt to the changing cultural economy of the region. As a result, television facilitated and mediated the gendered negotiations of modern domesticities.

The mediatory role of television in defining domesticities relies not only on the generation of a care economy which depends on the carefully calibrated distribution of affective labour, but also on the evocation of sanitised desires that reiterate the domestic space as a shared and nurturing space. Through the discourses and images circulated through television, it aimed to mould 'collective desires' that are consistent with the structure of the society and the family (Rajagopal 2014, 90). Since the private space of the family constitutes and stabilises the public sphere by serving as a space where the ideas, practices and discourses circulated in the public sphere are reproduced and negotiated (Punathambekar and Kumar 2014, 4), television's role in prescribing aspirational models in the intimate space of domesticity has a covert regulatory effect. Programmes like *Poomottukal* (Flower Buds), *Sindooram, Kaalveyppukal* (Innovations), *Yuvadarshanam* (The Vision of the Youth), *Naatinpuram* (Countryside) and *Krishidarshan* (Vision for Agriculture) were designed to address and inform various kinds of audience—children, women, students, youth and farmers, respectively.

Here, Doordarshan adheres to the 'Reithean philanthropic/ paternalist notions' of providing moral and informative content (Poduval 1999, 109). Through this seeming avuncularism, Doordarshan also instructs the viewing public about the significance of steering the citizen-subject's creative and constructive energies by instilling ideas of collective identity and shared responsibility. As Robin Jeffrey observes, the viewing publics were affectively moved by the televisual images, as some families noted that the representations aided them in regulating and nurturing their conjugal relationship (2010, 226). Since the discourses and images circulated through television tend to normalise and legitimise certain desires (Chakravarti 2000. 13), the televisual representations and narratives seem to construct idealised and sanitised conceptions of morality, desires and respectability by reinscribing the ambit of performance of femininity and by relying on some essentialist conceptions of gender.

Through the attempts to engage different sections of the viewing public through different programmes, not only for the extensive development of the society but also for endorsing inclusivity, Doordarshan is indirectly trying to categorise and address the gendered and classified desires associated with various sections of society. Here, the association of specific programmes with a specific audience, irrespective of whether they are viewed by the ideal-specific audience or a mixed and unsorted audience, reveals the tacit reproduction of hegemonic cultural discourses via mass media. This would in turn hint at the gendered responsibilities linked to various segments of viewers.

Since Doordarshan was a development-oriented public broadcasting service, the developmental modernity that it signified through the various programmes that were telecast in the early years differed considerably from the later versions of cosmopolitanisms facilitated through television. The modernity that television tried to mediate was 'Indianized' so as to establish a consensus between the nationalist interests and modernity (Mankekar 1998, 37). As a result, the television modernity initiated by the communicational revolution in India was non-Western in its essence (37). Nevertheless, at around the time when television was introduced in Kerala, Doordarshan underwent a paradigm shift due to commercial sponsorships offered by business conglomerates who were vying to reap profit out of its wide networks of audience (36). Thus, the national television gradually veered towards more entertainment and sponsored programmes without sacrificing its commitment towards the circulation of information (35).

The wide appeal of Doordarshan's programmes became evident as the viewers readily embraced Maggie 2-Minute Noodles, which was the product advertised during the commercial breaks of *Hum log* (Singhal and Rogers 2001, 88). At around the same time in Kerala, political organisations gave thrust to 'progress through modernization' as the period witnessed the region's accomplishments in the educational and health sectors, land reforms, and public distribution of food grains (Sreekumar and Parayil 2010, 245).

Despite the remarkable social development it achieved, the 'Kerala model of development' suffered due to an unstable economic base (Eapen and Kodoth 2002, 5). The large-scale migration to the Gulf countries was not only a result of the drastic rise in unemployment in Kerala, but it also solved the economic crisis that loomed large in Kerala (Sreekumar and Parayil 2010, 245). Thus, the consumption practices inaugurated in Kerala in the 1970s coincided with the discourses of development and regional modernity as the period witnessed the Kerala model of development and high levels of migration to the Gulf countries (Prakash 1998, 3209). Moreover, the rising middle class that started to gain ascendency through Gulf remittances and constituted consumerist aspirations, formed the formidable audience for television. In such a context, as class mobility became accessible to more and more people, television inaugurated a modernity that was closely tied to consumerist desires and aspirations.

At the time when Doordarshan broadcast was introduced in Kerala, the television was a prized possession that determined the social and economic standing of the family. In addition to inaugurating a consumption-oriented societal structuring through the representations and advertisements circulated through television, the television itself was a commodity that confirmed the commodity fetishism that characterised the consumerist desires in Kerala. In such a context, television-viewing becomes an act that is imbued with power hierarchies and socio-cultural significance as the control over the television set suggests women's power and negotiations within the domestic space (Brown 1990, 202–03). This becomes all the more relevant when one considers the fact that during the period under consideration, television was a 'new media', unlike in the present when it is regarded as an 'old media' owing to the presence of other digital technologies that has redefined the techniques of viewing.

Hence, at a time when television was the most luxurious indoor entertainment, it was regarded as a vaunted possession of the family as it self-evidently spoke about the socio-economic position of the family while also functioning as a site where/over which power relations were played out in the domestic sphere. Thus, the sitting room becomes the locale where the larger politics of gender and age are enacted (Morley 1995, 12). Since access to television among women and their consequent engagements with television were contingent on the disproportionate distribution of televisions across Kerala on socio-economic lines and the power equations within the family that ascribed the agency/privilege to control the television set to specific individuals, the modernity propagated by television had to waddle through the domestic and social power hierarchies before reaching the female audience.

As the possession of certain commodities served as a qualifier of one's relative socio-economic status, consumerism emerged as one among the many pedestals that mediated women's experience of television modernity. With the advent of television, family was transformed into 'viewing family', an entity that is embedded and implicated in the consumerist modernity buttressed by television (Mankekar 1998, 32). Thus, the family became a site wherein national and collective identities and collective desires were forged. The advent of television in Kerala also initiated the normalisation of culturally-rooted consumerist aspirations. Just as the fashioning of the modern citizen–subject was a cultural imperative, the creation of the consumer–citizen was a cultural necessity as it was an offshoot of socio-economic changes. Thus, modernity became a gendered experience through television's mediation of gender roles and creation of new gendered consumerist patterns.

By locating the female audience at the intersection of patriarchy and capitalism (Fiske 1989, 140; Felski 1995, 63), the gendered audience was conceptualised simultaneously as a consumer–citizen and citizen–subject. The shift towards sponsored programmes from 1983 in the national television marked its transformation from a 'revenue-guzzler to a prime money-spinner' (Poduval 1999, 110). In addition to the programmes telecast in the initial days of Doordarshan, the advertisements that were aired along with them also sought to define feminine moral and social roles. Feminist critics like Rita Felski have suggested that consumerist practices have a 'democratizing effect' in their ability to conceive all individuals as potential consumers (1995, 70).

Nevertheless, when television was introduced in Kerala, it was not a commodity that could be accessed by everyone. Its distribution was limited by structures of class, gender and locality. Though these commercials are hinged on the possibility that any viewer could be a potential consumer, the problem of accessibility draws a line between the viewer and non-viewer. The aspirational models produced by the advertisements sought to mould the consumerist desires and reiterate the gendered division of labour. These commercial advertisements not only professed to improve the family's quality of living but also sought to articulate modernity in the language of consumerism (Mankekar 1999, 48).

In the regional context, these commercials tried to fashion some idealised femininities premised on gendered moral economies. The 'capitalist language' of commercials 'couched in moral preaching' conceals the actual economic relations and intentions while stimulating certain consumerist desires which are feminine and culturally validated (Biju 2013, 26). Through the strategic marketing of commodities as objects not only of economic value but also of symbolic value that carry the mark of the family's socio-economic position in the social hierarchy, the viewing subject is coded with consumerist aspirations. Most often, these commercials target the female audience who are often lured through the promise of a reduction in domestic labour only to reinforce their traditional role within the domestic space (Fox 1990, 26). Viewed thus, the 'Kerala Model Woman', who is not only healthy and educated but also from an 'elite' family, is the ideal gendered consuming subject (Devika and Sukumar 2006, 4472). The literate woman, moored to traditional sociocultural codes, makes consumerist choices on behalf of the family, and negotiates the duality of modernity and tradition to qualify as a 'rational female consumer' who engages in consumerism as a 'familial and civic duty' (Felski 1995, 89). Women married to Gulf migrants and working women who have access to money and have consumerist agency are co-opted into new networks of patriarchal capitalism. As a result, the domestic space, and the feminine negotiations of modernity, are interwoven with larger discourses of desire, consumerism and power.

The gendered and mediated subject positions initiated by television modernity suggest new techniques of control that often operate through discreet modes in affirming various culturally validated performances of femininity. The modernity initiated by television that sought to mould the informed citizen moved beyond the interconnections of media and national identity, as the programmes that were telecast attempted to mediate the citizen-subject's negotiations with their everyday reality. One among the many ways in which television mediates the experience of modernity for women is through the 'colonization of leisure' (Robins and Webster 1993, 41). This colonisation of leisure is effected by reconfiguring the role of television as an instrument that leaps beyond its role as the state's mouthpiece, to become an instrument that has recreational value. Programmes like *Chithrageetham* (Film Songs), *Rainbow* and *Thamizhmalar* (Tamil Flower) were more for entertainment than for information. The programmes and advertisements telecast by Doordarshan clandestinely reiterated the gender hierarchies through the strategic gendering of leisure. Through the modernity initiated by television, women straddle between their identities as objects for consumption and subjects of consumption. On the one hand, the women viewers are conceived as consumer-subjects who have not only spatial and temporal access to the images on television but also the time and agency to indulge in the images. On the other hand, they are subjected to multiple levels of objectification—objects on the screen and objects of media manipulation. By defining women's relation with television through this helical interdependence between their status as subjects and objects, the discourses circulated via television reiterates the 'unspoken syllogism' about women's domestic duties (Oakley 1974, 25).

This, in turn, attempts to attain not only a gendered organisation of space but also time, through the strategic scheduling of female-oriented programmes. The programmes that aim at instructing women about useful engagements endeavour to insist on productive and creative activities. These programmes attempt to equip the female audiences with a skillset that would nurture their social skills and enable productive utilisation of leisure time. Programmes aimed at a female audience during the initial days of Doordarshan successfully adhered to this model. Even programmes like *Krishidarshan, Arogyavedi* (Health Forum) and *Kaalveppukal,* which anticipated a general audience, aimed at redefining leisure time. Thus, an economy of leisure, whereby the female audience is equipped with a skillset that would enable the productive utilisation of leisure time, is advocated through television. Here, leisure is not only colonised but also commodified.

The advent of television also marked new anxieties about the dwindling cultural sensibility through the proliferation of images. One of the concerns that were often associated with television was whether its influence could taint the progressive attitude and literacy in Kerala (Chandran 2014, 26). Moreover, television and other mass-media platforms were viewed with suspicion owing to the fear that it might adulterate 'good Malayalam' with colloquial idioms or augment the popularity of lowbrow, mass-circulated magazines (Jeffrey 2010, 224). In addition to this, some critics believed that television could lead to some regressive trends through the marginalisation of the region's social development in favour of pan-Indian forces (Chatterjee 1988, 214).

Such concerns about the quality and corrupting influence of mass media could not be misplaced given the region's literary history. Ancy Bay observes that the sustained dichotomy between the literary and the popular in Kerala solidified the hierarchical organisation of sensibilities wherein the popular was usually associated with women and the neo-literates (2015, 98). Hence, television and its vicarious pleasures were eyed with distrust owing to its potential to disrupt the idealised moral and social decorum.

As opposed to these general anxieties, the introduction of television had a constructive and levelling effect, as it undermined the traditional binary between the affluent literati and the neo-literate reader of Malayalam literature. Some of the programmes telecast in the early days of Doordarshan were adaptations of critically acclaimed literary works. The literary and cultural sensibility that was earlier associated with a privileged group of readers was made available to anyone who could access a television set. The first telefilm *Venalinte ozhivu* (Summer Vacation, 1988) was an adaptation of Kamala Das's story by the same name. Some of the literary works that were adapted into telefilms included N. Mohanan's *Peruvazhiyile kariyilakal* (Dry Leaves on the High

Road); Vaikom Muhammad Basheer's *Vishvavikhyaathamaaya mookku* (The World Famous Nose), *Mathilukal* (Walls) and *Poovampazham* (title refers to a specific variety of banana found in Kerala); Sara Joseph's *Nilaavariyunnu* (The Moonlight Knows); M. T. Vasudevan Nair's *Kariyilamoodiya vazhithaarakal* (roughly translated as The Bylanes Covered with Dry Leaves); and M. Govindan's *Money Order* (Santhoshkumar 2014, 65–66). Doordarshan continues this tradition of adapting literary works into television programmes in the twenty-first century as well, under a plan named *Kadhasaritha*. Thus, televisual modernity mediated and democratised literary taste and culture among a viewing-public that was stratified on the basis of gender, class and caste.

* * *

The arrival of television in Kerala introduced and reflected new 'ethnoscapes', 'mediascapes', 'technoscapes', 'financescapes' and 'ideoscapes' (Appadurai 1996, 33). From the 1970s onwards, the population of Kerala was in a state of flux. The migration to the Gulf and European countries that led to the transformation of the economic, social and political geographies of Kerala; new media technologies that facilitated communication; the economic impact of emigration and the consumerist practices initiated by these shifting cultural economies; and the discourses as well as the images circulated through television that defined the moral economies including domestic and social relations; suggest the ways in which Kerala endorsed new modernities even before the national boundaries were opened to global flows. These changes mediated and constituted women's experience of modernity in the last quarter of the twentieth century.

Lata Mani's observation that women have functioned as the site where the struggle between tradition and modernity is staged, would accurately describe Kerala's negotiations with modernity (1998, 2). By situating women at the intersection of domestic, social and economic hierarchies, the modernity introduced by television hints at the multiple axes of power that women have to navigate in order to engage/negotiate with the subject positions constructed by the new technologies of power. As the encounter between women and television is fraught with gendered anxieties, gendered desires and gendered spatial relations, the new terrains offered by television for articulating femininities tend to reflect, solidify and constitute the already existing gender hierarchies prevalent in society.

## References

Appadurai, Arjun. 1996. *Modernity at Large: Cultural Dimensions of Globalization*. Minneapolis: Minnesota UP.

Bay, Ancy. 2015. 'At the End of the Story: Popular Fiction, Readership and Modernity in Literary Malayalam'. In *Kerala Modernity: Ideas, Spaces and Practices in Transition*, edited by Satheesh Chandra Bose and Shiju Sam Varghese, 92–108. Hyderabad: Orient Blackswan.

Biju, B. L. 2013. 'Angels are Turning Red: Nurses' Strikes in Kerala'. *Economic and Political Weekly* 48(52): 25–28.

Brown, Mary Ellen, ed. 1990. *Television and Women's Culture*. London: Sage.

Chakravarti, Uma. 2000. 'State, Market and Freedom of Expression: Women and Electronic Media'. *Economic and Political Weekly* 35(18): 12–17.

Chandran, Baiju. 2014. 'Introduction'. In *Malayala Television Charithram: 1985–2013* by T. K. Sathoshkumar, 9–30. Kakkanad: Kerala P. Academy.

Chatterjee, Meera. 1988. *Implementing Health Policy*. New Delhi: Manohar.

Chatterjee, Partha. 1993. *The Nation and Its Fragments: Colonial and Postcolonial Histories*. New Jersey: Princeton UP.

Devika, J. 2002. 'Domesticating Malayalees: Family Planning, The Nation and Home-centred Anxieties in mid-20th Century Kerala'. *CDS Working Paper*, no. 340, 4–90.

———. 2009. 'Women's Labour, Patriarchy and Feminism in Twenty-first Century Kerala: Reflections on the Glocal Present'. *Review of Development and Change* 24(1): 79–99.

Devika, J., and Mini Sukumar. 2006. 'Making Space for Feminist Social Critique in Contemporary Kerala'. *Economic and Political Review* 41(42): 4469–75.

Eapen, Mridul, and Praveena Kodoth. 2002. 'Family Structure, Women's Education and Work: Re-examining the High Status of Women in Kerala'. *CDS Working Papers*, no. 341, 4–50.

Ellis, John. 1982. *Visible Fictions*. New York: Routledge.

Felski, Rita. 1995. *The Gender of Modernity*. Cambridge: Harvard UP.

Fiske, John. 1989. *Reading the Popular*. New York: Routledge.

Fox, Bonnie J. 1990. 'Selling the Mechanised Household: 70 Years of Ads in Ladies Home Journal'. *Gender and Society* 4(1): 25–40.

Gulati, Leela. 1983. 'Migration to Middle East and the Impact on Family'. *Economic and Political Weekly* 18(52/53): 2217–26.

Jeffrey, Robin. 2010. *Media and Modernity: Communications, Women and the State of India*. Ranikhet: Permanent Black.

Kumar, K. J. 2012. *Mass Communication in India*. Mumbai: Jaico Books.

Mani, Lata. 1998. *Contentious Traditions: The Debate on Sati in Colonial India*. Berkeley: U of California P.

Mankekar, Purnima. 1999. *Screening Culture, Viewing Politics: An Ethnography of Television, Womanhood and Nation in Postcolonial India*. Durham: Duke UP.

———. 1998. 'Entangled Spaces of Modernity: The Viewing Family, the Consuming Nation, and Television in India'. *Visual Anthropology Review* 14(2): 32–45.

Mathai, Shanthi. 2015. 'Indian Television in the Eras of Pre-liberalisation and Liberalisation'. *Media Watch* 6(2): 255–68.

Mattelart, Armand. 1980. *Mass, Media, Ideologies and the Revolutionary Movement*. Sussex: Harvester P.

Morley, David. 1995. 'Where the Global Meets the Local: Notes from the Sitting Room'. *Screen* 32(1): 1–15.

Mokkil, Navneetha. 2010. *Sexual Figures of Kerala: Cultural Practices, Regionality and the Politics of Sexuality*. Unpublished PhD Thesis, Michigan: University of Michigan.

Negt, Oskar. 1978. 'Tools of Domination or Instruments of Liberation: Aspects of the Frankfurt School's Communications Analysis'. *New German Critique* 17: 61–80.

Oakley, Ann. 1974. *The Sociology of Housework*. New York: Vintage.

Pillai, Meena T. 2014. 'Disciplining the Intimate: The Kerala Model'. *Economic and Political Weekly* 49(46): 10–13.

Poduval, Satish. 1999. 'The Possible Histories of Indian Television'. *The Journal of Arts and Ideas* 32–33: 107–18.

Prakash, B. A. 1998. 'Gulf Migration and Its Economic Impact'. *Economic and Political Weekly* 33(50): 3209–13.

Punathambekar, Aswin, and Shanti Kumar. 2014. 'Introduction: Television at Large'. In *Television at Large in South Asia*, edited by Aswin Punathambekar and Shanti Kumar, 1–8. Oxon: Routledge.

Rajagopal, Arvind. 2014. 'Television in India: Ideas, Institutions and Practices'. In *The Sage Handbook of Television Studies*, edited by Manuel Alvarado, Milly Buonanno, Herman Gray and Toby Miller, 83–104. London: Sage.

Robins, Kevin, and Frank Webster. 1993. 'Broadcasting Politics: Communications and Consumption'. *The Media Reader*, edited by Manuel Alvardo and John O. Thompson, 30–44. London: British Film Institute.

Santhoshkumar, T. K. 2014. *Malayala Television Charithram: 1985-2013*. Kakkanad: Kerala P. Academy.

Singhal, Arvind, and Everett M. Rogers. 2001. *India's Communication Revolution: From Bullock Carts to Cyber Marts*. New Delhi: Sage.

Sreekumar, T. T., and Govindan Parayil. 2010. 'Social Space, Civil Society and Transformative Politics of New Social Movements in Kerala'. In *Development, Democracy and the State: Critiquing the Kerala Model of Development,* edited by K. Ravi Raman, 237–50. Oxon: Routledge.

Vilanilam, John. 1996. 'The Social-cultural Dynamics of Indian Television'. *Contemporary Television: Eastern Perspectives*, edited by David French and Michael Richards, 61–90. New Delhi: Sage.

TEN

# Who is Afraid of the Raped Nun?

*Discourses, Contestations and Digital Publics*

Jobson Joshwa

'Modernity: An Unfinished Project', reads the title of Habermas' passionate rejoinder to the neoconservative rebuttal of the modernity project. While the specificities of this rebuttal remain deeply contentious, the title unambiguously captures the unrealised potential of modernity, a paradigm that is being reduced and reified as a shibboleth to signify and reminisce a long-lost historic-temporal rupture. The attempt here is not to break into a detailed appraisal of the trajectorial downswings that the project of modernity has undergone, because there is no singular version of modernity to speak of, and it would require a thorough emplacing of the many fault lines that vernacularised registers of modernity have opened up. Instead, an effort is being made to problematise and conceptualise the 'unfinishedness' of the modernity project by contextualising it within the matrices of Kerala's many modernities. Acknowledging the deep-seated ambivalences that have always been imprinted in the imaginings of Kerala modernity, this essay argues that envisionings of modernity in Kerala continue to be fraught with idioms of gender and that modernity remains an ongoing process, an ideal that is far from being realised.

To substantiate this argument, the contraventional digital engagements that arose in retaliation to the affective mobilisation garnered by a group of four nuns who extended their support to a fellow sister at the Kuravilangadu nunnery, who had levelled an accusation against Bishop Franco Mulakkal of raping her multiple times between 2014 and 2016, is subjected to scrutiny.

Before detailing the paradoxical undercurrents of these digital engagements evoked by the rape accusation, dissecting the differential vectors entangled in this is crucial. This essay assumes that this rape accusation converses with certain sedimented aspects of Kerala modernity. The radicalness of the critique thus lies in bringing these aspects to the fore, building a contextual terrain. Considering that this 'scandal' drew a specific kind of religious–moral public to the fore, the essay begins by engaging with the ambivalent dynamics that environ the intersections between religion and modernity.

## Religion, Secularism and Modernity: An Ambiguation

The dyad of religion and modernity evinces a modality that has not always been identified as cohabitational. This is primarily due to the standardised readings of modernity that have pigeonholed religion to the private sphere, presuming that it is antithetical to the spirit of modernity and would not survive its onslaught. Jürgen Habermas (1989), in his polemical work *The Structural Transformation of the Public Sphere,* shies away from factoring in religion as a category of inquiry, insulating it from the operational paradigms of the public sphere. The bifurcational logic of privatisation that denies religion of a strategic place in the functional terrains of the private sphere and the state, has further been ameliorated with the espousal of the secularism doctrine. A normative delineation of 'secularist regimes as bulwarks against religions' (Taylor 2011, 56) lays bare the debilitative renderings that fail to account for the fact that 'all significant concepts of the modern theory of the state are secularized theological concepts' (Schmitt 1985, 36).

It is worth noting that Habermas (2011), in what can be read as a recasting of his earlier theorisations, wrote that 'secular and religious citizens stand in a complementary relation' (27) in a democratic discourse. The idea here is to see religion and modernity as inhabitants of a 'common symbolic space', embodying an 'agonistic' consciousness rather than an 'antagonistic' one (Mouffe 2000, 13). These contentions make for an exciting read when they are located vis-à-vis the Indian context. Countervailing the supposedly trite conceptualisations of secularism in the West, a particular case for Indian secularism has been made, arguing that the 'interface between religion and modernity in postcolonial India' should be located at the 'constitutional notion of secularism' (Oommen 2017, 25). This conjecture essentially boils down to positing that 'the Indian constitution conceptualizes secularism as (a) the dignified coexistence of all religions and (b) the state keeping equal distance from all religions, notions which are in consonance with the empirical reality of India' (26).

This imbued exceptionalism of Indian secularism remains contentious, mainly owing to some of the 'praxiological aberrations' (Oommen 2017, 27) that seeped through the body politic. A detailed explication of these 'aberrations' is beyond the purview of this essay. However, it needs to be ascertained that the author is not trying to lend credence to the contentions of those scholars like Ashish Nandy who is summarily dismissive of the idea of secularism in India, claiming it to be a culturally inappropriate idea that might mutate into an ideology that breeds communalisation of politics (Nandy 1998, 326). Secularism might have 'failed to realize the objectives for which it was devised' (Bhargava 1998, 1), but that does not mean that it has to be abandoned once and for all. As Rajeev Bhargava (1998) points out, 'secularism in India, as elsewhere, is indispensable, and therefore that the critical need of the hour is to work out an alternative conception of secularism, not to seek an alternative' (2).

Curiously, the task of finding an alternative conceptualisation of secularism continues to be one of the most persistent commitments of the modernity project. The more the realisation of this commitment is delayed, the further the 'unfinishedness' of modernity is accentuated. As it stands, the polyphonic engagements of modernity that Kerala—an isle of land located at the southern tip of the Indian subcontinent—offers makes it a strategic eventscape to reflect on some of the complex crevices of modernity that have been previously discussed. The next section will briefly consider the anxieties that afflict Kerala's engagement with modernity, with a particular emphasis on the problematic dynamics that religious publics in Kerala share with the ideals of modernity.

## Religious Publics and Alternative Modernities: The Kerala Model?

Much has been said and made about the exemplarity with which Kerala 'asserted, challenged and reached out to a public world and a public political process' (Jeffrey 1992, 1). However, the tenability of a model based on a sole anchoring on indices of 'material wellbeing' is susceptible to questioning, especially when one considers the fact that an effort has not been made all these years to factor in the 'immaterial and intangible coordinates of gendered sociality and connectivity' into the discourses of developmentalism (Pillai 2021, 48). This is only one of the fissures in the much-vaunted 'Kerala Model'; there is plenty more to think of, particularly with respect to the claims of dispelling 'social autarky, religious orthodoxy and spiritual obscurantism' (Bijukumar 2019, 21) from infesting its visions of modernity. These claims are borne out of an overdetermination of what Dilip Menon (2002) terms a 'secular imagination of community' (1663).

Again, this should not be taken as an argument against the inclusion of religious imaginaries to the matrices of modernity; instead, the attempt here is to revoke the reified conceptualisations of defining a religious community in Kerala and to understand it as 'an unfixed, non-static constellation, which travels through times with inventions, deletions and renewals', without always bearing 'a stable relation of opposition to the "secular"' (Devika and Varghese 2011, 103). Even though the religious communities in Kerala have attempted to modernise themselves, the undercurrents of sectarianism and communalism remain to be moot points.

For J. Devika and V. J. Varghese (2011), the implications of the term 'communalism' in Kerala have undergone several alterations throughout the course of history. While in the early nineteenth and twentieth centuries, it evoked a sense of value-neutrality, with the term being associated with 'intense competition around rights and resources within the field of modern politics' between communities, and not 'fierce hatred and violence' (105). However, things have changed for the worse, especially with the events that unfolded after the 1950s. The Nilakkal controversy (1981) that erupted over the alleged defiling of Sabarimala Temple by Christian groups, the communal furore that P. M. Antony's play *Kristuvinte aaram thirumurivu* (1984) caused, and the Marad massacre of 2003 are some of the events that J. Devika and V. J. Varghese point out in reference to the burgeoning communalism in Kerala (106). There is no denying that these events have shapeshifted the patterns of understanding the communal dynamics in Kerala. But what is also interesting here is that most of these events coincided with the rise of far-right Hindutva groups in the political milieu of Kerala (106).

While it could be argued that the presence of Hindutva groups has not inflicted any substantial changes in the electoral politics in Kerala, with only a single MLA (2016–21) to speak of, such a longitudinal approach does not yield a tenable paradigm to gauge the socio-politico-cultural impact that they have in the Kerala context. They have managed to make significant inroads into Kerala's political economy, exposing the major crevices that have crept into the state's secular and modernist terrains. The Supreme Court verdict that sanctioned the entry of women into Sabarimala Temple is the most recent and glaring example of this infiltration. The kind of religious publics that partook in the violent protests against those women who attempted to enter the sanctum sanctorum of the temple bespeaks the ideological tenaciousness with which Hindutva forces have appropriated the discursive figurations of religion and faith in Kerala. With a tactful deployment of their political machinery and affectively charged evocation of religious morality, the Hindutva forces managed to institute events of magnitude such as the *Nama Japa* processions,[1] spectacularising reactionary values sedimented at the interstices of Kerala modernity.

While the discourses on Sabarimala brought the focus squarely on the debates between constitutional bindings of gender equality and religious freedom, the fact that the left government in Kerala went back on its promise of ensuring the entry of women into the temple meant that the vaunted Renaissance values that were supposedly enshrined in Kerala's polity are always fraught with the concerns of being delimited. This, however, does not mean that the growth of Hindutva forces is an offshoot of the Sabarimala Temple controversy. To glean that they have made their presence felt in the past without always resorting to a belligerent discourse of majoritarianism is what makes for a legitimate cause of concern. They have managed to make the minoritarian elements complicit in the 're-feudalisation of the public sphere' (Pillai 2014, 10). A case in point is made by Meena T. Pillai (2014) while looking at the wielding of discourses of morality by religious fundamentalists in the wake of the 'Kiss of Love' protest. She observes that minoritarian communities in Kerala have started to invoke the 'ideological commitments' of right-wing forces, a move that has had far-reaching implications:

> What is even more interesting is the manner in which this minoritarian politics invokes majoritarian Hindutva ideological commitments enshrining repressive and socially reactionary political forces. It is worthwhile to invoke here the Gramscian notion of hegemony, where minority religions and rights become the articulating principle whereby an entire set of social relations and practices, which by themselves do not form a fundamental class, is

[1] *Nama Japa Yatras* were a series of payer processions mainly organised by the Bharatiya Janata Party (BJP) in the wake of the Supreme Court verdict on Sabarimala. Condemning the state government's willingness to allow the entry of women into the temple, mass processions were held across the state, with massive footfall as Ayyappa devotees and religious women joined in. The processions were initiated by the Nair Service Society (NSS), with the BJP and RSS following suit.

> able to pave the way for the historical emergence of a bloc whose articulations of dominance and consent through political and civil society apparatuses help maintain the myth of democracy, secularism and common interest. (10)

This observation offers an interesting pathway to reflect on the minoritarian quandaries in constant tension with the secularist–modernist imaginations of the state of Kerala. The attempt here is not to engage in any theorisations of what it means to be a 'minority' in the current socio-political milieu. Instead, an effort is being made to rethink the saturated understandings of the term 'minority', especially in the context of Kerala. Talal Asad (2003), while talking about the articulation of minority rights in the political context of Europe, observes that '[m]inority rights are not derivable from general theories of citizenship: status is connected to membership in a specific historical group, not in the abstract class of citizens. In that sense, minorities are no different from majorities, also a historically constituted group' (175). To argue that the term 'minority' can only be defined as a derivative function of the 'hierarchical structures of power' (175) can raise quite a few eyebrows, at least in those parts of the world where minorities are subjected to political persecution. However, it does beget the debate in the Kerala context where the term 'minority' has been laden with multiple significations in varying contexts.

The focus of this essay will now shift to the analysis of ambiguations that discourses of/around Christianity—a powerful religious group in Kerala, and the third largest religious practice in the state, after Hinduism and Islam. The following section will focus on the ambivalences that have come to characterise the experiential terrains of modernity for the Christians in Kerala. The section will primarily focus on the 'woman' question in the Christian fold, explicating how they are curated as 'minors' within a 'minority' group. This section would end with specific pointers that would be taken up later to open the discussion on the rape case involving Bishop Franco Mulakkal.

## Christianity/Christianities and Modernities in Kerala: The 'Woman' Question

It is easy to slip into a monolithic fallaciousness while talking about Christianity in Kerala. The historical trajectories of Christianity in Kerala are rife with accounts of schisms, so much so that it becomes complicated to keep track of inner divisions and hierarchies, leading to the prevalence of all-consuming readings. Having said that, the discourses of Christianity in Kerala primarily centre around the figurations offered by Syrian Christianity and the concomitant readings on caste consciousness that curate marginal Christians within their fold. Even though marginal yet compelling academic scholarship on discourses of Christianity have been making efforts to look beyond the caste–sectarianism dyad as principal categories of analysis (Easo and Markose 2019), they have not yet had any significant bearings on the popular understandings of Christianity. Though there are multiple sites of inquiry that one can use to theorise on the structures of thought populated by the Christian-minority discourses in Kerala, this essay will limit its scope to the Catholic Church in Kerala—an ecclesiastical communion of three *sui iuris* Churches—Syro-Malabar, Latin and Syro-Malankara.

Of the three Churches, Syro-Malabar and Syro-Malankara factions are claimants of the Syrian Christian legacy, and the Latin Church is usually rendered by academic scholarship on Kerala Christianity as a 'subaltern' sect along with Dalit Christians. While the obvious question of caste dynamics gets projected here, it is essential to note that the Latin Church in Kerala bears the historical imprint of globalatinisation—a term Jacques Derrida (2002) uses to denote the Latinisation spree of the Roman Catholic Church. Though the author does not intend to gloss over the 'caste' question, he objects to the logic of placing both Latin Christians and Dalit Christians in a single category, especially when there is a discernible difference vis-à-vis social and symbolic capital.

Moreover, recent studies on Latin Christianity in Kerala have argued that 'Latinization of Christianity in Kerala does not fall in line with the "globalatinization" of the Universal Catholic church.

Rather, it has its own vernacular-cosmopolitan manifestation that demarcates its departure from "Western" Christian discourse, and affinity to "Eastern" Christian experiences' (Easo and Markose 2019, 27–28). When one takes into account powerful institutional structures like KCBC (Kerala Catholic Bishop Council), the confederation of bishops from the three Catholic denominations, it becomes apparent that one is dealing with a unique set of social equations that are markedly different from what the other Christian sects in Kerala bring to the fore.

The Christians in Kerala, particularly the Catholic fold, came in close contact with vectors of colonial modernity. They strategically combined pastoral theology and capitalist ethos in a Weberian sense to claim the perks of economic modernity, as evidenced by their monopoly in sectors like plantation agriculture and religious conversion—another significant modality of colonial modernity that has bred certain anxieties that continue to get articulated in varied forms. The religious–nationalist sensibilities that gained traction across India after the 1880s engineered certain social configurations that led to the bracketing of Indian Christianity as a Western element, along with Anglican missions (Carson 2008, 151).

Chandra Mallampalli (2004) argues that nationalist rhetoric curated a homogenised construct of Indian Christianity with 'pan-Christian' connections (87). 'Within the climate of Indian nationalism', Indian Christianity was ascribed 'an alternative national identity that stood at odds with a genuinely "Indian" one' (Mallampalli 2004, 87). This popular pan-Christian angle of Indian Christianity during the emergence of nationalist consciousness squarely brought the focus back onto the ecumenical connections that the Indian Christians had outside the national fold. Though it is not tenable to suggest that they made themselves available to be readily influenced by the 'normative or universal standards of Christian behaviour' (Mallampalli 2004, 87) laid down by the 'pan-Christian' networks that they had come in contact with, getting tagged with a nationalist pariahdom was almost inevitable. Thus, it is not difficult to see why Indian Christians followed a strain of conscience that could not be identified as something radically different from the codifications of cultural nationalism.

Gender was one of the principal sites where these anxieties of belongingness were articulated. In her bid to theorise the undercurrents of the patriarchal system in the lives of Catholic women, Kochurani Abraham (2019) observes that 'the hegemonic codes of gendered nationalism' form an essential frame of reference to understand the questions of gender and patriarchy within the Catholic apparatus. A division of the cultural domain marked the tenets of cultural nationalism into 'material and spiritual spheres' (73). The signification of 'home' as an embodiment of the spiritual dimension of the nation had catastrophic implications for Indian women, because the preoccupying emotion of 'the nationalist struggle was to protect, preserve and strengthen the inner core of the nationalist culture, its spiritual essence' (Abraham 2019, 74). This, however, does not imply that colonial modernity offered a starkly different worldview for Christian women. Their 'paternalistic and protectionist ways' (75) were equally problematic. The colonialists successfully evoked the 'images of Indian women as victims awaiting redress at the hands of imperialists' (76). Detailing these diverse, experiential terrains is beyond the scope of this essay. Instead, the attempt here is to draw attention to the gendering/genderedness of various spaces that women traverse and inhabit.

It has been argued that discourses on Kerala modernity and gender should do away with the rigid conceptualisation of the 'modern society as fundamentally divided into public and domestic domains' (Devika 2006, 172), because a specific kind of Malayali society anchored on a belief that 'the capacities attributed to ideal women had application in an ever-increasing number of institutions other than the home, situated in the public domain' has emerged. This conception draws its validity from the spatial inroads made by women 'into the public domain, particularly into institutions such as schools, hospitals, charity organisations, reform institutions or orphanages' (173). While it needs to be observed that the 'radical reconfiguration of the socio-spatial dynamics following the Kerala renaissance in the nineteenth century has covertly solidified the upper-caste and familial moorings of ideal femininities' (Pillai 2022, 178), it is also essential to talk about a particular 'omission' that characterises the discussions on gender and Kerala modernity.

Often, the discourses on gender and modernity revolve around well-defined notions of privatised/publicised femininities, un-accounting for specific categories of women, especially the ones who belong to religious structures like convents or nunneries. There are no theoretical engagements or scholarly consensus regarding the genderedness of the space they inhabit and the specific articulations of their femininities. This is where the path-breaking, first-of-its-kind public protest organised by a group of Catholic nuns against a bishop accused of rape, attains a discursive and affective potential that would allow one to reframe the fault lines of modernity discourses. The following section will look into this event in detail, explicating the nuns' transgression of their inhabited space, the implications that it had on the public conscience of Kerala, and finally, the affective transposition of the event in the digital sphere.

## Affective Articulations: Spaces, Gender and the Minority Question

In a bid to theorise the ideations offered by a convent space, Els De Paermentier (2008) argues that 'a religious community can also be considered as a "household" within society' (55). However, the implications of domesticity evoked by the term 'household' cannot always be 'equated to a private experience' (55). As Paermentier observes,

> [B]ecoming a nun and taking the monastic vows meant not only a renunciation of the nun's former social status, private property, and sexuality. Above all, it meant a denial of the nun's previous secular individuality in favor of a wish to assimilate into an alternative, collective identity that represented the ideal virtues of nun as a bride of god. When it is considered that they gave up or "depersonalized" their identity, it becomes understandable that there was not much

> space left for private experiences, since those potentially threatened the common identity and harmony within the religious community. (55–56)

While these observations make for a critical theoretical framework, it is equally important to problematise those readings that overdetermine the choice of asceticism as an enabling avenue that allows one to sidestep the patriarchal curation of gendered roles. Corinne G. Dempsey (2001), in her analysis of the Kerala Christian sainthood, offers an interesting perspective on this. Though she acknowledges that the female renunciate is a category produced 'within the narrow confines of institutionally recognized female sanctity' (140), she resorts to a 'middle ground' and posits that ascetic women cannot be wholly dismissed as 'passive empty vessels into which patriarchy simply places its goods' (142).

While this observation can make for an excellent contention, it must be stated that much of Dempsey's insights on female asceticism, particularly in the Kerala context, is drawn from the specific example of Saint Alphonsa.[2] This might not be a well-founded framework to analyse the experiential terrains of those women who suffer sexual and mental abuses within the papal enclosures. One such instance of alleged sexual abuse and the subsequent calling out of the perpetrator inform the central arguments of this essay.

In the year 2018, a nun who resides at the Kuravilangad convent, in Kottayam, lodged a complaint against Bishop Franco Mulakkal of the Jalandhar diocese, accusing him of raping her thirteen times between 2014 and 2016. While Bishop Franco was arrested on the basis of the FIR filed against him, prompting the larger public in Kerala to extend their support to the victim and

---

[2] Corinne G. Dempsey's work, 'Kerala Christian Sainthood: Collisions of Culture and Worldview in South India', attempts to trace the tangents of Kerala sainthood using the lens of postcolonial hybridisation. Rationalising the unrivalled popularity of Saint Alphonsa as a criteria marker, Dempsey uses her as a normative example to base her arguments on female sacrality.

the four nuns who stood by her, a court verdict that was pronounced on 14 January 2022, acquitting Bishop Franco of rape charges, came as a massive blow to the fight against sexual abuse in the Catholic Church. The verdict, however, sparked an overwhelming response from the public, evidenced by the tons of letters of support and solidarity that the nuns received. Though these events did not take their roots in the digital sphere per se, much of the unfoldings happened in the 'publicness' of digital media that constituted a 'hashtag' publics. The hashtags #WithTheNuns and #Avalkoppam (#WithHer) invoked an online counterpublics that rallied around the victim. These hashtags, as this essay argues, are iterations of the new modalities of female resistance abetted by contemporary idioms of digitality.

This essay does not intend to read this event as the originating point of female resistance within the Catholic Church in Kerala. Instead, it argues that the calling out of Bishop Franco Mulakkal and the subsequent public protest organised by the nuns need to be seen as an important node in a continuum of resistance that was instituted by the likes of Sister Jesme and Sister Lucy Kalapura, who spoke out against the sexual abuse in Catholic Church at various points in time. Their respective autobiographies—*Amen: The Autobiography of a Nun* and *In the Name of the Lord: A Nun's Tell-All*—are important textual artefacts that stand as a testament to the 'deviant' voices that have turned against the hypocrisy of the Church. The fact that both of them extended their solidarity to the protest organised by the nuns speaks of the tenability of this continuum. Expressing her dismay over the court judgement and defending the nuns' decision to stay at the convent, Sister Jesme said, 'They don't want to leave the convent because that means that they have to give up being a nun. Why should they do that?' (qtd. in Suresh). This remark is significant, considering that both she and Lucy Kalapura were technically ousted from their respective congregations for speaking out, making them outsiders to the inner mechanics of the Catholic Church.

However, being critical insiders alone is not what makes these nuns stand out. Their distinctiveness lies in what Butler (2015) would call a 'public assembly' of performative bodies. The reference here is to the fifteen-day strike that the nuns organised at Vanchi Square, in Kochi, in 2018, that eventually ended with the arrest of Bishop Franco Mulakkal. Even though the court judgement and the ensuant public outcry might have fomented significant public mobilisation, the criticalness and poignancy of the strike that preceded it cannot be overlooked. The 'publicness' of this protest and the public outreach that it garnered qualify as a critical claim of the 'right to appear' (Butler 2015, 51) in a public forum. This is where the earlier observations made on the particular 'spaces' the nuns inhabit and the question of transgressing them become significant. As Butler observes, 'no matter how "universal" the right to appear claims to be, its universalism is undercut by differential forms of power that qualify who can and cannot appear. For those who are considered "ineligible", the struggle to form alliances is paramount, and it involves a plural and performative positing of eligibility where it did not exist before' (51). The nuns who decided to 'assemble' in public, decrying the ignominy suffered by their fellow nun, thus rendered themselves a part of a 'political process', a function that can only be achieved by 'acting on terms of equality with others' (53).

What is remarkable about this 'assembling' is that it set the tone for a new modality of resistance that does not prioritise a corporeal presence, in the strictest sense of the term, or 'the metaphysics of presence' (55), as Butler would term it. This new modality of resistance referred to here is the affective–digital mobilisation that happened in the wake of the controversial court judgement that allowed the bishop to leave scot-free. The court judgement had a 'scandalising' impulse that fomented an immediate public outcry. Scandal, in lexical terms, is understood as any event that evokes a sharp moral repugnance. The Court was dismissive of the complainant, questioning her credibility as a 'sterling witness' (G. 2022, 245). The Court even went on to observe that 'there is no history of penetrative sex' (245), despite conceding that 'the hymen of the victim was found torn in her medical examination' (246). The judgement seemed to lend credence to allegations of promiscuity that the amorphous moral publics had made against the victim. An excerpt from the judgement reads:

> It is true that the hymen of the victim was found torn in her medical examination. But defence contends that there was a complaint against the victim, by her own cousin that she had indulged in sexual intercourse with her husband. Even if it is assumed that the complaint was a false complaint, from the mere fact that the victim's hymen was found torn, penile penetration or forceful sexual intercourse cannot be inferred. (G. 2022, 246)

The judgement also included a direct observation of the protest organised by the nuns in support of the victim. Vanchi Square, the venue of the protest, was a strategic location, considering that it was near the Kerala High Court. Understandably, the criticalness of the location contributed to the media attention that the event elicited. However, it appears the Court did not approve of this rightful claim to protest against injustice. It observed that 'a protest aimed solely for the arrest of a person cannot be regarded as a protest in good taste' (G. 2022, 205). It is obvious that the Court never really understood the concerns the victim had tried to raise. Also, the protest at Vanchi Square was not ill-conceived. As Butler (2015) observes, a struggle might be 'sometimes on the critical edge of the recognizable' or 'sometimes in the light of the dominant media', but what is essential is the 'assembly of bodies, plural, persisting, acting and laying claim to a public sphere by which one has been abandoned' (59).

To take the arguments on the 'scandal' further, it is critical to delve into the mechanics that impel scandals to mutate into variant forms of social action. In his theorisation of the 'scandal', Michael Warner (2005) draws a comparison between scandals and another form of public discourse—gossip—to arrive at a differentiation. Though this essay does not intend to invoke these theoretical conceptualisations into the present discussion, Warner's referencing of the 'appellative energy' (89) of modern publics that constitutes a 'demanding social phenomenology' (89) can be taken as a tenable paradigm to conceptualise the unfoldings that transpired in the digital media in the aftermath of the judgement. This essay argues that the complexities of the 'social phenomenology', constituted by modern publics, need to be situated in relation to the 'affective fabrics of digital culture' (Kuntsman 2012, 1).

It would be jarring to suggest that 'affect' is a new phenomenon that could be used in redefining discourses on/in humanities. Affect was always here, right from the age of Spinoza, who was among the first philosophers to theorise affect. In fact, 'affect is fundamental to human social coexistence and ... no discourse or debate can be conceived of as affect free' (Fleig and Scheve 2020, 2). A detailed exploration of the theoretical implications that affect offers is beyond the scope of this essay. However, dissecting the convergence points of affect and digitality is critical. While there is a larger scholarly consensus on the destabilising effects that new medialities offered by internet technologies have brought in in understanding media hierarchies, the transactions between affect and digitality have only been nominally studied. Apart from understanding the resonances of the 'fluid, unstable, fragile, and dynamic character of publics constituted via hashtags' (Lünenborg 2020, 33), the nuanced 'reflexivity' of the digital media that invokes 'feelings of community' (Dean qtd. in Papacharisi 2015, 9) also needs to be understood. This, then, can be read in conjunction with extant readings that conceptualise online engagements as 'inherently performative because it demands actors to negotiate predefined functionalities of media platforms within their specific social environment' (Lünenborg 2020, 35). Thus, it is not difficult to see why new modes of feminist engagements, particularly affective feminisms, have struck a chord with digital medialities. Meena T. Pillai (2022) has conceptualised this vividly in her analysis of the digital–affective feminisms in India:

> Where earlier homogenised mainstream media had limited visibility and voice of gendered players, such new enunciative paradigms contain possibilities for addressing discourses heretofore marginalised or subsumed under mainstream feminism and schemas of benevolent patriarchy, albeit under different levels of privilege. With no top-down mandates, the quotidian microaggressions and everyday othering in

> spaces of intimacy, which often fail to be addressed in mainstream feminist mobilizations, accrue the potential to constitute new loci of feminist dissent. (15)

Within this context, this essay would like to place the locutionary dynamics of the hashtags #WithTheNuns and #Avalkoppam. These hashtags were instituted after the pronouncement of the verdict that absolved Bishop Franco Mulakkal of the rape charges filed in the FIR. On 19 January 2022, Leena Gita Reghunath, a journalist, shared a Twitter post urging digital media users to write letters of solidarity to the nuns who were the face of the protest against the bishop. The post contained a letter she wrote herself with the hashtags #WithTheNuns and #Avalkoppam. The campaign, 'Write a letter to Our Sister', garnered tremendous traction, with thousands of people taking to social media platforms like Facebook and Twitter to share handwritten letters of solidarity. Many letters were sent directly to the nuns through conventional channels, enabling a 'coordination of online- and offline-activities', a feature shared by the publics that constituted the hashtags like #MeToo, #TimesUp, #blacklivesmatter and #MeTwo (Lünenborg 2020, 33).

The counterpublics that took to social media included people from all walks of life, reiterating the Warner-ian conceptualisation of performative publics marked for their 'dependence on the copresence of strangers' (2005, 76). For many users who shared their letters on Facebook, this campaign was a way of expressing solidarity.

Even though the Court refused to acknowledge the testimony of the nun, a host of men and women took to social media platforms to offer what could be viewed as counter-testimonials to rally around the nun. According to J. Devika, the order can only be described as 'judicial porn' (qtd. in Pandey). She goes on to observe that '[t]he order was not just to exonerate the bishop, it was also to demoralise the survivor and the other nuns who had supported her. It contains graphic descriptions of sexual acts and assaults narrated by the nun. The judge even details a breast examination she underwent. What was the need for any of that?'

(qtd. in Pandey). While the decision of the court to publicise the testimony of the victim is objectionable, there is also an alternative way to look at it. As Sara Ahmed (2014) observes, 'Healing does not cover over, but exposes the wound to others: the recovery is a form of exposure. The visibility produced by recognition is actually the visibility of what has been concealed under the sign of truth' (200). This essay, therefore, argues that the hashtag publics that were constituted after the judgement was also an attestation of the fact that, under modalities of affect, the digital has enabled the women to 'field shame dexterously, turning it into anger, reflexivity, and pride, in the process transforming its epistemic authority to garner more political legitimacy' (Pillai 2022, 127).

Now, the focus of the essay shifts to the contraventional cyber engagements that took place even as the victim was gaining significant public support. Since the implications of the term 'affect' do not automatically translate into a 'sense of togetherness or belonging' and involve 'an uneasy balancing of the sharp flames of anger and aggression in ways requiring boundary maintenance, moderation, content filtering, and other forms of intervention' (Paasonen 2020, 52), it is crucial to account for the significant digressions that have happened in connection with the case.

The modes of misogyny and victim-shaming that were in circulation with respect to this case can be broadly categorised into two: the first strain follows a pattern that could now be reckoned as prototypal, where the sterlingness of the victim is discredited on account of a shady implication of her promiscuity. It is precisely what P. C. George, a veteran politician from the state, did when he went on a rant defaming the victim. In a press conference held at Kottayam, he launched an assault on the victim's 'character', even dragging the other nuns into it: 'Is there any doubt that the nun is a prostitute? Twelve times it was pleasure, 13th time it became a rape? Where was she when it happened 12 times? Whom is she telling this to? Why did she not complain the first time it happened? … Let the three sisters be examined. Let us see if they are holy' (qtd. in 'MLA P. C. George calls nun …'). Though such instances of victim-shaming and character assassination cannot be glossed over, this essay intends to discuss a specific kind of misogyny that also transposes into a severe case of hate-mongering. Here, the reference is to some of the Facebook posts made by a Christian organisation called CASA (Christian Association and Alliance for Social Action). This outfit drew attention when they participated in a Hindu Maha Sammelan at Thiruvananthapuram, attending a panel discussion on 'love jihad', 'land jihad' and the 'halal economy' (Dutta). Though many aspects need detailing here, the essay's primary concern is to look at some of the Facebook posts of CASA made in connection with the Franco Mulakkal case.

CASA was one of the first groups to congratulate Bishop Franco Mulakkal after he was absolved of rape charges on 14 January 2022. In a Facebook post that appeared on the same date, a photo of the bishop and a caption expressing their satisfaction with the verdict were used. Even though there is nothing extraordinary about the caption, the description that followed it needs to be critically examined as it accused 'Jihadis', media and rebel clergy of forming a coterie to frame Bishop Franko Mulakkal. The usage of the word 'Jihadi' is not at all aberrational; it is a politically hideous usage targeted at a particular community. This becomes apparent in another Facebook post that was posted on 16 January. In a rather lengthy explanation of the judgement and its implications by Father Muthuplakkal, specific reference is made to a particular religious community that supposedly had vested interests in framing Bishop Franco Mulakkal in the rape case. It might appear that CASA made a deliberate attempt to efface the alleged act of sexual violence using hate-mongering.

However, it is not as straightforward as it seems; there is a deep strain of Islamophobia that is articulated. CASA shared a photo on 14 January 2022, the day of the verdict. The photo features a group of women holding a banner that reads, 'Prosecution has failed in Franco Mulakkal Case; protest march'. These women belong to an organisation called the 'Women Justice Movement' and could be identified as Muslim women from their attire. The post's description insinuates that the religious identity of the protesters is malevolently connected to their motives. It is evident that CASA is trying to bring in a communal angle and deflect the discussion from the fact that an alliance between minority women who are conjoined by their experiences of gender and religious precarity is being forged. The implications of this post by CASA holds much significance in the context of the larger themes that this essay has tried to raise in connection with gender and Kerala modernity, and modernity at large.

This essay briefly discussed how the Sabarimala debate punctured the ideations of/on Kerala Renaissance and *Navodhana moolyangal* (Renaissance values). As it stands, it has only deepened with the discursive matrices populated by words like 'love jihad', 'narcotic jihad' and '*Krisanghi*'. The term *Krisanghi* has become part of the popular parlance in Kerala, meaning a 'Christian Sanghi'. It is often used derogatorily to call out a Christian believer who advertently or inadvertently mirrors the ideology of the Sangh Parivar.

It is not surprising to see CASA resorting to a deeply Islamophobic vocabulary, considering that they had modelled this organisation after right-wing groups. In an interview, Kevin Peter, one of the seven founders of CASA, declared that the idea of forming a right-wing 'organisation for Christians led to its revival during the "love jihad" campaign in 2018' (qtd. in Surya). He also remarked that CASA and right-wing organisations 'have similar opinions on issues such as CAA-NRC, farmers' strike, surgical strike, etc.'. While CASA's open averral of its fundamentalism might seem surprising, it does not, in any way, lessen the gravitas of the situation. CASA is only following the suit of the top-tier of ecclesiastical hierarchy, who are increasingly beginning to speak in a majoritarian Hindutva rhetoric. Only recently, a Catholic Bishop of Kottayam district, Mar Joseph Kallarangatt, stirred up a controversy after alleging that youth from non-Muslim faiths are being preyed upon by jihadis by making them fall for drugs (Aswani).

However, as Bivita Easo (2022) writes, minority communities have an essential role to play in a social sphere which is overhauled by majoritarian Hindu nationalism. She observes that the present political climate calls for a reimagining of minority politics as a politics of 'becoming', which is intrinsically considerate towards those groups being curated as 'minor' (27). The espousal of such politics might not be easy. However, the urgency is pressing, especially with 'secularist' frames envisaged by Kerala modernity being subjected to questioning ever so often.

* * *

Now, the most critical question in the context of this volume looms large. How do all these discussions and trajectories, touched upon at various points in this essay, add to the complex transactions between modernity and gender? The answer is that all discursive iterations, including 'love jihad' and 'narcotic jihad', render women's bodies their site of articulation: 'Women's bodies which were co-opted by different movements and agendas in the history of Kerala, including conjugal, caste and agrarian reforms, are now co-opted by counter-democratic communal forces, in order to forge an emotional and ideological unity amongst themselves, at whatsoever minimal a level' (Pillai 2014, 11). Though the hashtag publics constituted by new forms of digitality hint at the possibility of having a 'women praxis', they will continue to occupy a liminal space in a lifeworld where fault lines of communal politics are ever widening. It makes modernity an unfinished project.

## References

Abraham, Kochurani. 2019. *Persisting Patriarchy: Intersectionalities, Negotiations, Subversions*. London: Palgrave Macmillan.

Ahmed, Sara. 2014. *The Cultural Politics of Emotion*. Edinburgh: Edinburgh UP.

Asad, Talal. 2003. *Formations of the Secular: Christianity, Islam, Modernity.* Stanford: Stanford UP.

Aswani, Tarushi. 'After "Love Jihad," India's Muslims are now being accused of "Narcotics Jihad"'. *The Diplomat*, 7 Oct. 2021, https://thediplomat.com/2021/10/after-love-jihad-indias-muslims-are-now-being-accused-of-narcotics-jihad/.

Bhargava, Rajeev, 1998. 'Introduction'. In *Secularism and Its Critics*, edited by Rajeev Bhargava, 1–30. Oxford: Oxford UP.

Bijukumar, V. 2019. 'Pungent Irrationality and Troubled Modernity in Kerala'. *History and Sociology of South Asia* 13(1): 19–35. https://doi.org/10.1177/2230807519836803.

Butler, Judith. 2015. *Notes Toward a Performative Theory of Assembly.* Cambridge: Harvard UP.

Carson, Penelope. 2008. 'Christianity, Colonialism, and Hinduism in Kerala: Integration, adaptation, or confrontation?'. In *Christians and Missionaries in India: Cross-cultural Communication Since 1500*, edited by Robert Eric Frykenberg, 127–55. London: Routledge.

CASA. 'Bishop Franco Mulakkal's innocence has been proven . . .'. *Facebook*, 14 Jan. 2022, https://m.facebook.com/photo.php?fbid=715748673162682&id=104019207668968&set=a.128648875206001&source=48&eav=AfYfH5AVefNmYfZPDslQei2r7Veoiygm1wURhO-YnmsNl8Xbesy5VSqgY6WgeETyvus&paipv=0.

———. 'Both questions and answers are there in this picture'. *Facebook*, 14 Jan. 2022, https://m.facebook.com/photo.php?fbid=716079156462967&id=104019207668968&set=a.128648875206001&source=48&eav=AfYas5no4cirEgNCyrvH0hVJPs6rpzi7x8b-9bbCNFpHdAkRDjVwALLDE36GbpDNHq0&paipv=0

Dempsey, Corinne G. 2001. *Kerala Christian Sainthood: Collisions of Culture and Worldview in South India.* Oxford: Oxford UP.

Derrida, Jacques. 2002. *Acts of Religion.* London: Routledge

Devika, J. 2006. *En-gendering Individuals: The Language of Re-forming in Twentieth-Century Keralam.* Hyderabad: Orient Blackswan.

Devika, J., and V. J. Varghese. 2011. 'To survive or To Flourish?: Minority Rights and Syrian Christian Community Assertions in Twentieth-century Travancore/Kerala'. *History and Sociology of South Asia* 5(2): 103–28. https://doi:10.1177/223080751100500202.

Dutta, Dibakar. 'Christian group CASA participates in Hindu Maha Sammelan: Read how the group is fighting "Love Jihad" in Kerala'. *OpIndia*, 27 Apr. 2022. https://www.opindia.com/2022/04/read-how-christian-outfit-casa-is-fighting-love-jihad-i n-kerala/.

Easo, Bivita. 2022. *Swayam Kuzhikunna Vishudha Chathikal. Pachakuthira* 19(6): 27–33.

Easo, Bivita, and Ambili Anna Markose. 2019. 'Worship Towards the East: Texts and Transitions of Christianity in Kerala'. *Nidān* 4(1): 19–38.

Fleig, Anne, and Christian von Scheve. 2020. 'Introduction: Public Spheres of Resonance—Constellations of Affect and Language'. In *Public Spheres of Resonance: Constellations of Affect and Language*, edited by Anne Fleig and Christian von Scheve, 1–17. London: Routledge.

G., Gopakumar. 2022. State of Kerala v. Bishop Franco Mulakkal. https://www.livelaw.in/pdf_upload/bishop-franco-mulakkal-case-judgment-407656.pdf. Accessed 21 Nov. 2022.

Habermas, Jürgen. 1989. *The Structural Transformation of the Public Sphere: An Inquiry into a Category of Bourgeois Society*. Cambridge: Polity Press.

———. 2011. '"The Political": The Rational Meaning of a Questionable Inheritance of Political Theology'. In *The Power of Religion in the Public Sphere*, edited by Eduardo Mendieta and Jonathan Van Antwerpen, 15–34. New York City: Columbia UP.

Jeffrey, Robin. 1992. *Politics, Women and Well-being: How Kerala Become 'A Model'*. London: Palgrave Macmillan.

Kuntsman, Adi. 2012. 'Introduction: Affective Fabrics of Digital Culture'. In *Digital Cultures and the Politics of Emotion: Feelings, Affect and Technological Change*, edited by Adi Kuntsman and Athina Karatzogianni, 1–21. London: Palgrave Macmillan.

Lunenborg, Margreth. 2020. 'Affective Publics: Understanding the Dynamic Formation of Public Articulations beyond the Public Sphere'. In *Public Spheres of Resonance: Constellations of Affect and Language*, edited by Anne Fleig and Christian von Scheve, 30–48. London: Routledge.

Mallampalli, Chandra. 2004. *Christians and Public Life in Colonial South India, 1863–1937: Contending with Marginality*. London: Routledge.

Menon, Dilip. 2002. 'Religion and Colonial Modernity: Rethinking Belief and Identity'. *Economic and Political Weekly* 37(17): 1662–67. https://www.epw.in/journal/2002/17/special-articles/religion-and-colonial-modernity.htmll.

'MLA P C George calls nun, who accused Bishop of rape, a "prostitute"; NCW demands action'. *The Indian Express*, 9 Sept. 2018, https://indianexpress.com/article/india/kerala-mla-pc-george-nun-raped-jalandhar-prostitute-5347122/lite.

Mouffe, Chantal. 2000. *The Democratic Paradox*. London: Verso.

Nandy, Ashish. 'The Politics of Secularism and the Recovery of Religious Toleration'. In *Secularism and Its Critics*, edited by Rajeev Bhargava, 321–44. Oxford: Oxford UP.

Oommen, T. K. 2017. 'Society, Religion, and Modernity in Postcolonial India'. In *Religion and Modernity in India*, edited by Sekhar Bandyopadhyay and Aloka Parasher Sen, 22–35. Oxford: Oxford UP.

Paasonen, Susanna. 2020. 'Resonant Networks: On Affect and Social Media'. In *Public Spheres of Resonance: Constellations of Affect and Language*, edited by Anne Fleig and Christian von Scheve, 49–63. London: Routledge.

Paermentier, Els De. 2008. 'Experiencing Space through Women's Convent Rules: The Rich Clares in Medieval Ghent (Thirteenth to Fourteenth Centuries)'. *Medieval Feminist Forum* 44(1): 53–68. https://www.medievalists.net/2011/05/experiencing-space-through-womens-convent-rules-the-rich-clares-in-medieval-ghent-thirteenth-to-fourteenth-centuries/.

Pandey, Geeta. 'Franco Mulakkal: Hundreds Write to Kerala Nun Who Lost Rape Case Against Bishop'. *BBC News*, 21 Jan. 2022, https://www.bbc.com/news/world-asia-india-60065287.

Papacharissi, Zizi. 2015. *Affective Publics: Sentiment, Technology, and Politics*. Oxford: Oxford UP.

Pillai, Meena T. 2014. 'Disciplining the Intimate: The Kerala Model'. *Economic and Political Weekly* 49(46): 10–13. https://www.epw.in/journal/2014/46/commentary/disciplining-intimate.html

———. 2021. 'Gendered Desire in Kerala: Affect and Assemblages as Development Indicators'. *Economic and Political Weekly* 56(7): 48–54. https://www.epw.in/journal/2021/7/special-articles/gendered-desire-kerala.html

———. 2022. *Affective Feminisms in Digital India: Intimate Rebels*. New York: Routledge.

Reghunath, Leena Gita [@leenaregunath]. 'Be a part of our small campaign ...'. *Twitter*, 19 Jan. 2022. twitter.com/leenareghunath/status/1483673478188630018?t=wTGVVNUdBqCaQEJ-bSuJdg&s=19.

Schmitt, Carl. 1985. *Political Theology: Four chapters on the Concept of Sovereignty*. Cambridge: MIT Press.

Suresh, Nidhi. '"What Will we Tell Other Nuns being Abused Who are Afraid?": Shock over Franco Mulakkal's Acquittal'. *Newslaundry*, 14 Jan. 2022, https://www.newslaundry.com/2022/01/14/what-will-we-tell-other-nuns-being-abused-who-are-afraid-shock-over-franco-mulakkals-acquittal.

Surya, Jisha. 'Inspired by RSS, CASA, a Christian outfit in Kerala is gaining popularity with "love jihad" interventions'. *News Nine*, 21 Apr. 2021, https://www.news9live.com/amp/state/kerala/inspired-by-rss-casa-a-christian-outfit-in-kerala-is-gaining-popularity-with-love-jihad-interventions-165774.

Taylor, Charles. 2011. 'Why We Need a Radical Redefinition of Secularism'. In *The Power of Religion in the Public Sphere*, edited by Eduardo Mendieta and Jonathan Van Antwerpen, 34–60. New York City: Columbia UP.

Warner, Michael. 2005. *Publics and Counterpublics*. New York: Zone Books.

# Contributors

**Meena T. Pillai** is Professor of English and Head at the Institute of English, University of Kerala. She is also Director of the Centre for Cultural Studies, University of Kerala. Widely published in the areas of gender studies, cultural studies and cinema, her latest book is *Affective Feminisms in Digital India: Intimate Rebels.*

**Muraleedharan Tharayil**'s research interests include cultural studies, gender, sexuality and cinema. His pioneering essays on gender and sexuality have been seminal in opening the field to new kinds of critical enquiries. He was Associate Professor and Head at the Department of English, St. Aloysius College (affiliated to the University of Calicut). He is currently Professor in Cinema and Culture, Chetana college of Media and Performing Arts, Thrissur.

**Arya K.** is Nava Kerala Post-Doctoral Fellow at the Institute of English, University of Kerala. She has a PhD in Malayalam Language and Literature from the Sree Sankaracharya University of Sanskrit on the topic 'Formation and Institutionalisation of Literature as Discourse in Malayalam: A Critique on Nineteenth Century Records'. Her research interests include discourses on literariness, Malayalam newspaper archives, and the relationship between the Malayali public sphere and literature.

**Maalavika Ajayakumar** is Assistant Professor at Mar Ivanios College (Self-Financing Wing), Kerala. Her doctoral research revolved around the gendered parameters of Kerala's public sphere(s) and its many transformations. Her thesis is titled 'Malayali Public Sphere and the Women's Question: A Study of Select Narratives'. She is interested in archival research, cultural studies, Kerala Studies, women's studies and narratives of resistance.

**Meera C.** is Assistant Professor of English at Sacred Heart College (East Campus), Ernakulam. She has a PhD in English from the Institute of English, University of Kerala, and is a former Fulbright Doctoral Fellow affiliated to the University of Wisconsin-Madison. Her areas of interest include Kerala Studies, Book History and women's studies.

**Sucheta Sankar V.** is Assistant Professor in the Department of English at Sreenarayanaguru Open University, Kureepuzha. Her areas of interest include travel studies, gender studies, cultural studies, and Kerala Studies. She was the recipient of the Fulbright–Nehru Doctoral Fellowship (2016–17), Kairali Gaveshaka Puraskaram for Postdoctoral Research (2021–23), and the Kerala Council for Historical Research Doctoral Fellowship (2015–16).

**Arya A.** is Senior Research Fellow at the Institute of English, University of Kerala, where she studies gender and sartorial politics in nineteenth-century Travancore. Her research interests include gender studies, critical theory, cultural studies and Kerala Studies.

**Gigy J. Alex** teaches in the Department of Humanities at the Indian Institute of Space Science and Technology (IIST), Department of Space, Thiruvananthapuram. Her areas of interest include food and cultural studies and science fiction. She writes a column on culinary memories, *Ruchiyorma*, in the online magazine *Grihalekshmi*. She is also Associate Editor of an in-house biannual journal, *Surabhi: Journal of Arts and Literature*, published by the Indian Institute of Space Science and Technology.

**Benita Acca Benjamin** is Senior Research Fellow at the Institute of English, University of Kerala. Her doctoral research attempts to understand the mediation of gender and the gendering of genres with specific focus on Malayalam soap operas. Her research interests include cultural studies, media studies, gender studies and Kerala modernity.

**Jobson Joshwa** is a research scholar at the Institute of English, University of Kerala. His doctoral research revolves around the discursivities of Syrian Christian identity politics, with specific focus on Syrian Christian family histories. His research interests include cultural studies, Kerala Studies, religious studies and critical theory.

# Publisher's Acknowledgements


Meena T. Pillai, 'Return of the Uncanny *Yakshi*: Gendering the "Spectres" of Kerala's Modernities', *Malayalam Research Journal*, vol. 14, issue 2, pp. 5251–69.

Muraleedharan Tharayil, 'Imaginations of Pleasure: Against a History of Desire in Kerala', *Malayalam Research Journal*, vol. 14, issue 3, pp. 5395–5423.

Arya K., 'Re-reading *Indulekha*: Intimate Hierarchies in the Ambiguities of Sanskritised Registers and Domesticated Social Space', *Malayalam Research Journal*, vol. 14, issue 2, pp. 5300–16.

Maalavika Ajayakumar, 'Sthree, Purushan, Napumsakan: Shaping Femininities and Effeminacies in Early-Nineteenth-Century Kerala', *Malayalam Research Journal*, vol. 14, issue 2, pp. 5317–36.

Meera C., 'Fashioning the Reading Woman in Colonial Kerala: A Woman Reader's Memoir in Perspective', *Malayalam Research Journal*, vol. 14, issue 3, pp. 5424–40.

Sucheta Sankar V., 'Liminal Modernities: At the Intersections of Travel Discourses, Gender and Kerala', *Malayalam Research Journal*, vol. 14, issue 2, pp. 5337–53.

Arya A., 'Sewing Malayali Christian Women: Missionary Makings of Sartorial Morality and "Modern" Domesticity in Travancore', *Malayalam Research Journal*, vol. 14, issue 2, pp. 5354–73.

Gigy J. Alex, 'Cookbooks from Kerala: Creative Adaptations and Inscriptions of Alternate Modernities', *Malayalam Research Journal*, vol. 14, issue 3, pp. 5467–84.

Benita Acca Benjamin, 'Television Modernity and Mediated Femininities in Kerala', *Malayalam Research Journal*, vol. 14, issue 3, pp. 5485–5502.

All essays reprinted by permission of *Malayalam Research Journal* and the Benjamin Bailey Foundation.